DISCARDED

D0083284

HIGHER EDUCATION IN TRANSITION

The Challenges of the New Millennium

Edited by
Joseph Losco
Brian L. Fife

BERGIN & GARVEY
Westport, Connecticut • London

Library of Congress Cataloging-in-Publication Data

Higher education in transition : the challenges of the new millennium
/ edited by Joseph Losco, Brian L. Fife.
    p.   cm.
Includes bibliographical references and index.
ISBN 0–89789–637–8 (alk. paper)
    1. Education, Higher—Aims and objectives—United States.
2. Higher education and state—United States.   I. Losco, Joseph.
II. Fife, Brian L.
LA227.4.H53   2000
378.73—dc21   99–33210

British Library Cataloguing in Publication Data is available.

Copyright © 2000 by Joseph Losco and Brian L. Fife

All rights reserved. No portion of this book may be
reproduced, by any process or technique, without the
express written consent of the publisher.

Library of Congress Catalog Card Number: 99–33210
ISBN: 0–89789–637–8

First published in 2000

Bergin & Garvey, 88 Post Road West, Westport, CT 06881
An imprint of Greenwood Publishing Group, Inc.
www.greenwood.com

Printed in the United States of America

The paper used in this book complies with the
Permanent Paper Standard issued by the National
Information Standards Organization (Z39.48–1984).

10   9   8   7   6   5   4   3   2   1

To
Mom and Dad
Who instilled in me the highest respect for education
—Joseph Losco

To
Samuel and Jackson
May your experience in higher education help promote a lifetime
of learning and knowledge exploration
—Brian L. Fife

Contents

Illustrations

TABLES

FIGURES

Acknowledgments

We would like to thank all the contributors for their willingness to share their expertise and opinions in this volume. Their participation in this project is greatly appreciated. We are indebted to them and to Jane Garry, our editor at Greenwood, who was very supportive of this project from the beginning. Further thanks go to David May, Tammy Davich, and Beth Hough of the School of Public and Environmental Affairs at Indiana University–Purdue University, Fort Wayne. Dave assisted with technical issues, Tammy with the manuscript preparation, and Beth with inputting the data for our chapter. Finally, we remain grateful to our respective immediate families: Marcia and Michael Losco; and Melissa, Samuel, and Jackson Fife, who were supportive of this project from its very infancy.

Introduction

It is very curious that so few care, or dare, to get their money's worth from the American college. . . . The typical parent of our undergraduates has stored up more or less capital; he has a position waiting for his son; his boy will be able to live comfortably, no matter what may be the efficiency of his mind. The ability to support himself, the power to make money is certainly not the most important quality for this boy to possess. Very commonly, especially in the endowed institutions of the East, money-making in his family has reached the saturation point. It is unnecessary, it may be inadvisable, or even wrong, for him to enter gainful pursuits. What the son of parents in comfortable circumstances requires is not so much a narrow training in the support of life as a broader one in how to utilize living. His interests, quite as much as his mental powers, need stimulus, development, and discipline.

—H. S. Canby. 1915: 72–73

The students Henry Seidel Canby taught at Yale in the early years of the twentieth century are markedly different from those who can be found walking the halls of the American university at century's end. Even at Yale, Canby would encounter far greater diversity on the basis of gender, race, and economic status. In fact, many of the changes that were to mark the democratization of higher education in the twentieth century were already underway as Canby wound his way through New Haven to teach English. The 1862 Morrill Land Grant Act was already responsible for opening higher education to a larger cross section of Americans. State aid opened opportunities for even more students, and a host of new colleges began opening their doors. Democratization of higher education continued in spurts and stops throughout the twentieth century, though few events made as big an impact as the G.I. Bill, which afforded hundreds of thousands of servicemen and women the opportunity to enter a world of higher education that they could otherwise not afford. The proof of such change is in the numbers, which demonstrate both a vast expansion of the higher education market and a dramatic change in the clientele. For example, in 1919, total fall enrollment at the nation's colleges was 597,880. Of the 27,410 bachelor's degrees conferred that year, fewer than one-fifth were received by women. By 1990, the number of college enrollees had increased dramatically to over 13.5 million, with the majority of the over one million bachelor's degrees received by women (U.S. Department of Education, 1999: tab. 168).

These changes should not obscure continuities in higher education that persist. Writing in 1919, Canby bemoaned the growing pressure for vocational training and insisted that the college graduate needed a more well-rounded liberal education: "[The college student] needs an honest knowledge of the great principles that underlie human thought and action, the principles that have been crystalized in the modern humanities—history, literature, social and natural science, art, and the rest (1915: 104)."

His concerns on this score continue to resound in the halls of academia and the floors of faculty senate meetings at the dawn of yet another century. Consider Canby's views on faculty compensation and lifestyle:

I do not wish to harp upon the ancient theme of the underpaid professor. That plaint has grown tiresome to academic as well as to unacademic ears, more so since it should never have been a complaint but a warning. . . . A college statistician has recently asserted that on the present salary basis the professor can hope to afford, on average, two fifths of a child! Again, if the professor lives a life apart in order that he may be thrown neither with his economic equals, who are culturally and educationally his inferiors, nor with his educational equals, who set a financial pace he cannot follow—if he lives a life apart, he must forfeit the place in the community that every self-respecting citizen desires; he must forfeit influence, and condemn himself to a narrow society. With all its minor hardships, his life is on the whole the most attractive that America offers. (1915: 59–61)

The modern academic would find little to fault with Canby's assessment.

While these comparisons between the early and late twentieth century are informative about the road higher education has traversed, this volume is not about the changes that have occurred over the last century. Rather, it is meant to record the current state of higher education at century's end and to chart the current challenges it faces in the new millennium. To that end, we have assembled in this volume contributions highlighting major trends and forks in the road. Neither is the volume intended to be an exercise in arcane academic discourse. Each chapter raises significant questions about the future of higher education in America that must be addressed by the largest possible audience.

The first two chapters survey the dramatic changes occurring on college campuses across the nation at the end of the twentieth century that will have a dramatic impact on the operation of the higher education community in the twenty-first century. Alexander W. Astin begins in Chapter 1 by examining demographic shifts in the student population. Among the most significant changes are increasing numbers of nontraditional, minority, and female students along with a sharp reorientation toward career training and a precipitous decline in political interest. In Chapter 2, Gary Rhoades explores the equally dramatic changes occurring in the role of the professorate. In addition to performing the traditional functions of teaching, research, and service, faculty are increasingly asked to intensify their contact with students as mentors outside of the classroom, demonstrate new competencies in technology, act as entrepreneurs attracting external funds, serve as liaisons for alumni fundraising, infuse their research and teaching with real-world applications, engage in interdisciplinary endeavors, and interact with a myriad of nonfaculty professionals whose ranks have swelled within the university in recent years while the proportion of full-time faculty has dwindled. These two introductory chapters demonstrate that when baby-boomer alums visit their children at college today, they are stepping foot on very different campuses than the ones they had known as students. The authors also highlight the nature of the challenges that await the campus of tomorrow in adjusting to the seismic demographic changes already underway.

The next three chapters examine the changing economic and political landscape of higher education. In Chapter 3, Joseph Losco and Brian L. Fife assess changing expenditure patterns in higher education. While there is great diversity across categories of higher-education institutions, several general trends emerge. Among these is the finding that college spending on traditional operations including instruction and libraries has been declining as a proportion of overall budgets, while costs associated with scholarships, research, technology, and administration are on the rise. In the face of mounting political pressures to control the cost of attending college and continued demands on public resources from competing constituents in the fields of health care and criminal justice, the higher education community is likely to face increasing difficulty meeting the demands for new initiatives driven by the competition for students, while preserving quality education.

Chapters 4 and 5 illustrate the reasons why the higher-education community is unlikely to be rescued from its financial dilemma by either federal or state governments. In his chapter, Michael D. Parsons finds an association between the declining support for federal programs to aid higher education and a realignment in the membership of the higher education community in Washington, D.C. The constellation of persons and opportunities that gave rise to consensus for an expanded federal role in the mid-twentieth century is no longer in place. In the last decade of the twentieth century, fluidity in higher-education leadership was accompanied by a significant shift in the political and ideological landscape, producing potent changes in the higher-education policy arena. Perhaps the most significant change is the shift in values away from the notion that higher education is a social good whose expense is warranted by the social benefits it produces to the notion that higher education is a consumer product whose costs must be born increasingly by the beneficiary and whose public financial investment must be protected by increased oversight and accountability requirements. These developments portend significant changes in higher education policy in the years to come.

In Chapter 5, Cheryl D. Lovell paints a similar portrait of static funding and increased regulation emerging at the state level for higher education. Despite surpluses in state coffers at the end of the twentieth century, additional funding for higher education continues to be incremental while accountability measures appear to be growing exponentially. Together, Parsons and Lovell signal a changed environment in higher-education policy at the dawn of the twenty-first century, one that is far less congenial to higher education than the seemingly halcyon days of the mid-twentieth century.

College sports have often been perceived as a positive force in higher education. Changes in broadcast technology and the sports and entertainment industries have given higher visibility and revenue to colleges that compete nationally. Yet, as Richard G. Sheehan points out in Chapter 6, the financial benefits of the professionalization of college sports do not extend very far. Sheehan calculates that once the true costs are identified, very few institutions benefit directly from national competition in the most visible college sports: football and basketball. Greater promotion of sports that are less expensive to provide, including women's sports, may prove more lucrative for most colleges. However, Sheehan concludes that auxiliary and nonfinancial benefits, including alumni support, may nevertheless sustain revenue-losing activities well into the next century.

If the task of running a college or university in the twentieth century appeared challenging, it seems especially daunting in the new millennium. Still, Richard L. Pattenaude, president of the University of Southern Maine, reminds us in Chapter 7 that the traditions and values of higher education need not be sacrificed in accommodating the changing needs of the university. While a prospective college CEO is well advised to obtain some training in management and accounting, his/her job will continue primarily to be that of providing vision for the college community. Pattenaude believes those schooled in the ways of academia and attentive to its values are likely to have fewer problems managing their campuses than those trained outside of these traditions.

Reginald Wilson of the American Council on Education examines the issues of desegregation and diversity in higher education in Chapter 8. He points out that the growing level of conservatism in court decisions concerning desegregation at the elementary and secondary school levels in the past few decades has also occurred in higher education. This conservative retrenchment is not only indicative of the federal judiciary, but public opinion as well, where many have come to conclude that policies such as affirmative action are no longer plausible. Wilson concludes that a dramatic policy similar to the G.I. Bill is needed to continue to enhance diversity in higher education and to provide equal opportunities for all citizens.

Finally, no volume on the challenges awaiting higher education would be complete without a discussion of the impact of technology. As in most endeavors, technological innovation is changing the way higher education operates. Opportunities to enhance teaching in the classroom, to offer courses over long distances, and to conduct research across continents have the potential of enriching all aspects of higher education in the new millennium. In Chapter 9, Karen Hardy Cárdenas offers a framework for evaluating the impact of technology in higher education. While educators, often seen as traditionalists, must not shy away from technology, neither should they embrace it uncritically. Cárdenas reminds us that modern technology like any tool must be assessed in terms of its usefulness in helping educators and researchers do a better job of teaching and researching.

It is the hope of the authors and editors that the issues addressed in these pages will begin a policy discussion about the future direction and course of American higher education. This discussion must be broadly engaged. While those inside the academy seemingly have the largest stake in the outcome of the debate to come, they must be mindful of the larger community and goals they serve. The public, too, must become part of the dialogue. Whether in their role as parents of college students, taxpayers who support significant federal and state investments (even at private colleges), or members of the business community who rely on the academy for advances in knowledge and the training of the work force, the stakes of this debate for all Americans are significant. Policy makers are already engaged in considering these issues. They must be aware of competing interests and be alert to generating consensus in bridging the significant accomplishments of the past with the challenges of the future.

BIBLIOGRAPHY

Canby, Henry S. 1915. *College Sons and College Fathers*. New York: Harper & Brothers.
U. S. Department of Education. 1999. *The Digest of Education Statistics, 1996*. http://nces.ed.gov/pubs/d96/D96T168.html.

1

The American College Student: Three Decades of Change

Alexander W. Astin

The Cooperative Institutional Research Program (CIRP) was founded in 1966 as a national longitudinal study of undergraduates attending different types of colleges and universities.[1] While the basic design of the study is to examine the comparative impact of different college environments by means of periodic longitudinal follow-ups of students who were initially assessed as entering freshmen (see, for example, Astin, 1977, 1982, 1993; Pascarella and Terenzini, 1991), the entering freshman survey tends to attract more media attention than do the longitudinal studies because the "trends" associated with each new survey are seen as a kind of "Gallup Poll" that makes interesting copy and "sound bites" for the various news media. Media attention notwithstanding, a careful examination of the results from the first thirty-one surveys (1966–1996) provides an extremely interesting and informative portrait of the changing character of American college students. While reflecting changes that directly affect higher education, the trend data generated by these surveys can also be viewed as indicators of our changing society. In this essay I will provide an overview of these three decades of data from the CIRP, highlighting key findings and discussing the possible significance that these findings may have for higher education and for American society at large.

Between 1966 and 1996 the entering freshman survey was completed by more than 9 million entering freshmen at more than 1,500 accredited colleges and universities.[2] A complete tabulation of the data from each of these annual surveys was recently published by the Higher Education Research Institute (Astin, Parrott, Korn, and Sax, 1997).

THE WOMEN'S MOVEMENT

A close examination of the diverse changes that have occurred in the characteristics of entering freshmen during the past three decades reveals the effects of many different social, political, and economic changes in the larger society. None of these larger societal forces, however, stands out as clearly in the data as does the Women's Movement. For this reason, I will begin the discussion of trends by looking at the many changes that appear to be attributable, at least in part, to the effects of this major social movement in American society. The impact of the Women's Movement is most obvious in three areas: the educational plans and career aspirations of women, and the attitudes of both sexes towards the role of women in society.

Women's Educational Plans and Aspirations

One of the most obvious effects of the Women's Movement during the past thirty years can be seen in the greatly increased interest of women in pursuing advanced degrees (see Table 1.1). Whereas only two women in five (40.3 percent) aspired to graduate degrees in 1966, fully two-thirds (67.7 percent) are seeking such degrees among today's freshmen women. Women show increased interest in every type of graduate degree, but especially in doctorate and advanced professional degrees, where their interest has increased by between 188 and 411 percent. By contrast, during the same time men have shown decreased interest in law degrees (-38 percent) and only small increases in interest in the other graduate degrees (1 to 23 percent). Because of these differential gender trends, women are now more interested in pursuing graduate degrees (67.7 percent) than are the men (65.3 percent). By contrast, in 1966 the men were much more likely than were the women to aspire to graduate degrees: 58.4 percent versus only 40.3 percent.

Table 1.1
Changes in Aspirations for Advanced Degrees among Freshmen, 1966 to 1996

Highest Degree Planned	Women			Men		
	1966	1996	Relative % Change	1966	1996	Relative % Change
Master's	32.3	39.3	+22	31.2	38.3	+23
Ph.D./Ed.D.	5.2	15.0	+188	13.7	15.1	+10
Medical/Dental[1]	1.9	9.7	+411	7.4	7.5	+1
Law	.9[2]	3.7	+311	5.6[2]	3.5	-38

[1]Includes optometry, veterinary, and pharmacy.

[2]Data from 1970 (1966 to 1969 not available).

Figure 1.1
Aspirations for Ph.D.–Ed.D. Degrees

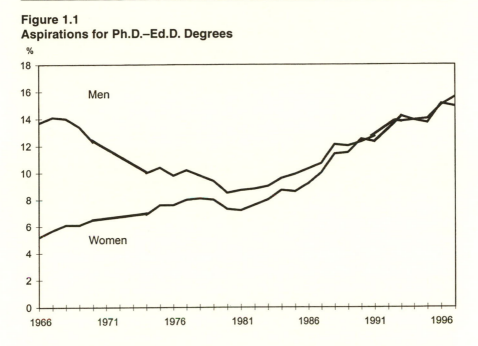

These differential gender trends for doctorate degrees are shown in Figure 1.1. Note that the women began to show increasing interest in doctoral degrees at a time when men's interest in such degrees was on the decline—the late 1960s and early 1970s, which is precisely the time that the Women's Movement was beginning to gain momentum. Men's and women's interests continued to converge until 1990, by which time they had become virtually identical. In fact, today's freshman men and women show very similar levels of interest in all types of graduate degrees (the largest difference being in medical–dental degrees, which are sought by 9.7 percent of the women but only 7.4 percent of the men).

Consider for a moment the implications of these trends for the future of the labor force: It seems probable that the proportion of women in virtually all jobs that require advanced training beyond the baccalaureate will continue to increase in the foreseeable future. What will happen to the legal and medical professions in this country when the women outnumber the men? Indeed, if we were to convert these percentages into absolute numbers, the projected effects on the labor force appear to be even more pronounced, given that between 1966 and 1996 the representation of women among entering college freshmen has switched from a minority of 45.7 percent to a majority of 55.3 percent. This latter trend is no doubt still another manifestation of the Women's Movement. That is, the increasing educational aspirations of young women in this country are reflected not only in their greater interest in postgraduate degrees, but also in their increasing interest simply in attending college.

Career Plans of Men and Women

Trends in the career aspirations of men and women freshmen during the three decades are summarized in Table 1.2. The last two columns of the table show the gender differences (in absolute percentages) in 1966 and 1996, respectively.

With only minor exceptions, the relative career interests of men and women during the thirty-year period show increasing convergence in all fields. Indeed, 1966 gender differences for six of the careers—physician–dentist, lawyer, secondary-school teacher, college teacher, research scientist, and artist—had been virtually eliminated by 1996! Moreover, substantial reductions in gender differences have occurred for four other careers: business (two-thirds reduction between 1966 and 1996), farmer–rancher (50 percent reduction), primary-school teacher (40 percent reduction), and engineer (one-third reduction). The three exceptions are as follows: The relative interest of men and women in nursing careers has shown very little change since 1966, and the gender differences for two careers—allied health and the clergy—have actually widened slightly since 1966.

What is especially interesting from the perspective of the Women's Movement is that this convergence of men's and women's career interests has been caused primarily by changes in *women's* interests: dramatically increased interest in the traditionally "male" careers of medicine, law, as well as business, and rapidly declining interest in careers in school teaching and the arts. While

Table 1.2
Changes in Career Plans among Freshmen, 1966 to 1996

Career Aspiration	Women		Men		Gender Difference[1]	
	1966	1996	1966	1996	1966	1996
Teacher (primary)	15.7	9.3	.8	1.6	+14.9	+7.7
Teacher (secondary)	18.4	4.4	10.5	4.1	+7.9	+.3
Nurse	5.3	5.5	.1	.5	+5.2	+5.0
Artist (inc. performance)	8.9	6.8	4.6	6.5	+4.3	+.3
Allied health	6.6	9.4	3.1	4.6	+3.5	+4.8
Clergy	.8	.1	.6	1.2	+.2	-1.1
College teacher	1.5	.5	2.1	.6	-.6	-.1
Research scientist	1.9	1.8	4.9	1.8	-3.0	0
Farmer/rancher	.2	.8	3.2	2.4	-3.0	-1.6
Physician/dentist	1.7	6.9	7.4	5.8	-5.7	+1.1
Lawyer	.7	3.5	6.7	3.1	-6.0	+.4
Business	3.3	11.8	18.5	16.8	-15.2	-5.0
Engineer	.2	2.4	16.3	12.8	-16.1	-10.4

[1]This difference is expressed as percentage of the women minus the percentage of men.

the women's interest in engineering careers has also shown modest increases, the gender convergence on this career has been caused more by declining interest among the men. Gender convergence on college teaching and especially on research-science careers is also mainly attributable to declining interest among the men. In the case of careers in the arts, gender convergence is equally attributable to decreasing interest among women and increasing interest among men. The largest remaining gender gaps are associated with some of the most sex-stereotypic careers: engineering (10.4 percent), primary-school teaching (7.7 percent), allied health (5.1 percent), business (5 percent), and nursing (5 percent).

Thirty-year trends in the aspirations of men and women for careers in law (as a lawyer or judge) are shown in Figure 1.2. In 1966, men were nine times more likely than women to aspire to legal careers. Gender convergence begins in the early 1970s and was complete by the late 1980s, after which women actually began to show more interest in legal careers. In looking at thirty-year trends for other careers where there has been significant gender convergence, it would appear that the Women's Movement had its greatest effect during the 1970s, although in a few instances (most notably medicine and law) the effects persisted well into the 1980s.

In summary, these data on career changes suggest that one of the most dramatic effects of the Women's Movement has been to encourage more young women to forgo careers in school teaching and the arts in favor of careers in

Figure 1.2
Aspirations for a Career in Law

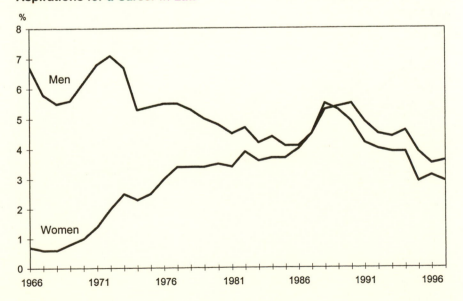

medicine, law, business, and engineering. The net consequence of these effects is that the patterns of career choices for college men and women are much more alike today than they were in the 1960s. Gender-stereotyping of careers, it would seem, is rapidly disappearing.

Student Attitudes toward Women

Students' attitudes toward women have been assessed by means of two items from the CIRP surveys. The first of these, "The activities of married women are best confined to the home and family," was first asked in 1967. Since that time, the proportions of both men and women who endorse such a view have declined dramatically to less than half the 1967 levels (see Figure 1.3). Considering that there is now such widespread acceptance of working mothers and wives in contemporary U.S. society, it is difficult to believe that a majority of college students in 1967 (56.6 percent) agreed with the view expressed in this item. Indeed, fully two-thirds (66.5 percent) of the men in 1967 agreed, as did better than two in five (44.3 percent) of the women. By 1996 these figures dropped to three out of every ten men (30.8 percent) and two out of every ten women (19 percent). Since 1967, the gender gap on this attitude has also narrowed (from 22.2 percent to 11.2 percent).

The second attitudinal item has to do with sex equity in the workplace: "Women should receive the same salary and opportunities for advancement

Figure 1.3
"The Activities of Married Women Are Best Confined to the Home and Family"

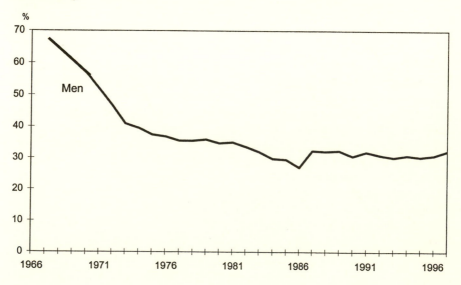

as men in comparable positions." Between 1970 and 1980 student agreement increased among both men (from 76.5 to 89.9 percent) and women (from 87.1 to 96.4 percent). However, unlike the first attitudinal item, the gender gap with respect to work-place equity has remained quite stable (at about 7 to 9 percent).

Gender "Convergence"

One effect of the Women's Movement, as we have already seen, has been the increasing similarity between men and women in their educational aspirations, career plans, and attitudes toward the role of married women. In effect, the sexes have become more alike in these areas (nearly identical, in fact, when it comes to educational aspirations). A careful inspection of other items in the CIRP survey reveals that there are a great many other ways in which the sexes have become more alike since the late 1960s. This is especially true in the case of values. Of the eighteen value questions that have been regularly included in CIRP surveys since 1966, men and women have shown a substantial degree of convergence on twelve of the items, maintained their distance on four, and shown a slight divergence on two. More significantly, of the ten items that produced gender differences of at least ten percent in the late 1960s, the sexes have shown significant convergence on all ten. In fact, gender convergence has been virtually complete on five of these items: creating artistic works, raising a family, obtaining recognition from colleagues, having administrative responsibility for the work of others, and being very well-off financially. Men used to endorse these last three values more often than did women; the first two were previously more often endorsed by women. Although both men and women have contributed to this convergence process, the women have, with few exceptions, changed more than have the men. In other words, gender convergence in values has come about primarily as a result of changes in women's values. Additional evidence of gender convergence is seen in the attitudes of men and women on certain social and political issues. In the area of defense spending, for example, a 1980 gender gap of 18.0 percent in support for increasing defense spending has been narrowed to only 4.5 percent. At the same time, the largest gap of all—in support of "casual sex," or, the notion that "if two people really like each other, it's all right for them to have sex even if they've known each other for only a very short time"—has been reduced from 31.1 percent to 21.9 percent since 1974. And most recently, the gender gap in support of the question that expresses opposition to "date rape"— "just because a man thinks that a woman has 'led him on' does not entitle him to have sex with her"—has been narrowed from 15.7 percent to 10.5 percent just since 1988, the first year it was included in the CIRP survey.

A substantial amount of gender convergence can also be observed in what might be called "bad habits," such as smoking and drinking. In 1966 the men were substantially more likely than were the women to drink beer and to smoke cigarettes frequently. Since that time the gender gap has been reduced from 22.6 percent to only 9.9 percent in the case of beer drinking. In the case of frequent smoking, the gap has actually been reversed. In 1966 the men were nearly 50 percent more likely than were the women to be frequent smokers (19.4 versus 13.2 percent); by 1978 the sex differences had been reversed, with the women more than 50 percent more likely to be frequent smokers (17.1 versus 10.6 percent). Apparently, during the same time that concerns about smoking and health were causing more men to avoid smoking, women's growing sense of autonomy and independence was causing more of them to take up smoking ("You've Come a Long Way, Baby!"). (Indeed, since it seems fair to assume that women were likewise becoming aware of the health risks during this same period, these figures probably underestimate the true effect of the Women's Movement on women's smoking habits.) After 1978, health concerns apparently prevailed for both women and men, as the rates declined to 11.3 percent and 6.6 percent respectively. Since that time the rate of smoking for both sexes has increased steadily, and the gender gap has once again narrowed. Although the absolute size of the gender gap has been reduced since 1966 (from 6.2 to 2.5 percent), the direction of the sex difference has been reversed, so that the women are more likely than are the men to be frequent smokers among contemporary college freshmen (15.6 versus 13.1 percent).

The students' political self-identification provides one of the most interesting examples of gender convergence and divergence. In 1970 (the first year the question was asked), men were more likely than were the women to identify themselves as either liberal or far left: 38.8 percent versus 33.9 percent. By 1981 the percentages were virtually identical: 20 percent and 19.5 percent for men and women respectively. The sexes have diverged since then, with women now significantly more likely to identify themselves as either liberal or far left: 26.6 percent versus 22.3 percent for men. When it comes to identifying themselves as conservative and far right, however, the pattern has been pure divergence: in 1970 men were significantly more likely than were the women to identify themselves in this way (19.3 versus 16.7 percent), and since then the gap has gradually widened to 27.1 versus 19.0 percent.

In effect, these differential gender trends have produced a major change in the political balance as it relates to the two sexes. Among men, the left–right balance in 1970 favored the left by fully 2 to 1 (38.8 versus 19.3 percent); today the men lean significantly to the right (27.1 percent versus 22.3 percent left). By contrast, women, who also leaned to the left by a 2 to 1 margin in 1970 (33.9 versus 16.7 percent right), continue to favor the left today: 26.6 versus 19.0 percent. In short, college men and women today differ in their political leanings much more than they did in the 1970s.

What are some of the possible causes of this gender divergence in political leanings? Has the Women's Movement served to polarize men and women politically? Or has the ascendance of the political right in the United States also played a role? Certainly the position of the right in general, and the Republican Party in particular, on issues such as the Equal Rights Amendment, reproductive rights, welfare, handgun control, and other so-called "women's issues" may well have deterred many young women from embracing this side of the political spectrum. This political polarization is reflected in the fact that since the early 1970s men and women have shown a modest amount of divergence in their degree of support for a national health-care plan and for such governmental policies as environmental protection and consumer protection.

Gender Differences among Today's Freshmen

Despite the considerable amount of gender convergence that we have observed during the past thirty years, there are still a few areas remaining where college men and women continue to show differences. In addition to the career-plan differences already discussed (i.e., women's greater interest in nursing, allied health, and primary-school teaching and men's greater interest in business and engineering), the areas of largest difference are attitudinal: Women are much more supportive than are men of increased governmental efforts to promote disarmament (a 19 percentage point difference) and handgun control (an 18 percentage point difference), and much less supportive of casual sex (a 22 percentage point difference) and outlawing homosexuality (a 21 percentage point difference). Also, in a new item introduced in the 1995 survey—hours per week spent playing video games—we find one of the largest gender differences in the history of the CIRP survey: Men are more than three times more likely than women to spend at least some time playing such games (59.5 percent versus 18.3 percent), six times as likely to spend at least one hour per week playing (36.0 versus 6.2 percent), and *eleven* times more likely to spend six hours or more per week—8.0 versus only 0.7 percent for the women!

Impact of the Women's Movement: An Overview

These three decades of CIRP trends make it clear that the Women's Movement has had dramatic effects on the educational aspirations, career plans, behavior, and values of young women entering college. The movement has had equally dramatic effects on the attitudes of both sexes toward the role of women. One major consequence of these trends is that *men and women freshmen are in general much more alike today than they were thirty years ago.*

As would be expected, many of these effects of the Women's Movement are also reflected in changes in the students' families. Thus, we find that today's freshmen, compared to those in earlier decades, have much more highly educated parents (especially their mothers, where there has been a two-thirds drop in the percentage who are homemakers.) Freshmen are also more likely to come from families where both parents are working and much more likely to have parents who are divorced or separated.

TRENDS IN VALUES

Some of the most pronounced changes during the past thirty years are students' values. Especially notable are changes in two contrasting value statements: "the importance of developing a meaningful philosophy of life" and "the importance of being very well-off financially" (see Figure 1.4). In the late 1960s developing a meaningful philosophy of life was the top value, being endorsed as an "essential" or "very important" goal by more than 80 percent of the entering freshmen. Being very well-off financially, on the other hand, lagged far behind, ranking fifth or sixth on the list with less than 45 percent of the freshmen endorsing it as a very important or essential goal in life. Since that time these two values have basically traded places, with being very well off financially now the top value (at 74.1 percent endorsement) and developing a meaningful philosophy of life now occupying sixth place (at only 42.1 percent endorsement). These contrasting trends began in the early 1970s, continued through the decade (crossing paths in 1977), and reached their opposite extremes in the late 1980s. Since then, they have pretty much maintained their respective positions.

Trends on two other CIRP items suggest that these value trends do indeed reflect increased student materialism: Agreement with the statement that "the chief benefit of a college education is to increase one's earning power" increased from 53.6 percent to 70.9 percent between 1969 and 1989, and the percent of

Figure 1.4
Contrasting Value Trends

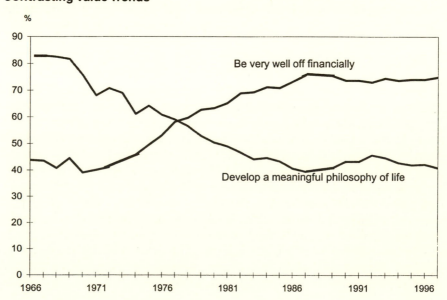

students who say they are attending college "to be able to make more money" increased from 49.9 percent to 74.7 percent between 1971 and 1991.

Why should these two values—being very well-off financially and developing a meaningful philosophy of life—show such profound and contrasting patterns of change during the first two decades of the CIRP surveys? In some unpublished analyses done several years ago at the Higher Education Research Institute (HERI), we determined that these two values were associated with the number of hours per week that students watched television during the past year (for most freshmen, this would be the senior year in high school). The more television watched, the stronger the endorsement of the goal of being very well-off financially, and the weaker the endorsement of the goal of developing a meaningful philosophy of life. While such correlations obviously cannot prove causation, they raise some interesting possibilities. Could these trends be attributed, at least in part, to changes in the television-viewing habits of our young people? When the earliest cohorts from the late 1960s were old enough to start watching television—say, in the early 1950s—relatively few homes had even black-and-white television sets. By contrast, when the freshmen from the late 1980s were old enough to start watching—that is, in the early 1970s—American homes were pretty much saturated with color television, and many homes had several sets. Television had become the "electronic baby sitter." In other words, it seems safe to assume that freshmen from the late 1960s had been exposed to much less television by the time they entered college than had freshmen from the late 1980s. It also seems safe to assume that today's freshmen and those from the late 1980s differ much less, if at all, in their degree of precollege exposure to television, a fact which would help to explain why there has been relatively little change in these values during the past nine years.

Given that television's commercial message is, almost by definition, materialistic, and given that much of the programming itself celebrates materialistic values (e.g., *Beverly Hills 90210, Melrose Place*), it is perhaps to be expected that watching a lot of television would tend to promote materialistic values among young persons. Why it would simultaneously weaken the young person's commitment to "developing a meaningful philosophy of life" is not as clear. We consider this statement to reflect an "existential" perspective, where the student is seeking to find a meaning or purpose that can guide major life decisions. (The idea for this item initially came from student focus groups that I was conducting in the early 1960s. While reviewing drafts of our questionnaires, several students pointed out that the "most important" value was missing: "These are the questions we talk about in late-night bull sessions." We subsequently decided to include such a value in the CIRP surveys, and it did indeed turn out to be the most important one for students in the late 1960s.)

Television, with its materialistic message and its emphasis on rapidly changing visual imagery, certainly does not promote contemplation or reflection on the great questions of life. In a sense, committing oneself to making money as a major goal in life and as a major reason for attending college may obviate the need to "develop a meaningful philosophy of life." Indeed, it could be argued that for many young people today, the making of money has become a kind of "philosophy of life" in itself.

Such speculations about television's possible role in helping to produce these value changes is supported by recent longitudinal studies of entering freshman classes (Astin, 1993), which show that television viewing during college is associated with increased commitment to the goal of being very well off financially and decreased commitment to the goal of developing a meaningful philosophy of life. In other words, *changes* in these same values during college are affected by how much television students watch during their undergraduate years.

Student endorsement of some of the other value questions has also changed during the past three decades, but none of these changes has been as marked or as consistent as the ones just discussed. Some of these other trends are summarized in this chapter in the section on "Eras of Rapid Change."

OTHER TRENDS

Other major trends observed during the past three decades can be briefly summarized under two general headings: student attitudes and academics.

Student Attitudes

- Avoidance of the "liberal" political label.
- Increased liberalism on issues of students' rights, gay rights, and gender equality.
- Increased conservatism on law-and-order issues.
- Political disengagement.

Academics

- Severe inflation of secondary-school grades.
- Increased competitiveness.
- Increased optimism about academic performance in college.
- Growing interest in postbaccalaureate education.
- Declining interest in liberal-arts majors and in teaching careers.

More details on some of these long-term trends are given in the next section.

TWO ERAS OF RAPID CHANGE

While each of the thirty freshman surveys conducted since the initial 1966 survey has revealed significant changes from the previous year's survey, there have been two periods during which students have shown particularly rapid and widespread change: the late 1960s through the early 1970s, and the past eight to ten years covering the end of the 1980s to the present time. Many of the thirty-year changes in freshmen can be best understood by looking in some depth at these two eras.

From the Late 1960s to the Early 1970s

This period in American history comprises the peak years of the Student Movement and the early years of the Women's Movement. While pundits like to talk about "The Sixties," the fact is that the diverse phenomena implied by this label really became salient only in the latter part of that infamous decade and spilled over well into the 1970s. The CIRP surveys during this era reveal that practically everything in the survey was changing during this six-to-eight year period. To simplify what could be a very long and detailed presentation, only the highlights will be briefly summarized.

Greater Support for Students' Rights

Practically all of the substantial change in support for students' rights during the past three decades occurred between 1967 and 1974, the period of time when American college campuses experienced most of the so-called "Sixties protests." The popular conception of this period is that the protests were mainly about civil rights and the war in Vietnam. The fact is, however, that most of the protests—including most of the mass protests—had to do with more general issues of students' rights (Astin, Astin, Bayer, and Bisconti, 1975). It is thus not surprising that changes between 1967 and 1974 in the views of freshmen were all in the direction of greater support for student autonomy and rights: greater support for the use of student evaluations of teaching in the faculty personnel process (20 percent increase) and less support for the idea that institutional officials should be able either to censor student publications (41 percent decrease) or to ban controversial speakers from the campus (43 percent decrease).

Marriage, Family, and Women's Role

The profound changes in students' views about the role of women actually occurred in a very brief time span. Thus, when it comes to the notion that "married women should confine their activities to the home and family," most of the change in student attitudes occurred in just seven years: from 1967 (56.6 percent) to 1974 (28.3 percent), a 50 percent reduction in support. During this same period, endorsement of the value of "raising a family" dropped by one-fourth (from 71.4 to 55.0 percent), as did the percentage of students who planned to marry within a year after finishing college (from 22.9 to 16.6 percent). Also, between 1967 and 1971 student agreement with the notion that "parents should be discouraged from having large families" increased by three-fifths (from 42.2 to 68.5 percent).

Disengagement from Politics

Between 1966 and 1974 the students' level of commitment to "keeping up with political affairs" declined by more than one-third (from 57.8 to 36.6 percent), and commitment to "developing a meaningful philosophy of life" declined by one-fourth (from 82.9 to 61.1 percent). At the same time, the percentage of students who reported no religious preference more than doubled, the percentage of those desiring to "become a community leader" fell by two-fifths, and the percentage indicating an interest in joining an organization such as the Peace Corps or VISTA dropped by one-fourth. Finally, between 1967 and 1974 the percent of freshmen indicating that they planned to join a social fraternity or sorority declined by more than half (from 30.8 to 13.0 percent).

Several other findings suggest a trend toward disengagement in general: a one-fourth decline between 1967 and 1971 in the percent of students who played a musical instrument during the past year (from 51.4 to 37.7), and declines in the percentages of students who participated in high school activities such as student government, theater, and debate. Although it may not necessarily be another indication of disengagement, support for legalization of marijuana also more than doubled (from 19.4 to 48.2 percent) between 1966 and 1973.

Student Uncertainty

Between 1967 and 1972 the percent of freshmen who were "undecided" about their career plans increased by more than one-third (from 10.1 to 13.9 percent). Also, between 1966 and 1973 the percent who expressed "major concern" about their ability to pay for college nearly doubled (from 8.6 percent to 16.6 percent).

Career Changes

Most of the precipitous decline in students' interest in teaching careers (from 23.5 to only 6.5 percent) occurred in the relatively brief interval between 1968 and 1975. This loss of nearly three-fourths was also accompanied by a two-thirds decline in the percent of freshmen indicating that they wanted to become college teachers and a one-third drop in the percent desiring to become scientific researchers. Interest in careers in engineering and in the clergy also declined by about half. Careers showing increased student interest during this same period included farmer–forester, which more than doubled in popularity, and all of the health-related careers: physician (three-fifths increase), nurse (three-fourths increase), and allied health, which more than doubled in popularity.

Grade Inflation

The three-decade trend in grade inflation got off to a flying start in the late 1960s: between 1969 and 1974 the percent of "A-" or higher grades increased by half (from 12.5 to 18.8 percent), and the percent of "C+" or lower grades declined by one-third (from 32.5 to 21.9 percent) (see Figure 1.5).

From the Late 1980s to the Present

Since the late 1980s we have once again witnessed wide-ranging changes in students' interests, values, attitudes, and aspirations. While some of these changes—for example, grade inflation and political disengagement—resemble those just discussed for the late 1960s–early 1970s, most others are unique. Since these are the most recent trends, they will be discussed in the context of contemporary higher-education issues.

Concerns about Finances

Recent classes of entering freshman show a clear pattern of increasing concern about financing college: record-high percentages of students expressed "major concern" about their ability to pay for college, and record-high percentages indicated they picked their college either because of "low tuition"

Figure 1.5
Grade Inflation

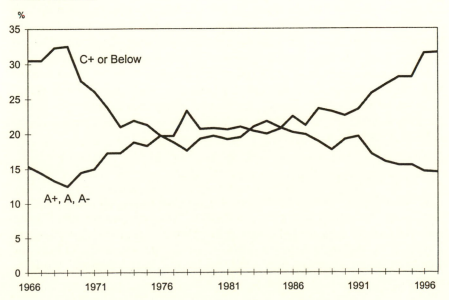

(31.3 percent, compared to only 20.9 percent in 1987) or because of "financial aid offers" (33.1 percent, compared to 20.2 percent in 1987). At the same time, record high percentages of freshmen said that they will have to "get a job to help pay for college expenses," and record numbers said they plan to work full time while attending college. These latter trends are especially troubling in light of recent studies suggesting that working off campus, especially full-time work, increases the likelihood that the student will drop out of college (Astin, 1993; Astin, Tsui, and Avalos, 1996).

That these trends may have been brought about at least in part by an increasing inability of federal financial aid to keep pace with the rising cost of college is suggested by other CIRP data. Thus, in spite of rising college costs, the percentages of students who receive at least $1,500 per year from Pell Grants or Stafford Loans (the principal need-based federal aid programs) have actually declined since 1990: from 7.1 to 5.1 for Pell Grants and from 13.6 to 13.1 for Stafford Loans. Indeed, the percentage of students receiving any support from a Pell Grant has also declined (from 23.2 to 20.1) during the same period. At the same time, the percentage of students who rely on nonfederal and nonstate sources—parents, savings from summer work, other savings, part-time work, and full-time work—for at least $1,500 of support for college expenses had gone up in virtually every category. Changes in federal aid have also apparently required colleges to provide more support to needy students out of their own resources, as evidenced by the substantial increase in student reliance on grants or scholarships from the college—from 5.2 percent to 16.8 percent since 1987—for at least $1,500 of support during the freshman year.

These trends suggest that the failure of federal aid to keep up with the rising cost of college has not only forced more needy students and parents to carry a greater share of the financial burden, but has also contributed to a greater sense of concern about paying for college and caused more students to pick their college on the basis of costs and available financial aid rather than because of the quality of programs offered. These findings also provide at least a partial explanation for rising college costs: Since a good deal of "internal" institutional aid for students comes from tuition revenues (especially in the private institutions), the failure of government aid to cover increasing student need puts greater pressure on the institution to make up the difference with internal funds.

Greater Levels of Stress

Recent trends in several other items suggest that today's freshmen are experiencing more stress than previous classes. Thus, the percentage of freshmen who report "being overwhelmed by everything I have to do" has increased steadily from 16.4 to 29.4 since 1987 (the first year it was asked). At the same time, the percentage reporting that they frequently "feel depressed" has been increasing (from 8.3 to 10.0), and the percentage rating themselves above average in "emotional health" has been on the decline (from 59.0 to 52.7). Not surprisingly, since 1989 the inclination of entering freshmen to "seek personal counseling" after they enter college has also been on the rise—from 34.7 to 41.1 percent.

Competition, Grade Inflation, and Academic Disengagement

While these heightened financial pressures may well have contributed to increased stress, there is good reason to believe that student stress may also have been exacerbated by competitiveness. Multiple applications to college have reached an all-time high, and grade inflation has once again been accelerating (see Figure 1.5). In just the six years since 1990, the proportion of freshmen with "A-" or higher grade averages has increased by nearly half (from 22.6 to 31.5 percent), and the percent with "C+" or lower grade averages has declined from 19.2 to only 14.6 percent. That this grade inflation has had an effect on students' expectations is revealed by the fact that record-high proportions of 1996 freshmen believe that they will make at least a "B" average, graduate with honors, and be elected to an academic honor society.

Record high numbers of students are also aspiring to graduate degrees. That these increased aspirations may also reflect competitiveness rather than changes in career aspirations is suggested by the fact that, although interest in the Ph.D. degree is at an all-time high, interest in the two careers for which such a degree would be most appropriate—college teaching and scientific research—remains near its all-time low.

More students than ever before are also taking more college-preparatory courses. That these trends may also be reflective of a desire to gain a competitive edge in the college admissions process is indicated by several other lines of evidence. For example, despite the increased involvement in college-prep courses, students show signs of increasing academic disengagement: Since 1989 the percent who report spending at least six hours per week studying or doing homework has dropped from 42.3 to 35.7. Further, the percentages reporting that they either asked a teacher for advice after class or visited a teacher's home have also been on the decline.

Another relevant trend is the recent increase in engagement in volunteer work at the precollegiate level: Since 1987 the percentage of students who report spending at least some time in volunteer service during the year before entering college has increased from 42.0 to 59.0 percent, an all-time high. While it might be argued that this increase is yet another sign of students' increasing desire to gain a competitive edge in the college-admissions process, it should be noted that this rise in precollege volunteerism has also been accompanied by a parallel increase in students' intentions to volunteer during college: Since 1990 the inclination of students to say that there is a "very good chance" that they will be volunteers in college has risen from 14.2 to 19.3 percent. Still, it must be acknowledged that these percentages lag far behind the percentage who volunteer before entering college.

Disengagement from Politics

Among the 1996 freshmen, only 16.2 percent say that they had frequently "discussed politics" during the past year. Although this is a slight increase over the record low of 14.8 percent recorded in 1995, it is considerably lower than the 1992 level of 24.6 percent and the lowest level ever recorded for an election year. Similarly, in 1996 only 29.4 percent of the freshmen (compared to 42.4 percent in 1990) say that "keeping up with political affairs" is an important goal in life, once again the lowest figure ever recorded in an election year (see Figure 1.6).

Political disengagement is also suggested by results from an infrequently-asked item, "voted in a student election." In just the five years between 1991 and 1996, the percentage of students reporting that they frequently voted in a student election dropped by nearly one-third (from 32.7 to 23.0 percent), and the percentage that never voted in such an election increased by a third (from 22.0 to 28.3 percent). As Figure 1.6 shows, these recent trends are really a continuation of a process of long-term political disengagement by students that began in the late 1960s.

Figure 1.6
Importance of "Keeping up to Date with Political Affairs"

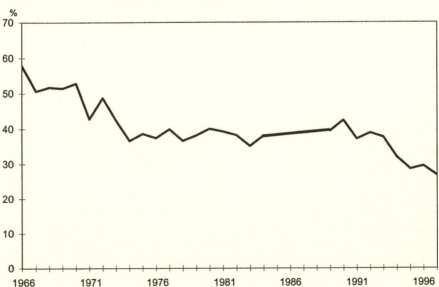

Another indicator of disengagement is the sharp decline just since 1992 in the inclination of students to rate "becoming involved in programs to clean up the environment" as an important goal in life: from 35.6 percent to only 20.7 percent in the 1996 survey. During this same brief period there have also been significant declines in the percentages of students who are willing to commit themselves to "participating in a community action program" (from 26.1 to 23.7 percent), "promoting racial understanding" (from 42.0 to 34.7 percent), and "developing a meaningful philosophy of life" (from 45.6 to 42.1 percent). Finally, the percent of students who report "none" as their religious preference has also been on the rise, increasing from 10.1 to 14.0 percent since 1987.

Decreased Reliance on Government

Since 1992 there has been a slow but steady decline in the tendency for students to support governmental action as a means of dealing with social and economic issues. Thus, we see modest declines in agreement that the federal government "should be doing more" to control environmental pollution, encourage energy conservation, or protect consumers. There have also been declines in support for the notions that the federal government should increase taxes on the wealthy, develop a national health-care plan, or raise taxes to reduce the deficit.

It is perhaps somewhat ironic that these trends should have occurred during the first term of a democratic administration. Perhaps they reflect the rightward shift of President Bill Clinton and his assertion that "the era of big government is over." Even so, it should be emphasized that throughout the first thirty-one years of freshman surveys, the students have in general been strong supporters of governmental action to deal with social and economic problems. Thus, even among 1996 freshmen, large majorities continue to support increased governmental action in the areas of environmental protection (81.9 percent), consumer protection (71.8 percent), and energy conservation (71.9 percent). And large majorities also support the ideas of a national health-care plan that covers everyone's health-care costs (72.3 percent) and increasing taxes on the wealthy (65.7 percent). The only such proposition that is not supported by a majority of students is to increase taxes as a means of reducing the deficit (23.6 percent).

Social Issues: Mixed Trends

A mixed pattern is suggested by recent trends on other social issues. Perhaps most dramatic is the declining tendency for students to agree that "it is important to have laws prohibiting homosexual relationships," which since 1987 has dropped steadily from 53.1 percent to 33.5 percent. Also moving in a "liberal" direction is the recent rapid increase since 1989 in agreement with the proposition that marijuana should be legalized, up from 16.7 to 33.0 percent.

A very recent conservative trend is revealed in support for legal abortion: although support reached a high point of 64.1 percent in the 1992 survey, it has fallen off somewhat in recent years to 56.3 percent. Also, perhaps because of the AIDS epidemic, support for "casual sex" has declined from its high point of 51.9 percent in 1987 to 41.6 percent in 1996. Finally, students are more inclined than ever before to agree that "there is too much concern in the courts for the rights of criminals" (from 65.3 to 71.6 percent since 1991). Agreement with the idea of outlawing capital punishment remains near its lowest point (20.1 percent in 1994) at 22.2 percent in the 1996 survey.

SUMMARY AND CONCLUSIONS

This detailed examination of trends in the CIRP freshman survey results during the past three decades shows that college freshmen today are very different from freshmen of the late 1960s. Highlights and possible implications of these trends, which are based on data from more than 9 million freshmen at over 1,500 institutions, can be summarized as follows:

- The profound effects of the Women's Movement are reflected in (1) changes in the attitudes of both men and women toward the role of women in society, and (2) the dramatic changes in the women themselves. Compared to their counterparts of the late 1960s, freshmen women today have much higher educational aspirations and are much more interested in careers in the traditionally "male" professions (business, law, medicine, and engineering).

- The fact that women now account for 45 percent of the freshmen planning careers in business and the *majority* of those pursuing doctorate degrees and careers in law and medicine will almost certainly have profound effects on our society in the years to come.

- The effect of the Women's Movement is also apparent in the "gender convergence" that we have observed during the past three decades: Women and men today are much more alike in their interests, aspirations, values, and behavior than they were in the 1960s. About the only area where the sexes have diverged is politics: Whereas men and women were very similar in their politics during the late 1960s, today the women lean to the left, while the men lean to the right.

- Between the late 1960s and the mid-1980s students became much more committed to materialistic values and much less committed to "developing a meaningful philosophy of life." Other analyses suggest that these value changes may be attributable, at least in part, to the effects of television.

- Two periods during the past three decades have produced especially rapid and widespread change: from the late 1960s to the early 1970s and from the late 1980s to the present.

- Between the late 1960s and early 1970s, the so-called "student protest" era, there was rapid grade inflation in the high schools, disengagement of students from traditional politics, increasing uncertainty about college finances and careers, decreasing interest in getting married and raising a family, and increasing support for gender equality, student autonomy, and students' rights.

• Since the late 1980s grade inflation has reached new heights, and students are showing signs of increased competitiveness, heightened concern about college finances,
and increased stress. The growing inability of federal and state aid to meet the
student's financial need is forcing students to borrow more and forcing colleges to
rely more on their own resources (primarily tuition) to help pay for college. Although engagement in the political process has reached new lows, student interest
and engagement in volunteer and community service work has reached new highs.

NOTES

1. This chapter has been adapted from Astin (1998). The author is indebted to
Sarah Parrott, William Korn, Helen Astin, and Linda Sax for their assistance in preparing this chapter.

2. Each year the CIRP surveys some 350,000 full-time students who constitute
the entering freshman classes at a nationally representative sample of some 700 two-
year and four-year colleges and universities across the United States. The first seven
freshman surveys were conducted at the American Council on Education, with support from the Carnegie Corporation of New York and the Ford Foundation. Since
1972, the annual CIRP freshman surveys have been conducted by the Higher Education Research Institute at the University of California, Los Angeles, with the continuing sponsorship of the American Council on Education (see Sax, Astin, Korn, and
Mahoney, 1996).

BIBLIOGRAPHY

Astin, Alexander W. 1998. The Changing American College Student: Thirty-Year
    Trends, 1966–1996. *The Review of Higher Education*, 21:2, 115–135.
———. 1993. *What Matters in College?* San Francisco: Jossey-Bass.
———. 1982. *Minorities in American Higher Education*. San Francisco: Jossey-Bass.
———. 1977. *Four Critical Years*. San Francisco: Jossey-Bass.
Astin, Alexander W.; Helen S. Astin; Alan E. Bayer; and Ann S. Bisconti. 1975. *The
    Power of Protest*. San Francisco: Jossey-Bass.
Astin, Alexander W.; Kenneth C. Green; and William S. Korn. 1987. *The American
    Freshman: Twenty Year Trends*. Los Angeles: Higher Education Research In-
    stitute, UCLA.
Astin, Alexander W.; Sarah A. Parrott; William S. Korn; and Linda J. Sax. 1997. *The
    American Freshman: Thirty Year Trends*. Los Angeles: Higher Education Re-
    search Institute, UCLA.
Astin, Alexander W.; Lisa Tsui; and Juan Avalos. 1996. *Degree Attainment Rates at
    American Colleges and Universities: Effects on Race, Gender, and Institu-
    tional Type*. Los Angeles: Higher Education Research Institute, UCLA.
Pascarella, Ernest T., and Patrick T. Terenzini. 1991. *How College Affects Students*.
    San Francisco: Jossey-Bass.
Sax, Linda J.; Alexander W. Astin; William S. Korn; and Kathryn M. Mahoney. 1996.
    The American Freshman: National Norms for Fall 1996. Los Angeles: Higher
    Education Research Institute, UCLA.

2

The Changing Role of Faculty

Gary Rhoades

According to many in the policy arena, the role of faculty should change by spending more time teaching more lower-division undergraduates and by spending less time doing so much irrelevant research. Yet, according to many of these same critics, faculty have been changing their roles in quite the opposite direction over the past two decades. They have been spending less time teaching, (and when they do, teaching increasingly irrelevant material to students) and spending more time doing research that nobody reads. According to many managers and policy makers, and some higher-education scholars, that is how the role of faculty has been changing.

In this chapter, I address several dimensions of the changing role of faculty, of which the foregrounded policy discussion is but one. I begin by considering faculty's involvement in teaching and research activities over time. In doing so, I go beyond the oversimplified dichotomy and universalization found in prevailing views. Faculty work is more complex than doing teaching *or* research. And, an accurate understanding of faculty work must recognize that there is no such thing as a typical university faculty member. The work of faculty in research universities is not the same as of faculty in masters granting comprehensive institutions. Work in both of those institutions is different still from that of faculty in highly selective liberal-arts colleges, which is also not the same as of faculty in unselective liberal-arts colleges. The institutional setting matters, shaping the nature of faculty work in fundamental ways. So, too, departmental and college settings shape faculty work. The work of faculty in sociology is different than the work of microbiology and immunology faculty in a medical school, which is different from the work of teacher education faculty, which is different from the work of electrical engineering faculty, and so on. Layer those differences on top of institutional differences, and one begins to get a sense of the variety and complexity of faculty work.

The first section of the chapter examines teaching and research in fairly traditional terms. By contrast, the second section explores the changes in the production processes of universities that impact the nature of teaching and research. The most apparent of such changes is the changing technologies with which faculty must work in teaching and in doing research. The ways in which faculty members teach and advise students have been altered by the introduction of computers into most faculty offices. Similarly, the ways in which faculty conduct and disseminate research have been altered by rapidly changing technologies. More than just technologies that impact individual faculty, there are new production units that are emerging as more central parts of universities. Over time, there has been a substantial increase in the numbers and types of interdisciplinary units on campuses, with implications for the teaching and research of faculty. Finally, there has been a proliferation of new production workers on university campuses. There are increasingly large numbers of nonfaculty professionals who are involved in teaching and research in various ways. More and more, faculty are interacting with such "support" professionals, who I call "managerial professionals," in their basic academic activities.

Finally, I conclude by discussing yet another dimension of change that is fast changing the role of faculty. Universities themselves are changing in significant ways that are both transforming the teaching and research activities of faculty and are pushing faculty well beyond these traditional roles. Universities are becoming more managerial and increasingly emphasizing accountability processes which increase both the demands on faculty to interact in new ways with students and the time faculty spend on reporting and reviewing activities. Universities have become more market oriented, with attendant implications for faculty to change their teaching and research activities and to become more like entrepreneurs who contribute revenue to the institution.

TEACHING AND RESEARCH:
THE COMPLEXITIES OF TIME AND PLACE

The most tangible dimension of faculty work, and the one of most interest to most players in the policy arena, is classroom teaching. That activity is familiar and understandable to almost anyone. A less tangible dimension of faculty work, and the target of much criticism by many players in the policy arena, is research. That activity is unfamiliar and unclear to most everyone outside academe. In the two-dimensional view of faculty work which prevails in the policy arena and the literature, teaching and research are seen as competing for faculty's time, and the teaching activity is seen as losing out over time, so much so that policy makers and managers are questioning how hard faculty work, when the heaviest-average teaching loads are fifteen hours a week. The critique is that faculty do not work hard enough, and that they work more doing research than teaching.

In this section, I briefly review this critique, exploring the empirical phenomena that support such a view of faculty work. I then review longitudinal, national empirical data regarding faculty's allocation of their time between teaching and research. In addition, I offer some evidence of the significance of "joint-production" activities in the lives of typical faculty, challenging the view of teaching and research as distinct and purely competitive activities. Finally, I examine the importance of location. Whether by institutional type or by discipline, the nature and extent of teaching and research vary.

The Critique of Faculty Teaching and Research Activity

Much of the critique of how faculty spend their time is built on premises about how faculty would prefer to spend their time and about which activity they are more rewarded for doing. With regard to the first premise, one of the central conceptions in the literature is of the "academic ratchet" (Massy and Zemsky, 1994; Zemsky, Massy, and Oedel, 1993), a process whereby faculty act on their preferences to do more research by encouraging the increased recruitment of new colleagues and reduced teaching loads of existing colleagues. With regard to the second premise, one of the central conceptions is that university reward systems favor research, not teaching, in tenure, promotion, and salaries (Fairweather, 1996; Finkelstein, 1995). Faculty are rational actors responding to incentives that encourage research and discourage teaching.

These premises are flawed in two regards. First, the empirical support for them is limited in either scope or power. For all their writing about the academic ratchet, Massy and Zemsky offer limited empirical evidence. Their 1994 study is based on data from four private liberal-arts colleges and two private research universities—a curious focus, in that most of the criticism nationally is of public research universities. Moreover, their data are cross-sectional, although the ratchet operates longitudinally over time. The ratchet involves faculty pressuring departments to hire more faculty (who remain when enrollments do not rise) and to reduce teaching loads. Faculty gradually "ratchet" their departments to add faculty, reduce faculty teaching loads, and enable faculty to spend more and more time on research. To adequately substantiate the operation of the process, some time dimension is essential in the data.

The stronger evidence nationally is that faculty preferences have been moving toward research. National surveys indicate that in every institutional sector from 1960 to 1989 the percentage of faculty saying that their interests lie primarily in teaching declined (Finkelstein, 1995). The decline has been greatest in research universities (37%), but is evident as well in doctoral granting institutions (20%), masters granting universities (9%), and even in liberal arts colleges (7%). Still, in 1989, the interests of most faculty in all sectors except research universities lay primarily in teaching. Even in research universities, over one-third of faculty had interests primarily in teaching.

In a different way—not in scope, but in power—evidence about reward systems that favor research over teaching is limited. Fairweather (1996) documents a national pattern of higher salaries for faculty who rate higher on the criteria of time on research and publishing. That pattern holds for all types of four-year institutions and for all field areas. Moreover, the effects of teaching activity and productivity are consistently found to be either neutral or negative, again across institutional types and field areas. Even in institutions that have teaching-oriented missions, research is rewarded more than teaching. These findings are obtained from analysis of 1988 survey data. More recently, Fairweather (1997) has obtained similar findings based on 1993 data.

How are such findings limited? Throughout, Fairweather dramatizes his case by identifying faculty salaries associated with different levels of research and teaching activity. However, such differences are misleading. Faculty salaries vary dramatically by field: Entry level salaries in some fields are higher than salaries of full professors in other fields (Rhoades, 1998a). Moreover, there are obvious and major differences in salary by rank and seniority. Further, gender significantly impacts faculty salaries, both as an individual and a structural variable (the "feminization" of the field is described by Bellas, 1994.) Yet when Fairweather factors in rank, seniority, and program area, he provides no reading of the magnitude of salary differences. Earlier research that he builds upon finds such differences to be small in magnitude—in the hundreds of dollars (Konrad and Pfeffer, 1990). Moreover, in no case does Fairweather's model account for more than 50 percent of the variance in faculty salaries. As a final note, Fairweather's analysis focuses on the amount rather than on the quality of teaching. Teaching more is obviously not teaching better. If quality of teaching is a factor in the reward system, as measured by student evaluations, then we would not expect to find, nor would we want to find, that salaries are simply a function of how much a faculty member teaches.

Another aspect of the reward system is promotion and tenure. National survey data reveal that over time, growing numbers of faculty report the primary significance of research in tenure decisions. From 1969 to 1989, the percentage of faculty saying that it is difficult to gain tenure without publishing increased from 40 percent in 1969 to about 60 percent in 1989 (Finkelstein, 1995). That does not mean faculty are teaching less—only that more of them are having to publish in order to advance in their academic careers.

Indeed, the premises about faculty workload ignore the basic power structure of universities, in which deans and central administrators, not faculty, shape and make decisions about faculty positions, workloads, and salaries. When faculty retire, leave, or do not obtain tenure, department heads must gain the approval of deans, who in turn must gain the approval of the provost, to replace the vacancy. Similarly, whatever faculty preferences are about workload and salaries, and whatever peer review is involved, the authority lies not just in the hands of department heads, but of deans and sometimes even provosts. Even if the premises are true in terms of faculty preferences and reward systems, they would not necessarily lead to reduced teaching loads and instructional activity—not without the active complicity of administrators. Massy and Zemsky go no further than the department head in assessing blame or responsibility for the alleged pattern of reduced teaching loads. Fairweather, too, targets department chairs for blame, in noting the disparity between their stated views about the value of teaching and patterns in faculty compensation. (However, he sees the solution to the problem as lying in the actions of senior academic officials.)

If the premises about faculty activities that lead to reduced teaching activity are flawed, what of the conclusions? What do national data tell us about faculty activity in teaching and research, and to what extent have the patterns of activity changed over time? What is the relationship of teaching and research activity? And what do the data tell us about the variations in such activity by institutional type and by field?

Teaching versus Research over Time

Over time, has teaching become a less significant part of the role of faculty? It depends on the measure. If the measure is time spent on instructional activities, then survey evidence suggests that from 1987 to 1992, faculty spent less time on teaching and more time on research, in every type of four-year institution (Allen, 1996). But, if the measure is classroom hours and student contact hours, or instruction of undergraduates, the evidence is quite the contrary. From 1987 to 1992, classroom hours increased in all types of four-year institution except liberal-arts colleges, where they remained the same (Allen, 1996). During this same time, faculty's student-contact hours (the number of students a faculty member contacts in and out of class) increased in all types of four-year institution except liberal-arts colleges. Finally, going further back in time, from 1975 to 1989, and focusing on median undergraduate hours per week, full-time faculty involvement in teaching undergraduates has remained much the same in research and doctoral-granting universities (increasing slightly in the latter); has declined by about one hour in comprehensive universities; and has slightly declined in liberal arts colleges (Finkelstein, 1995). Such findings challenge the public critique of faculty. Whatever faculty *prefer*, they are teaching either the same or heavier courseloads and are spending more time with students.

Given the data on faculty preferences and on faculty spending more time on research, these findings call into question the oversimplified view of a zero-sum competition between teaching and research for faculty's time. If faculty are spending somewhat less time on instructional matters in their workweek, they are maintaining or increasing their teaching loads and contact hours with students. Such data suggest it is time to stop conceiving of the faculty role in terms of teaching *versus* research.

The mid-1970s witnessed a national critique of faculty work that is much like the current one. The major study of the subject at the time (Fulton and Trow, 1974) found that research-oriented faculty did as much or more teaching and administration as did less research-oriented faculty. High achievers were hard workers across the board. Fairweather challenges the current relevance and accuracy of this view: "The NSOPF data reveal that in 1987–88 faculty in research universities who focused on research spent less time on teaching, administration, and service than their peers. *The integrated picture described by Fulton and Trow . . . no longer exists* (1996: 39, emphasis in original)."

Yet Fairweather fails to control for all the factors that affect teaching load. For example, research-oriented faculty tend to be younger, with fewer years of service. It is common practice, as Fairweather knows, for first-year faculty to have reduced teaching loads, at least for a semester, in order to ease the transition. It is misleading to compare them with associate professors who have been at the institution six to twelve years. Moreover, what has changed most since 1975 is differences not between research-oriented and other faculty, but between the teaching loads of faculty in different fields. Internal stratification has heightened, further explaining Fairweather's results.

Let me offer some initial findings from a current National Science Foundation (NSF)-supported study that I am conducting with Larry Leslie and Ron Oaxaca to illustrate my point. Data from 133 departments and 414 faculty in 11 public research universities in physical science, life science, engineering, math and computer science, and social science confirm what is fairly standard knowledge within the academy: teaching loads vary across fields. In the social sciences and in math and some fields of engineering, the standard teaching load for research-active faculty is two courses per semester. By contrast, the standard load in some physical-science departments is two courses per year. In other science and engineering departments, it is no more than three courses per year. Yet, the total time spent on instructional activity, including preparation time, grading, and contact with students, runs about the same across fields, and this time *outweighs* research time. Such data challenge the operation of an academic ratchet across fields—there are field differences, and time on instruction is greater than time on research.

Unfortunately, our time allocation data are cross-sectional. However, there is a time dimension in our data on courseload and on the import of student evaluations and teaching in promotion, tenure, and salary decisions. Our interview schedules with department heads (and faculty) included a question about whether courseloads had changed in the past five years, and whether student evaluations and teaching counted more, less, or the same as they had five years earlier in promotion, tenure, and salary decisions. Less than 10 percent of the department heads indicated that course loads had decreased or that student evaluations and teaching were less important than before in reviewing faculty. A substantial minority (over one-third) indicated that loads had increased, and a majority indicated that student evaluations and teaching were more important than they had been. In short, the evidence from these eleven public research universities directly contradicts the operation of an academic ratchet by faculty. Quite the contrary, instruction is becoming an increasingly important part of faculty's role.

As a final note, it is a false formulation to pit teaching against research, as if they were purely competitive and distinct activities. As any faculty member will attest, there are times when they are engaged in more than one activity. For example, when they work in a lab or on a research project with a student, often the interaction involves teaching *and* research. Economists refer to this as joint production. Survey data on faculty has been constructed in such a way as to overlook this dimension of faculty work. Respondents must choose between time spent on one versus the other. The outcomes are necessarily that respondents who do more of one activity do less of the other. The interview data we have gathered from over 400 faculty at 11 public research universities indicates that most faculty engage in such joint production. And it is not an insignificant proportion of their time. Upward of 10 percent of total faculty time is spent in joint-production activities, most of which combine research and teaching and graduate and undergraduate instruction. The construction of faculty work as teaching versus research seriously misrepresents the nature of faculty work.

Teaching and Research by Institutional Type and Discipline

Higher education in the United States is an enormous and complex system. It consists of a large number (over 3,600) of institutions and a wide variety of institutional types. Each of these institutions consists of a large number and variety of disciplines, departments, and colleges. Most scholars recognize what policy makers do not: Institutional and disciplinary differences shape faculty work. Fairweather (1996) notes and documents variations in faculty workload by such dimensions. By contrast, Massy and Zemsky (1994) universalize the "academic ratchet," overlooking fundamentally important institution and field-based variations in faculty workload and allocation of time. More than this, there are variations other than institutional type and field area that are significantly correlated with faculty workload and allocation of effort. In closing this section, I focus on the public–private dimension of institutions and on gender as it relates to faculty work. My point is that there is no such thing as a typical faculty member with a typical workload. To understand faculty work, one must disaggregate.

Typically, for institutional type, higher-education data are disaggregated by categories of the Carnegie classification of institutions—that is, by research universities (type I and II), doctoral granting universities (type I and II), comprehensive universities (type I and II), liberal-arts colleges (selective and nonselective), and community colleges. Fairweather (1996) focuses on four-year schools. He finds that although the average number of hours that faculty spend in class per week is 9.4, the number ranges from 7.7 hours for research-university faculty to 11.1 hours for comprehensive-university faculty. For two-year college faculty, the average is over 15 hours per week (Finkelstein, 1995). There is similar variation for time spent on research: The average is 22 percent for faculty in four-year institutions, ranging from 10.5 percent for liberal-arts college faculty to 31.4 percent for research-university faculty (Fairweather, 1996). The percentage is even smaller (3%) for faculty in two-year institutions (Allen, 1994).

Program area also impacts faculty workload and time allocation. Fairweather (1996) finds that the average hours in class for faculty in four-year institutions in 1986 and 1987 ranged from 7.7 in agriculture and home economics and 8.1 in natural science to 11.6 in fine arts and 12.7 in health sciences. Student contact hours ranged from 227.2 in education to 488 in health sciences. Time allocation on teaching ranged from 36 percent in health sciences to 63 percent in humanities; time allocation on research ranged from 13.6 percent in education to 31.6 percent in agriculture and home economics.

The above findings of variations in faculty work are important. There may be a pattern across institutions and fields of research being rewarded. There may be a pattern across time of faculty interest in research increasing. But there are substantial differences in faculty's workload and time allocation in regard to teaching. Such findings challenge the view that faculty are able to translate their preferences into practice and that patterns of reward translate directly into patterns of workload. In short, such findings refute the existence of an academic ratchet.

Beyond the conventional variables of institutional type and discipline, there is evidence that the variables of gender and of public–private status also influence faculty workload and time allocation. In a multivariate analysis of 1993 national-survey data, Allen (1998) finds that gender is significantly correlated with time devoted to teaching and research: Women spend more time on teaching and less time on research. Such differences are independent of differences by institutional type and field (this is also a dimension of gender variation: Women are more concentrated in institutional types and fields that have heavier teaching loads). Gender influences faculty workload.

Faculty workload is also affected by whether the institution in which they work is public or private. In 1987, classroom hours and contact hours were higher for faculty in public than in private research and doctoral-granting universities: Classroom hours in public research universities were 6.6, compared to 5.9 for privates; classroom hours for public doctoral universities were 8, compared to 6.9 for privates; contact hours in public research universities were 259, compared to 229 for privates; contact hours in public doctoral universities were 285, compared to 201 for privates (Allen, 1994, 1996). The pattern is much the same for 1992 national-survey data on faculty.

So, too, there are differences between publics and privates in the percentage of time spent on research and teaching. In research and doctoral universities, faculty in publics spend a larger percentage of their time on teaching and a lower percentage on research. In 1987, the percentage of time on teaching was 43 percent in public versus 40 percent in private research and 47 percent in public versus 39 percent in private doctoral universities. In 1992, the percentage of time on teaching was 36 percent in public versus 30 percent in private research and 43 percent in public versus 41 percent in private doctoral universities. Similarly, the percentage of time faculty spend on research is greater in privates than in publics. In fact, there is only one sector in which faculty spend more time on research than on teaching: independent research universities in 1992 (39% of their time on research, 30% on teaching). Given the public criticism of public research universities, this is remarkable. It underscores the necessity of disaggregating when examining faculty work, not just by institutional type, but by institutional status.

Summary

These data suggest that the critique of faculty involvement in teaching is way out of proportion to the reality of faculty work. That is the case even when only teaching and research in conventional terms are considered. As I shall indicate subsequently, there are significant changes in production processes within universities that are currently impacting faculty work. Such changes have implications for our understanding of faculty's role in teaching and research, both qualitatively, in terms of the nature of that work, and quantitatively, in terms of the time involved in that work.

CHANGES IN PRODUCTION PROCESSES
WITHIN UNIVERSITIES

In the past twenty years, universities have experienced significant changes in the processes by which they "produce" their teaching and research outcomes. This flies in the face of public mythology surrounding the internal inertia and unresponsiveness of the "ivory tower" to the "real world." However, the reality of universities in the last two decades is that they have increasingly introduced new technologies that have impacted faculty teaching and research. The conduct of teaching (and advising) and of research now involves new technologies that faculty have had to learn and with which they now commonly work. At the same time, the units in which teaching and research are produced have become increasingly complex and variegated. At one time, discipline-based departmental units dominated the university landscape. Now, the terrain is filled with not only such departments, but with interdisciplinary, problem-based centers and institutes that are becoming increasingly central players in teaching and research-production processes. Finally, along with these changes in technology and structure has come a significant change in the configuration of professional personnel in universities. With the changes in production processes have come new professions—growing numbers of personnel who monitor and manage new technologies and who interact with faculty. Each of these changes has changed the role of faculty in ways that are reflected in their daily work lives.

New Technology That Change the Role of Faculty

It is a truism in organizational studies that changing technology affects various and contingent changes in the organization and in the conduct of work within the organization. The truism applies no less to universities and to faculty than to other organizations and employees. Remarkably, this has yet to be understood by most people outside the academy and by many inside as well.

Most observers of and commentators on higher education believe universities are labor intensive and suffer from a "cost disease" (Baumol and Blackman, 1983). That is, the costs of production cannot be reduced by introducing new, labor-saving technologies because higher-education production processes are labor intensive and labor contingent. Classrooms need teachers. Research requires faculty investigators. As the costs of faculty labor keep rising, so do the costs of production.

Many within higher education subscribe to this view in ways that translate into criticism of faculty who are resistant to new technology. Presidents, provosts, deans, and directors of technology complain about faculty who resist change, and innovation. If we are to believe them, the role of faculty has not changed.

Is it true that new technology has not impacted the daily lives of faculty—that their basic role and work remain much the same as before? One easy way to answer this question is to concentrate on the traditional faculty roles of teaching and research. Holding constant these familiar dimensions of faculty's lives, with the introduction and proliferation of new technology, faculty work is in fact changing, at least in its form, in the daily production processes that are attached to teaching and research. The standard national surveys do not enable us to tap into such changes: Questionnaires provide little detail as to faculty's teaching and research activities. Thus, I rely upon other surveys, work that is in progress, and on personal observations.

Teaching, broadly conceived, has always involved not just classroom teaching but class preparation and various forms of student advising and contact. In each of these areas of instructional activity, computers and the Internet have impacted faculty work. It is not that the functions of faculty have changed dramatically. But the forms of instructional work are impacted by new technology.

Obviously, there are still traditional classrooms, with the old technology of chalkboards and overheads. However, classroom teaching and course materials are becoming more sophisticated and complex in ways that translate into new forms of faculty work. From the standpoint of workload, perhaps most important is the fact that such new forms are not replacing the old ones, but instead are layered on top of them, making for more work. Consider the use of Power Point and multimedia approaches to presenting material in class-rooms. Although the majority of faculty may not yet utilize such technology, its use is expanding. More widespread is the practice of putting syllabi and class notes on line, making them available in various forms. Interviews with faculty in science and engineering at eleven public research universities suggest that this is an increasingly common practice (Leslie, Rhoades, and Oaxaca, 1996). Nor is it only a practice at research universities. A 1998 survey of National Education Association (NEA) members in colleges and universities (a few being research universities) revealed that almost 30 percent use a website for their classes (Abacus Associates, 1998; Maitland and Rhoades, 1999). In some settings, this has become a policy governing faculty work. Less common is another practice that is increasingly encouraged as a means for enhancing interaction among faculty and students: the use of Listservs and electronic bulletin boards.

Each of these practices blurs the lines between what is classroom activity and what is preparation and out-of-class contact. Putting class notes and syllabi on line means faculty must prepare them in a form that can be inputted onto the Internet—in a way that reduces or discourages extemporaneous activity sometimes triggered by student questions and/or input. Moreover, it was once students who were responsible for taking notes. Over the past two decades it has become relatively common for class notes to be provided by off-campus companies. Now it is becoming the faculty's responsibility to not only prepare the lecture or seminar, but to prepare the notes for the students in a form that they can use. New technology represents yet another medium through which faculty must interact with students. And with the new technology, the old responsibilities do not die off. Instead, new ones are added on.

Another area of technology's impact on faculty's instructional load is advising. Typically, faculty have at least five office hours per week in which they are available for student consultation, in addition to whatever time they make available by appointment. New technology has expanded that time in ways that essentially mean faculty are "on call," because they are "on line." In interviews with over 400 faculty at 11 public research universities, Larry Leslie and I found a pattern that was nearly universal: Faculty spend an hour or more a day on e-mail, and a substantial proportion of this time is spent interacting with students. Of course, faculty interact with colleagues, and they receive various communications from the administration through e-mail. But a good deal of e-mail time is spent setting up appointments with students, responding to their questions, and advising them. Such consultation is "hidden," in that it is not formally set-aside time. Faculty check their e-mail upon coming into the office and then repeatedly check it throughout the day. Again, this time is layered on top of the traditional forms (such as office hours) through which faculty interact with students.

The introduction of new technology into higher education has also impacted faculty's conduct and dissemination of research. Here the differences are not so much a matter of layering on new responsibilities in addition to old ones. Rather, faculty are required to master new technologies to perform their ongoing research activities. One obvious example of such changes is the library system of most campuses, which has become computerized. Libraries have become more sophisticated in their technology, such as making databases available online. The amount of data available through governmental and private sources online is proliferating. Such changes have altered the work of those faculty who conduct library and archive-based research. It has also enabled and facilitated the research of those who gather documentary and archival data in the field. For faculty in engineering and science, technological changes are even more dramatic. Some scientists and engineers that I have interviewed suggest that computers represent a basic addition to and change in the experimental method. Thus, there are geologists who go not so much into the field as into the virtual world.

The changes identified above represent technological changes that impact the process of gathering data. There are also significant changes that computers have effected in the analysis of data due to their ability to conduct sophisticated calculations. With each advance, faculty retrain themselves in new data-analysis software packages.

Further, new technologies have broadened the scope of faculty's "invisible college" in conducting research. With e-mail, collaborations across state and national borders have been facilitated. By virtue of making connections with any university in the world immediate, new information technologies have enabled and encouraged the growth of collaborations across greater geographical distances. In subtle, powerful ways such collaborations impact faculty work. It has long been known that faculty have mixed loyalties between the local campus and their national professional peers. E-mail expands the invisible college of professional peers to encompass the world.

Finally, in the past two decades new technologies have impacted how research is written up. Not fifteen years ago, when I started as a faculty member, our college and department had manuscript typists, secretaries responsible for typing up faculty manuscripts. Now faculty prepare their own manuscripts on their computers. Faculty have had to train themselves on not just word processing, but on all the tools that accompany the preparation of manuscripts. Technology has reshaped the research production process, from beginning to end.

New Production Units That Change the Role of Faculty

The production process is changing by virtue not just of technological change, but of changing the structures within which teaching and research are produced. The scale of these structural changes is such that some scholars write of a "new mode of production" (Gibbons et al., 1994). This new mode is characterized by interdisciplinary organizational sites that are focused on a context of application, and of solving real-world problems. Such sites represent a direct contrast to the traditional mode of production, which is concentrated in discipline-based departments, the work of which is driven by the academic imperatives of the disciplines. Within universities, they take the form of centers and institutes that draw on faculty from various discipline-based departments. Such units are more likely than traditional departments to be linked in a variety of ways to sites outside the university, promoting interaction between faculty and people in the external world. Moreover, such transdisciplinary units are more transient than are departments. Thus, faculty may find themselves combining and recombining in various work teams surrounding particular projects.

The proliferation of interdisciplinary units within universities has been a defining feature of research universities in the 1980s and 1990s (Geiger 1993, 1996). Indeed, the faster growing research universities conduct more research in centers and institutes than do the slower growing research universities (Stahler and Tash, 1994). Federal agencies that fund research have contributed to this pattern: for example, in the 1980s, an increasingly large proportion of NSF funds went to teams and centers, and a declining proportion (though still the majority) went to individual investigators.

What does this mean for faculty? It means that both the form and function of their research is changing. To the extent that research monies are concentrated more and more on interdisciplinary teams, the pressure is for faculty to work more and more in cooperative groups with other academics. To the extent that these cooperative units link up more and more with organizations external to the university, the pressure is for faculty to work more and more with people outside the university. To the extent that research monies are concentrated more and more on "useful" research that is oriented to practical outcomes, the pressure is for faculty to reorient their research to uses that are relevant to the external world. Each of these pressures pushes faculty beyond the confines of their discipline and their "ivory tower." The more that these new patterns of research production take hold, the less that faculty can follow old patterns of work.

As with research, so with teaching. However, the pattern in teaching is much less pronounced. To the extent that research centers and institutes are involved in instructional activity, it is largely graduate education. Overwhelmingly, undergraduate teaching continues to take place within traditional, discipline-based departments. Yet even in this regard, the development of new modes of production of research leads to changes in the role of faculty. As individual faculty get pulled into various centers and institutes for their research and graduate instruction, the task of (re)organizing and undertaking reform initiatives in undergraduate education becomes more complicated, and the task of staffing undergraduate courses also becomes more complicated by the increased growth of specialization within and across the disciplines.

If the growth of interdisciplinary units in undergraduate education has been far less pronounced (and studied) than the proliferation of interdisciplinary research units, the 1980s nevertheless saw an increase in interdisciplinary instructional units. The most obvious examples are ethnic and women's studies programs and departments that draw on the faculty resources of various other programs and departments. The implication for the role of faculty is that there are growing numbers of faculty with multiple ties and affiliations *within* the university—faculty who are connected in their teaching as well as research responsibilities to more than one academic unit.

Changes in the Professional Work Force That Change the Role of Faculty

There is yet another way in which the production process in universities is changing, thereby impacting the role of faculty. The configuration of the professional work force on campus is changing substantially. To some extent, these changes are linked to the types of technological changes referred to above. In addition, however, the changes are linked to the changing functions and activities of universities and their faculty, discussed in the next section of the chapter. In any case, the changes mean the emergence and proliferation of nonfaculty, professional workers and of new categories of employees. This, in turn, means a whole new set of social relationships in which faculty find themselves involved.

With technological change has come substantial changes in the work force of universities mainly in two ways. First, there are ever increasing numbers of nonfaculty professionals. Second, a new category of worker—the technician—is emerging, with which existing professionals, faculty and nonfaculty alike, must interact.

Twenty-five years ago, faculty represented nearly two-thirds of the professional workers on campuses nationwide. Today, that proportion has dropped to just over half the professional workforce (Rhoades, 1998b). What accounts for such a change? In part, it is a function of the growing ranks of administrators. From 1975 to the present, the growth rate of administrative positions outpaced that of faculty positions. However, the major growth category of professional employee during this time period has been "other professionals," "support professionals," or what I have called "managerial professionals" (Rhoades, 1998b). These employees are not administrators, but are closely linked to management in their work days, contracts, and conditions of work. At the same time, though not faculty, they follow the faculty model of professionalization in their professional associations, journals, and technical bodies of knowledge. From 1975 to 1985, these managerial professionals grew in numbers at a rate ten times that of faculty. From 1985 to 1990, their numbers grew at a rate three times that of faculty. What does that mean for faculty work? Apart from the obvious work-force implications—trading off the hiring of more managerial professionals for less faculty—the implication of growing numbers of nonfaculty professionals is that increasingly faculty must interact with these professionals in their daily work lives. Indeed, faculty find themselves working in an increasingly interdependent environment. Ever-increasing numbers of managerial professionals do work that directly involves faculty. For example, as the use of innovative instructional technologies and distance education expands, faculty production of teaching increasingly involves working with professionals who specialize in the construction and delivery of these new modalities of teaching and learning. Faculty cannot perform all the new functions involved in delivering instruction with technology. They need the support, assistance, and the expertise of other professionals. Other examples abound in the area not just of instructional but of new information (and research) technology. Faculty no longer conduct their work as lone professionals. And increasingly, the conduct of that work involves the support, expertise and even the monitoring of other professionals—most campuses, for example, now have some variation of teaching centers and assessment centers that gather data on and provide advice and support for improving teaching.

It is not just other professionals with whom faculty increasingly must interact and upon whom they increasingly depend. It is growing numbers of technicians who monitor and manipulate new technologies. There was a time when the distinction between white- and blue-collar work, between mental and manual labor, made not only analytical sense, but concrete sense in the real world. That is no longer the case. Today, there are large numbers of occupations and employees who fall betwixt and between the categories of mental and manual labor. Their work combines significant analytical (mental) components, and accompanying educational requirements, with considerable sensory–motor (manual) components, with the accompanying importance of contextual experience. These skills are combined into a new archetype occupation: the technician (Barley 1996b). In Barley's words, "As advanced technologies infuse technical content into traditional jobs, more and more work is likely to come to resemble the work of a technician" (1996a: 41). The percentage of positions in the national work force classified as technicians has expanded significantly.

As with the national work force, so with the university work force. At one time, within universities there were essentially faculty and administrators, the (white-collar) professionals, and clerical, maintenance, and trades personnel, the (blue-collar) workers. Not so anymore. Today, there are rapidly growing numbers of technicians, and their work intersects with that of faculty, whether in faculty's research labs, in the classrooms and computer labs, or in faculty offices.

Summary

Over time, universities have become more complex, in terms of their technology, their organizational structures, and their professional work force. With that growing complexity has come growing interdependence. So it is with most organizations, and so it is with universities. The myth about universities is that they are slow to change, and that they are isolated and insulated from developments and demands in the external world. The reality of universities is quite the contrary. New technologies have been introduced, impacting the daily work of faculty. Various new sorts of structures and units have been created to better articulate with the external world. Such structures reflect the emergence of new functions and partnerships taken on by the university. In turn, that has meant the emergence of new roles and realities for faculty. Finally, the proliferation of new professionals and technicians has meant for faculty a more interdependent and collective production process.

CONCLUSION: CHANGING UNIVERSITIES CHANGE THE ROLE OF FACULTY

In the past two decades, universities have changed significantly, in their management and in their functions. The external challenges confronted by central administrations throughout the country, in both public and private institutions, have led to an increased centralization of management, as presidents, provosts, vice presidents, and deans have struggled to address criticisms regarding tuition, quality and relevance of teaching and curricula, and workload and productivity of the faculty. Heightened demands for accountability and economic relevance and reduced levels of state support for higher education have led universities to develop new structures and functions, layered on top of the old. Today, most campuses have offices devoted to various accountability demands, from risk management to affirmative action to institutional research and assessment. Similarly, most public universities today are undertaking significant fundraising and development efforts, whereas such activity in the public sector was limited in the early 1980s. Moreover, many universities have developed various structures to intersect more effectively with the private sector, from advisory boards in various colleges to technology-transfer offices geared to getting commercially relevant faculty research from the labs to the marketplace.

Could such changes occur without substantially impacting the role of faculty? To those who are critical of intransigent faculty, the answer is yes. Thus, despite the magnitude of such changes in universities, Massy and Zemsky (1994) characterize the principal process related to faculty work as an academic ratchet, in which a strong faculty systematically wrench the system from below to further their purposes: researching more and teaching less, hiring more faculty, and reducing instructional workload. From a different theoretical vantage point, the answer is also yes. Institutional theory holds that the formal structures of an organization (in this case, the administration and bureaucratic structures of the university) protect and enable the preservation of the ongoing technical activities of the organization, as they are patterned by professionals (Meyer and Rowan, 1977; Meyer and Scott, 1983; Powell and DiMaggio, 1991). The formal structures of an organization may change even as the technical activities of professionals within the organization persist. In this schema, faculty are buffered from the external world by adjustments in the formal structure of the university.

There is too much evidence to the contrary to accept either of the above views. I have already drawn on data to demonstrate that rather than faculty ratcheting the system, quite the contrary holds true: Faculty are being ratcheted by external and internal pressures (Rhoades, Leslie, and Oaxaca, 1999). Instructional time exceeds research time even in research universities, and the pressure to teach more, teach better, and adopt technological innovations has increased throughout the 1990s. As for being buffered from external pressures by the university's formal structures, the evidence again leads to the opposite conclusion.

Structural changes in universities are transforming faculty's teaching and research, and are pushing faculty well beyond these traditional roles. External forces that lead universities to become more managerial and to increasingly emphasize accountability translate into increased demands on faculty. External forces that lead universities to become more market oriented and to focus on revenue generation translate into demands for faculty to orient their teaching and research more towards external, commercial concerns, and for them to take on new, entrepreneurial roles.

At one and the same time, faculty are being told to be more productive, and they are being forced to spend more time proving that they are productive. The productivity paradox is multifaceted. The press for increased instructional productivity promotes larger classes. Yet there is also a press for faculty to spend more individualized time with students in one on one settings. Moreover, there is a press for faculty to take on a new role vis-à-vis students—that of mentor. That role demands not just quantitatively more individualized interaction with and support of students, but qualitatively different sorts of interaction that move faculty–student relations into sensitive affective domains at the same time that faculty must be more aware of not crossing certain interpersonal boundaries. As these demands on instructional effort increase, of course, faculty are expected to maintain and indeed to increase their scholarly output. No time trade-off is allowed. Finally, in the third main domain of faculty activity—service—there are also at the same time increased demands. More and more faculty are being required to not only engage in professional service—largely within the academy—but to perform outreach that takes them into the external community. In an increasingly managed university, faculty are being asked to spend more time in more arenas of work.

Amidst these pressures to increase productivity across the board, faculty are in work places where their work is monitored more, individually and collectively. Faculty have long been evaluated as individuals. Yet the timing of the individual evaluation of faculty has been stepped up. More of them are done, and with the advent of processes such as posttenure review, the complexity and the time demands embedded in these evaluations have been heightened. It is not just that faculty's instructional activity, including student evaluations, now count for more in the faculty evaluation process. It is that more goes into the dossier that is reviewed. For example, there is growing emphasis on peer review of classroom activities. Syllabi, exams, examples of student work, letters from students, and even videotapes may be included in the dossier. And it is becoming more common for faculty to speak to the extent to which they have incorporated innovations—often meaning utilizing technology—into their teaching. Much time and effort goes into preparing, not to mention reviewing, these dossiers.

But more than just the review of individual faculty in the managed university, data on faculty productivity and evaluation in departments are being gathered and reported, in some cases to assess and demonstrate quality, and in other cases, to guide internal budgetary allocations. Thus, the review of faculty in collectivities—generally departments—is becoming a more common dimension of university life. And each such review places further demands on faculty to record and report their activities in standardized formats, both as individuals and in faculty committees. Assessment, then, can be seen as a considerable encumbrance on faculty time, not just in their role as an individual being reviewed, but in their service role as evaluators–assessors.

New and expanded roles for faculty stem not just from the managerial university and its push for accountability, but from the market-oriented university that focuses on connections to the private sector and on revenue generation. In their teaching and research, faculty are being encouraged to make their work relevant to the private sector. In teaching, this may mean revising and developing courses and curricula that articulate more clearly with the world of work. For example, our study of eleven public research universities (Leslie, Rhoades, and Oaxaca, 1996) found that a great majority of science and engineering departments had implemented or were planning master's degrees focused on preparing students for private sector employment. Such efforts marked a significant shift in the orientation of these graduate departments, a shift also evident in the research activity of faculty. The 1980s and 1990s have witnessed a "renorming" of faculty and of universities, with growing emphasis on commercially relevant research, at the institutional and state levels, and at the level of funding agencies that support academic science and technology (Slaughter and Rhoades, 1990, 1993, 1996). Such pressures have meant that in addition to conducting research oriented to publication, faculty have increasingly been encouraged to do work oriented to the marketplace and to revenue generation. Such encouragement and pursuit of commercially exploitable knowledge have led to contests over faculty's and universities' ownership of intellectual property (Rhoades and Slaughter, 1991a).

These changes go beyond the addition of particular roles for faculty and additions to their workload. They go to the heart of the definition and purposes of universities, and therefore of faculty. When everyone is a customer and/or a consumer, education, and the faculty, are commodified. As a faculty member, I am now not principally an intellectual but an economic being. In my teaching I am now focused not on intellectual development but on preparation for employment. In my connections to alumni, I am now not a concerned professor following up with my students, but a fund-raiser, expected to play a role in the capital campaign of my university by tapping my former students. In my research activities I am pursuing discoveries not to advance knowledge in the public domain but to pursue economic interests in the private marketplace. Moreover, I am now an entrepreneur, seeking venture capital from foundations and corporations and private parties to support revenue generating activities. And in cultivating connections in the community I seek to engage in outreach as a service not for free, but for a fee. In this configuration of values, the public interest is served by professors working not as a public servants in an institution oriented to knowledge growth, but as private entrepreneurs in an enterprise oriented to revenue generation (Rhoades and Slaughter, 1991b).

With the changes described above, the increasingly managed and market-oriented university becomes an increasingly internally divided university (Rhoades, 1998a). Over time, the gap between salaries of faculty in different fields has increased. So, too, has the gap between faculty in different employment categories. At one time, not too long ago, the overwhelming majority of faculty were full time and on the tenure track. One of the most dramatic changes in the faculty role over the past two decades has been the substantial shift away from this standard role (Breneman and Leslie, 1999). In some sense the growth of other categories of faculty (off the tenure track) renders the tenure debate (if the reader will forgive the pun) "academic."

Not only are the numbers of part-time faculty increasing—to about 43 percent of all faculty—but so are the numbers of full-time faculty who are not on the tenure track. As a result, the collective context of the faculty, and of institutional life, is undermined.

In closing, I want to come full circle—back to the classroom and to the students, who, like faculty, are an increasingly complex and stratified body. As faculty salaries are stratified by field, so, too, student career earnings are stratified and correlated with differences in students' race, class, and gender. Although the student body today represents a richer mix of ethnicities, for example, the preponderance of students of color (and of so-called first generation students and female students) are concentrated within a few fields in the university. On top of these variations by student demographic characteristics are increased variation in age and in attendance status, with the student profile getting older and including more part-time students.

In short, the role of faculty has been changing significantly in recent years and not in the ways that the public debate features. The technologies that faculty use to conduct their work have changed. The units in which they work have changed. The range of professionals and technicians with whom they interact has changed. The organizations in which they work have changed. And the clientele that they teach has changed. Such developments have led to heightened demands on the traditional faculty roles of teaching and research, the transformation of these roles, and the addition of new roles that fundamentally alter the work and overall role of faculty.

BIBLIOGRAPHY

Abacus Associates. 1998. *A Survey of Higher Education Members and Leaders.* Washington, D.C.: National Education Association.

Allen, Henry L. 1998. Faculty Workload and Productivity: Gender Comparisons. In *The NEA 1998 Almanac of Higher Education.* Washington, D.C.: National Education Association, 29–44.

———. 1996. Faculty Workload and Productivity in the 1990s: Preliminary Findings. In *The NEA 1996 Almanac of Higher Education.* Washington, D.C.: National Education Association, 21–34.

———. 1994. Workload and Productivity in an Accountability Era. In *The NEA 1994 Almanac of Higher Education.* Washington, D.C.: National Education Association, 25–38.

Barley, Stephen R. 1996a. *The New World of Work.* London: British–North American Committee.

———. 1996b. Technicians in the Workplace: Ethnographic Evidence for Bringing Work into Organization Studies. *Administrative Science Quarterly* 41:3, 404–441.

Baumol, W., and S.A.B. Blackman. 1983. Electronics, the Cost Disease, and the Operation of Libraries. *Journal of the American Society for Information Sciences* 34, 181–191.

Bellas, Marcia L. 1994. Comparable Worth in Academia: The Effect on Faculty Salaries of the Sex Composition and Labor Market Conditions of Academic Disciplines. *American Sociological Review* 59:6, 807–821.

Breneman, David W., and David W. Leslie. 1999. The Other Faculty. Paper presented at the annual meeting of the American Association for the Advancement of Science, January, Anaheim, California.

Fairweather, James. 1997. The Relative Value of Teaching and Research. In *The NEA 1997 Almanac of Higher Education.* Washington, D.C.: National Education Association, 43–62.

———. 1996. *Faculty Work and Public Trust: Restoring the Value of Teaching and Public Service in American Academic Life.* Boston: Allyn and Bacon.

Finkelstein, Martin. 1995. College Faculty as Teacher. In *The NEA 1995 Almanac of Higher Education.* Washington, D.C.: National Education Association, 33–48.

Fulton, Oliver, and Martin Trow. 1974. Research Activity in Higher Education. *Sociology of Education* 47, 29–73.

Geiger, Roger. 1996. Making the Grade: Institutional Enhancement of Research Competitiveness. In *Competitiveness in Academic Research,* ed. Albert H. Teich. New York: American Association for the Advancement of Science, 113–136.

———. 1993. *Research and Relevant Knowledge: American Research Universities since World War II*. New York: Oxford University Press.

Gibbons, Michael; Camille Limoges; Helga Nowotny; Simon Schwartzman; Peter Scott; and Martin Trow. 1994. *The New Production of Knowledge: The Dynamics of Science and Research in Contemporary Societies*. London: Sage.

Konrad, Alison M., and Jeffrey Pfeffer. 1990. Do You Get What You Deserve?: Factors Affecting the Relationship between Productivity and Pay. *Administrative Science Quarterly* 35:2, 258–285.

Leslie, Larry L.; Gary Rhoades; and Ronald Oaxaca. 1996. Research Related Revenues and Undergraduate Education in Public Research Universities. Grant funded by the National Science Foundation.

Maitland, Christine, and Gary Rhoades. 1999. Technology Issues in Bargaining: The New Unionism. *The NEA 1999 Almanac of Higher Education*. Washington, D.C.: National Education Association, 55–70.

Massy, William F., and Robert Zemsky. 1994. Faculty Discretionary Time: Departments and the "Academic Ratchet." *The Journal of Higher Education* 65:1, 1–22.

Meyer, John W., and Brian Rowan. 1977. Institutionalized Organizations: Formal Structure as Myth and Ceremony. *American Journal of Sociology* 83, 340–363.

Meyer, John W., and W. Richard Scott, eds. 1983. *Organizational Environments: Ritual and Rationality*. Beverly Hills: Sage.

Powell, Walter W., and Paul DiMaggio, eds. 1991. *The New Institutionalism in Organizational Analysis*. Chicago: University of Chicago Press.

Rhoades, Gary. 1998a. *Managed Professionals: Unionized Faculty and Restructuring Academic Labor*. Albany: State University of New York Press.

———. 1998b. Reviewing and Rethinking Administrative Costs. In *Higher Education: Handbook of Theory and Research*, ed. John C. Smart. New York: Agathon, 111–147.

Rhoades, Gary; Larry L. Leslie; and Ronald Oaxaca. 1999. Who's Ratcheting Whom? Paper presented at the annual meeting of the American Association for the Advancement of Science, January, Anaheim, California.

Rhoades, Gary, and Sheila Slaughter. 1991a. Professors, Administrators, and Patents: The Negotiation of Technology Transfer. *Sociology of Education* 64:2, 65–77.

———. 1991b. The Public Interest and Professional Labor: Research Universities. In *Culture and Ideology in Higher Education: Advancing a Critical Agenda*, ed. William G. Tierney. New York: Praeger, 187–211.

Slaughter, Sheila, and Gary Rhoades. 1996. The Emergence of a Competitiveness Research and Development Policy Coalition and the Commercialization of Academic Science and Technology. *Science, Technology, and Human Values* 21:3, 303–339.

———. 1993. Changes in Intellectual Property Statutes and Policies at a Public University: Revising the Terms of Professional Labor. *Higher Education* 26, 287–312.

———. 1990. Renorming the Social Relations of Academic Science. *Educational Policy* 4, 4: 341–361.

Stahler, G. J., and W. R. Tash. 1994. Center and Institutes in the Research University: Issues, Problems, and Prospects. *The Journal of Higher Education* 65:5, 540–554.

Zemsky, Robert; William F. Massy; and P. Oedel. 1993. On Reversing the Ratchet. *Change* 25, 56–62.

3

Higher Education Spending: Assessing Policy Priorities

Joseph Losco and Brian L. Fife

Every September, the College Board issues a report on the cost of a year of college education.[1] The public reaction is typically quite predictable: sticker shock. The price of a college degree has grown consistently above the average level of inflation since the 1960s, with the most significant increases in the 1980s. Since 1980, the dollar cost for tuition at all types of institutions of higher education has tripled. Even controlling for inflation, the price of a college education doubled since 1980, making education costs rise faster than the cost of virtually all other consumer goods and services, rivaling the dramatic increases in the cost of medical care over this period (National Commission on the Cost of Higher Education, 1998: 160–161 [hereinafter referred to as NCCHE]). At the same time, the ability of average Americans to pay for higher education diminished, as wages, especially for low-skill workers, stagnated or decreased. Those who can most benefit from a college education are finding it is most inaccessible. Ironically, while twentieth-century citizens witnessed a democratization of higher education as it ceased to remain the prerogative of a wealthy elite, increases in the price of attaining a college degree threaten to reverse this trend at the dawn of the new millennium.

College officials are quick to point out that not everyone pays the sticker price for tuition. Scholarships, grants, and other types of financial aid reduce the "net" price for many attendees. In fact, during the 1995–1996 academic year, 66 percent of four-year students in public institutions and 63 percent of two-year students in public institutions received some form of financial aid. The figure for private institutions was 80 percent at four-year schools and 82 percent for two-year schools (NCCHE, 1998: 3). Still, after factoring in the impact of aid, the total price of attending college at public four-year institutions increased by 95 percent from 1987 to 1996. The figure was 64 percent for private four-year colleges and 169 percent for public two-year institutions (NCCHE, 1998: 7).[2]

Exacerbating the problem of rising costs was the fact that in the 1980s and early 1990s state spending for public higher education fell. Between 1984 and 1994, government appropriations per full-time equivalent (FTE) students at public universities fell both in constant dollars, from $8,327 to $7,393, and as a share of all revenues, from 53 percent to 42 percent (U.S. Department of Education, 1997a: 172). As a result, tuition and fees per FTE increased at all types of institutions of higher education, although increases at private institutions were much steeper. Some states have more recently increased spending for higher education, beginning to make up for ground lost in the 1980s when funding levels diminished. Yet, the cost of educating the college population continues to rise faster than the willingness or ability of the nation to pay for it. Recent trends in federal financing also reveal less willingness to support higher education as a social good and greater reliance on individual initiative in paying one's way (see discussion by Parsons, this volume). These features of the financial landscape of American higher education have led some researchers examining college spending and funding patterns to conclude that our "present course . . . is unsustainable" (Council for Aid to Education, 1997: 1).

The effect of increases in the price of college for the typical American family was dramatic. Between 1980 and 1995, tuition, room, and board at public institutions increased from 11 percent to 15 percent of median family income. This increase was larger for lower-income families whose incomes failed to keep pace with the cost of living generally. It increased from 22 percent to 32 percent for families at the twentieth percentile of family income compared to an increase of from 7 percent to 9 percent for families at the eightieth percentile. The pattern of increases at private institutions was comparable but steeper, as tuition, room, and board rose to 42 percent of median family income over this period (U.S. Department of Education, 1997b: 50–51).

Public reaction to this set of conditions has begun to mount. While 75 percent of Americans surveyed said they believed college education was necessary "to get ahead in life," 40 percent said the cost of a college education today is not justified by what people get out of it (*The New York Times*, August 31, 1997). Parents' groups like College Parents of America have begun to organize to pressure government officials to devise ways to curb costs. Congress responded in 1996 by forming a special commission to investigate rising costs. The question, it seems, more and more Americans are beginning to ask is, "Where does all the money go?" Presumably, an answer to this question could lead to meaningful cost containment.

As will become apparent, the range of higher-education institutions in the United States is diverse, and spending patterns will diverge on the basis of institutional mission and populations served. Still, it is possible to describe a range of spending patterns both for the higher education community in general and for a subset of institutions to which we will pay special attention. Once patterns of spending can be identified, policy questions can be raised regarding the means of controlling these in order to make higher education a commodity that is within the reach of a majority of Americans in the twenty-first century.

THE COSTS OF HIGHER EDUCATION

Controlling for inflation by utilizing the Consumer Price Index (the conventional measure of inflation), college costs[3] have increased at more than double the inflation rate since the 1970s. Educators prefer, however, to use an alternative tool, the Higher Education Price Index (HEPI), in measuring the effects of inflation. This measure takes into consideration rises in the costs of a typical market basket of educational goods, including utilities, facilities, personnel costs, and campus services. Even if this measure developed by educators (and much more friendly to their interests) is used, however, the cost for providing a college education has consistently outpaced inflation. The Council for Aid to Education (CAE) has determined that between 1980 and 1995, the annual average rate of growth in the costs of providing higher education (as measured by the HEPI) exceeded the general rate of inflation by a full percentage point. The greatest increase in costs occurred over the years 1983–1984 and 1985–1986 when total spending per student rose at 7 percent per year above inflation (Getz and Siegfried, 1991: 323). According to the CAE, while college spending slowed slightly since 1995, the rate of spending is still likely to continue to outpace inflation for the foreseeable future (CAE, 1997: 10).

College spending actually increased at a higher rate during the boom years of the 1960s than in recent years, but at that time, there was a burgeoning student population to absorb unit costs. For example, spending in the second half of the 1960s increased by an average of 12 percent per year, but per student spending grew by only 3 percent. By contrast, between 1975 and 1980, overall spending grew at a somewhat more moderate rate, but declining student population resulted in increased per pupil spending. From 1980 to 1985, overall spending and per-pupil expenditures grew at roughly the same rates (Hauptman and Merisotis, 1990: 41). Similar though less dramatic growth at private institutions during this period led to corresponding increases in per-pupil spending, but the decline in enrollments in the private sector in recent years has not been as dramatic as in the public sector (Snyder and Galambos, 1988: 4; Hauptman and Merisotis, 1990: 45).

One way to approach an understanding of "where the money goes" is to examine summary figures on broad areas of institutional expenditure. The U.S. Department of Education receives data from all postsecondary institutions including colleges and universities as well as technical and vocational schools. The current data collection system, IPEDS (Integrated Postsecondary

Education Data System), began in 1986, replacing and expanding an earlier system called Higher Education General Information Survey (HEGIS), which dated back to 1966. Categories used in the collection of financial data have been revised several times over the history of these surveys. However, beginning in 1974, the Department of Education has employed the standard categories for reporting financial data outlined by the National Association of College and University Business Officers, yielding comparable data at least from the period of 1977 to the present. The categories utilized to collect data are defined in Appendix A.

For the purposes of this chapter, we focus exclusively on four year institutions of higher education. While the two-year market is important and growing, there are a host of vocational issues associated with their operation that complicate their study. In addition, these institutions have not borne the type of criticism for cost increases that have accompanied discussion of more traditional four-year institutions. As will shortly be demonstrated, given the diversity of educational institutions in America, even the four-year market needs to be segmented by university mission and population in order to insure accurate evaluation.

IPEDS and HEGIS figures illustrate that instruction predictably accounts for the largest percentage of total spending (total current fund expenditures and transfers—see Appendix A). Additional spending varies by type of institution, with public and private doctoral universities expending a higher percentage on research while four-year colleges spend varying amounts on research, scholarships, and operations. Yet, while spending increased in almost all categories between 1977 and 1995, increases were smallest in traditional areas of instruction, libraries, and plant operations (see Getz and Siegfried, 1991: 298). Important differences surface, however, when we distinguish among types of institution. Included in Table 3.1 are the relevant data on expenditures per FTE.

Although the dollar amount of instructional expenditures per FTE increased between 1977 and 1995, instructional spending as a percentage of total expenditures fell at public universities (from 38.6 to 35.4), public four-year colleges (from 45.1 to 41.8) and private four-year colleges (from 37.3 to 32.3). Instructional spending as a percentage of total spending at private universities increased marginally over this period from 38 percent to 38.3 percent. Expenditures for research increased by 22 percent in dollar figures at private universities but fell in relation to other expenditure categories by over 3 percent. Research spending at public universities took up a larger fraction of expenditures rising from approximately 18 percent in 1977 to over 22 percent in 1994. Scholarships,[4] mandatory transfers,[5] administration, and public service accounted for the largest increases at private universities, followed in order by spending for instruction and student services. Decreases came in research, operations, and libraries. At public universities, spending increased most for research, scholarships, administration, and mandatory transfers. Per-

Table 3.1
Educational and General Expenditures by Institution Type per FTE Student

Private Universities

	Instruction	Administration	Student Services	Research	Libraries	Public Service	Operations	Scholarships	Mandatory Transfers
% Distribution 1995	38.3	13.7	3.6	17.9	3.3	2.7	7.1	11.6	1.9
% Change 1977-1995	+.3	+.5	+.3	-3.2	-.9	+.5	-1.7	+3.5	+.8

Public Universities

	Instruction	Administration	Student Services	Research	Libraries	Public Service	Operations	Scholarships	Mandatory Transfers
% Distribution 1995	35.4	13.3	3.7	22.3	3.0	8.1	7.0	5.7	1.5
% Change 1977-1995	-3.6	+.3	0	+3.9	-.5	0	-2.1	+1.7	+.3

Private 4 Year Colleges

	Instruction	Administration	Student Services	Research	Libraries	Public Service	Operations	Scholarships	Mandatory Transfers
% Distribution 1995	32.3	20.1	8.7	4.3	2.8	3.9	8.1	17.6	2.2
% Change 1977-1995	-5.0	-.3	+1.3	-.7	-1.1	+1.5	-3.1	+7.6	-.1

Public 4 Year Colleges

	Instruction	Administration	Student Services	Research	Libraries	Public Service	Operations	Scholarships	Mandatory Transfers
% Distribution 1995	41.8	18.8	6.1	10.1	3.0	4.5	8.7	5.1	1.9
% Change 1977-1995	-4.6	+2.1	+.3	+3.1	-.9	+1.6	-2.8	+1.2	-.1

Sources: The figures for 1977 to 1994 were derived from the U.S. Department of Education, *The Condition of Education 1997*. Washington, D.C.: U.S. Government Printing Office. Figures may not total 100 percent due to rounding. Figures for 1995 emanated from a preliminary report of the U.S. Department of Education, *Preliminary Report on the Condition of Education 1998*. http://nces.ed.gov/pubs98/condition98/index.html.

Note: The Higher Education Price Index was used to calculate constant dollars. This may understate the rise in costs.

centage decreases occurred for instruction, operations, and libraries. Private four-year colleges experienced the highest gains in scholarships, public service, and student services. Allocation decreases occurred in instruction, operations, libraries, research, administration and mandatory transfers. Public four-year colleges experienced the largest growth in research, administration, public service, scholarships, and student services, with decreases in allocation distributions for instruction, operations, libraries, and mandatory transfers.

Our analysis of the macrolevel data from IPEDS for the period from 1977 to 1995 confirms the findings of Getz and Siegfried in their study, which stops in 1988: "The most obvious trend in expenditure patterns is the declining importance of the core areas of a college or university—instruction, academic support and plant operations" (1991: 298). By way of contrast, the evidence points to college-supported financial aid, research, public service, and administration as among the fastest-growing cost components.

As the data suggest, however, differences in spending patterns arise with regard to type of institution, that is, whether it is public or private, a comprehensive university, or a four-year college. Because these categories themselves may mask more important differences on the basis of university mission and populations served, it is necessary to refine the analysis further by examining more coherent institutional categories.

AN EXAMINATION OF SELECT
CARNEGIE INSTITUTIONS

The Carnegie Foundation for the Advancement of Teaching, beginning in 1970, created categories of similar institutions of higher education based on several criteria: the highest level of degree offering, the number of degrees conferred by discipline, and the amount of federal support for research received by the institution. There are currently eleven categories in the new classification scheme; we examine doctoral-lending institutions in this section only. While there are only 236 institutions in these categories (out of about 3,600 institutions in the United States), they account for 26.1 percent of all students in higher education (almost 4 million people). This is the second largest category, only behind associate of arts colleges (42.8%). In addition, the total budgets of the doctorate-granting institutions are significantly larger than all other institutional types (master's colleges and universities, baccalaureate colleges, associate of arts colleges, specialized institutions, and tribal colleges and universities) (Carnegie Foundation, 1998). Simply put, the executive leaders of these institutions exert a tremendous amount of political, economic, and social power and truly play an instrumental role in molding and shaping the politics of higher education. There are four such categories using this system: Carnegie 11–Research Universities I, Carnegie 12–Research Universities II, Carnegie 13–Doctoral Universities I, and Carnegie 14–Doctoral Universities II (see Appendix B for a more detailed discussion). Bear in mind that both public and private institutions are included in this category. Thus, there are eight different groupings of higher education institutions employed in this analysis. Included in Appendix C is a complete list of institutions in each category.

The Data

Data for this analysis only exist from 1988–1989 through 1994–1995 (U.S. Department of Education, 1998a). Thus, the time-series analysis is limited, though it appears that the IPEDS finance data will be updated on an annual basis by the Department of Education, which will certainly facilitate further empirical inquiry into higher-education spending.

There are fourteen variables included in the IPEDS finance data related to expenditures and transfers: total current expenditures and transfers; instruction; research; public service; academic support; student services; institutional support; operation and maintenance of the physical plant; scholarships and fellowships; mandatory transfers; nonmandatory transfers; auxiliary enterprises; hospitals; and independent operations. Definitions of these categories are available in Appendix A.

Analyzing Budgetary Spending Patterns

In order to compare spending patterns in the Carnegie 11, 12, 13, and 14 institutions (both public and private), simple descriptive statistics can assist in analyzing spending patterns from 1988–1989 to 1994–1995. For each category of expenditures, means and standard deviations were calculated to determine proportionate changes from the first year of data to the last (excluding total expenditures, of course). Included in Tables 3.2 through 3.9 are the mean figures for institutional expenditures, as well as the change in budgetary proportions from 1988–1989 to 1994–1995, for the eight groups in this investigation. The results of four of the variables are not reported in the tables (mandatory and nonmandatory transfers, hospitals, and independent operations). There are two compelling reasons by way of justification. First, many of the institutions, particularly those not in the Carnegie 11 category, do not have hospitals, rendering the statistics in question fairly meaningless. Second, the data for most of the categories were widely dispersed for mandatory transfers, nonmandatory transfers, and independent operations. In many cases, the standard deviation was larger than the mean. Indeed, some institutions allocated relatively nominal amounts in these categories (or in some cases, nothing), while the expenditures for others tallied in the millions of dollars. Thus discernible patterns were most elusive for these variables.

The mean represents the sum of the values of each category divided by the number of values. The standard deviation is the most common measure of dispersion for interval data. It is reflective of the dispersion of data points about the mean. The smaller the standard deviation, the more the data cluster about the mean. The results of this limited time-series analysis suggest that,

Table 3.2
Mean and Proportional Institutional Expenditures, Carnegie 11 Public Institutions

	1988/89		1994/95		
	M	(SD)	*M*	(SD)	% Change
Instruction	140,663,300	(67,282,920)	185,958,600	(82,602,940)	
	26.5%	(5.5)	25.3%	(5.5)	-1.2
Research	92,789,140	(54,564,190)	136,501,300	(79,880,940)	
	17.7%	(7.6)	18.3%	(6.9)	+0.7
Public Service	29,176,910	(23,688,680)	40,908,160	(31,125,370)	
	5.9%	(4.5)	6.0%	(4.3)	+0.1
Academic Support	37,665,380	(24,669,930)	52,345,120	(33,533,630)	
	6.8%	(2.6)	6.8%	(2.2)	0
Student Services	13,462,650	(8,407,796)	18,319,070	(10,024,730)	
	2.7%	(1.5)	2.6%	(1.4)	-0.1
Institutional Support	27,350,700	(16,621,290)	35,577,320	(16,905,570)	
	5.3%	(2.6)	5.0%	(1.8)	-0.3
Physical Plant	28,731,690	(14,060,000)	36,037,300	(16,248,310)	
	5.6%	(2.2)	5.0%	(1.6)	-0.6
Scholarships/Fellowships	21,694,440	(12,574,000)	36,872,450	(20,734,320)	
	4.1%	(1.6)	5.0%	(1.9)	+0.9
Auxiliary Enterprises	52,427,730	(29,781,520)	78,518,820	(54,820,720)	
	10.5%	(5.3)	10.9%	(5.4)	+0.4
Total Expenditures	545,610,200	(276,181,300)	770,296,800	(394,509,500)	

Note: N = 59. Data missing for Rutgers University–New Brunswick (1994–1995).

not surprisingly, incrementalism (see Lindbloom, 1959) is the dominant budgetary mode for the categories of institutions reviewed.

Proportional Changes in Budgetary Expenditures, 1988–1989 to 1994–1995

Since there are eight categories of institutions and nine budgetary expenditures in each, our examination includes seventy-two differential categories in the aggregate. Incrementalism was certainly apparent in that of these seventy-two categories, only twenty-four resulted in a change in excess of 1 percent or higher from 1988–1989 to 1994–1995. The largest proportionate change

Table 3.3
Mean and Proportional Institutional Expenditures, Carnegie 12 Public Institutions

	1988/89		1994/95		
	M	(SD)	M	(SD)	% Change
Instruction	65,498,600	(20,485,030)	88,262,010	(30,924,670)	
	31.5%	(5.3)	31.0%	(6.0)	-0.5
Research	28,197,720	(13,443,780)	41,463,260	(18,921,910)	
	13.7%	(6.3)	14.7%	(6.4)	+1.0
Public Service	13,978,750	(11,428,240)	19,085,650	(14,807,680)	
	6.4%	(4.8)	6.4%	(4.6)	0
Academic Support	16,496,170	(7,557,661)	23,237,400	(10,110,730)	
	7.9%	(2.4)	8.2%	(2.4)	+0.3
Student Services	7,440,199	(3,409,763)	10,761,000	(4,843,045)	
	3.7%	(1.8)	3.9%	(1.9)	+0.2
Institutional Support	15,118,370	(6,596,688)	18,415,530	(7,770,854)	
	7.2%	(2.1)	6.4%	(1.8)	-0.8
Physical Plant	14,527,620	(4,696,410)	16,870,560	(4,903,550)	
	7.0%	(1.6)	5.9%	(.01)	-1.1
Scholarships/Fellowships	11,013,920	(3,303,246)	17,810,390	(4,916,197)	
	5.4%	(1.5)	6.4%	(1.6)	+1.0
Auxiliary Enterprises	29,526,410	(9,351,814)	39,563,280	(12,361,570)	
	14.4%	(4.2)	14.1%	(3.7)	-0.3
Total Expenditures	207,461,500	(48,476,990)	283,605,500	(68,829,450)	

Note: N = 26.

was an increase in mean expenditures for scholarships and fellowships in Carnegie 12 private institutions of 4.2 percent. Yet in two-thirds of all cases, the proportionate change was less than 1 percent. As the IPEDS data set expands longitudinally, however, more consistent budgetary patterns can be assessed over longer periods of time.

DISCUSSION

A comparison of Table 3.1 with Tables 3.2 through 3.9 illustrates that differences in expenditure patterns between the whole universe of higher education institutions and the Carnegie categories we selected for particular attention

Table 3.4
Mean and Proportional Institutional Expenditures, Carnegie 13 Public Institutions

	1988/89		1994/95		
	M	(SD)	*M*	(SD)	% Change
Instruction	47,372,500	(18,308,040)	63,883,270	(21,507,140)	
	35.1%	(10.5)	37.3%	(5.6)	+2.1
Research	6,003,944	(5,350,946)	9,382,081	(6,730,992)	
	4.3%	(4.0)	5.5%	(4.3)	+1.2
Public Service	4,058,401	(5,388,778)	7,251,805	(8,832,604)	
	2.4%	(2.2)	3.9%	(4.4)	+1.5
Academic Support	11,414,560	(5,217,361)	15,236,820	(7,195,712)	
	8.2%	(2.6)	8.4%	(1.8)	+0.2
Student Services	6,156,058	(3,306,265)	8,722,808	(4,357,671)	
	4.5%	(2.5)	5.2%	(2.4)	+0.7
Institutional Support	10,710,960	(6,243,972)	13,891,020	(5,213,721)	
	7.8%	(3.4)	8.0%	(1.3)	+0.2
Physical Plant	9,418,796	(3,980,674)	11,651,400	(4,478,233)	
	7.2%	(2.9)	6.9%	(1.9)	-0.3
Scholarships/Fellowships	7,394,960	(4,079,410)	13,344,620	(5,798,816)	
	5.3%	(2.4)	7.6%	(2.3)	+2.3
Auxiliary Enterprises	19,364,710	(11,877,360)	26,094,960	(16,206,970)	
	14.4%	(7.8)	14.4%	(6.9)	0
Total Expenditures	153,323,300	(95,783,310)	175,781,600	(67,035,830)	

Note: N = 28.

are subtle. Spending for scholarships and research went up for all public Carnegie categories we examined, while public service, student services, and academic support increased in three of the four categories. There was less uniformity in areas where spending went down. Only spending on the operation and maintenance of the physical plant decreased for all categories, while decreases in instruction, institutional support, and auxiliary enterprises went down on average for institutions in three of four categories examined. Among private institutions in these categories, there was less uniformity, with the exception of spending for scholarships, which went up across the board, and spending on institutional support, which went down.

Perhaps the best way to evaluate the data is by focusing on expenditure categories. In our analysis, we will relate our findings from the Carnegie cat-

Table 3.5
Mean and Proportional Institutional Expenditures, Carnegie 14 Public Institutions

	1988/89		1994/95		
	M	(SD)	*M*	(SD)	% Change
Instruction	36,664,590	(23,221,570)	50,117,310	(24,442,520)	
	35.8%	(7.0)	34.4%	(7.3)	-1.4
Research	10,133,250	(10,131,110)	18,046,980	(15,623,420)	
	9.9%	(8.0)	12.0%	(8.3)	+2.1
Public Service	3,898,516	(6,035,791)	6,580,809	(8,859,200)	
	3.2%	(3.4)	3.8%	(3.9)	+0.6
Academic Support	8,385,389	(4,400,541)	13,763,080	(11,745,740)	
	8.4%	(2.4)	8.8%	(2.6)	+0.4
Student Services	4,633,403	(2,420,608)	7,012,893	(3,507,368)	
	4.8%	(1.7)	5.0%	(1.9)	+0.2
Institutional Support	7,723,937	(4,347,384)	11,337,000	(5,593,045)	
	8.0%	(3.1)	7.9%	(2.3)	-0.1
Physical Plant	8,249,045	(4,482,968)	9,993,979	(6,179,821)	
	8.4%	(3.4)	6.7%	(1.9)	-1.7
Scholarships/Fellowships	6,443,900	(3,390,154)	10,869,190	(5,133,495)	
	6.9%	(3.0)	7.8%	(2.3)	+0.9
Auxiliary Enterprises	11,662,770	(8,181,559)	18,216,260	(17,931,970)	
	11.3%	(6.5)	10.9%	(6.2)	-0.4
Total Expenditures	106,024,000	(78,094,770)	156,746,500	(121,646,400)	

Note: N = 38. Data missing for Rutgers University–Newark (1994–1995 and 1988–1989), University of Central Florida (1988–1989), Florida Atlantic University (1988–1989), and Florida International University (1988–1989).

egories we examined to overall patterns in the four-year higher-education universe (Table 3.1) where appropriate. The most significant spending categories will be treated separately, while others will be aggregated.

Instruction

Instruction includes a myriad of activities and expenses comprising the primary mission of the academy. What is most notable from our analysis is that for the majority of categories (five of eight) of higher-education institu-

Table 3.6
Mean and Proportional Institutional Expenditures, Carnegie 11 Private Institutions

	1988/89		1994/95		
	M	(SD)	*M*	(SD)	% Change
Instruction	145,309,500	(87,163,340)	225,113,600	(136,438,500)	
	23.6%	(9.4)	24.4%	(9.8)	+0.8
Research	92,192,790	(60,365,030)	133,053,500	(84,462,860)	
	17.1%	(10.6)	16.5%	(10.4)	-0.6
Public Service	17,334,610	(34,232,510)	18,589,990	(50,111,000)	
	3.3%	(5.9)	2.3%	(5.1)	-1.0
Academic Support	33,164,940	(24,945,260)	41,078,490	(26,668,040)	
	5.9%	(3.8)	5.0%	(2.9)	-0.9
Student Services	12,995,260	(6,330,217)	17,898,980	(9,396,617)	
	2.4%	(1.3)	2.2%	(1.3)	-0.2
Institutional Support	36,714,400	(22,618,420)	53,648,480	(30,507,360)	
	6.5%	(3.1)	6.3%	(2.7)	-0.2
Physical Plant	29,717,550	(16,893,150)	43,490,870	(30,679,010)	
	5.3%	(2.5)	5.1%	(2.7)	-0.2
Scholarships/Fellowships	37,095,400	(20,362,630)	63,527,360	(34,554,000)	
	6.2%	(2.9)	7.2%	(3.2)	+1.0
Auxiliary Enterprises	45,111,240	(30,284,340)	59,431,810	(35,783,580)	
	7.8%	(3.9)	7.1%	(3.5)	-0.7
Total Expenditures	623,413,800	(319,601,200)	924,123,000	(460,812,700)	

Note: N = 29.

tions, the share of expenditures devoted to this mission has fallen, despite the fact that both college costs and prices have risen substantially. For all institutions nationally, instruction expenditures as a percentage of overall spending have either stagnated (private universities) or substantially decreased (a decline of 3.6% of expenditures at public universities and of approximately 5% at public and private four-year colleges—see Table 3.1).

What is most astonishing is that this reduction has occurred as the number of disciplinary specialties and subspecialties has increased at modern universities and colleges. As the National Commission on the Cost of Higher Education notes, "The curriculum has become more specialized and institutions now support disciplines that did not exist a generation or two ago" (1998: 12).

Table 3.7
Mean and Proportional Institutional Expenditures, Carnegie 12 Private Institutions

	1988/89		1994/95		
	M	(SD)	*M*	(SD)	% Change
Instruction	69,267,730	(27,676,190)	102,808,500	(45,595,850)	
	30.3%	(9.0)	28.6%	(5.9)	-1.7
Research	16,361,920	(9,092,945)	28,657,130	(13,931,230)	
	7.9%	(5.8)	9.8%	(5.8)	+1.9
Public Service	2,454,875	(2,082,906)	1,756,535	(2,399,708)	
	0.9%	(0.6)	0.5%	(0.6)	-0.4
Academic Support	9,903,705	(4,680,401)	20,022,540	(11,821,750)	
	4.6%	(1.9)	5.7%	(2.0)	+1.1
Student Services	7,849,907	(6,332,137)	10,765,740	(5,376,046)	
	3.5%	(2.5)	3.3%	(1.7)	-0.2
Institutional Support	17,183,400	(9,843,140)	25,472,480	(9,978,075)	
	7.8%	(4.5)	7.7%	(3.1)	-0.1
Physical Plant	10,590,870	(6,232,296)	17,578,650	(6,546,056)	
	4.7%	(2.5)	5.5%	(2.1)	+0.8
Scholarships/Fellowships	18,416,480	(10,811,250)	40,960,520	(17,919,650)	
	8.6%	(4.6)	12.8%	(5.5)	+4.2
Auxiliary Enterprises	26,371,130	(18,308,710)	45,959,800	(45,133,700)	
	12.0%	(7.5)	12.6%	(9.1)	+0.6
Total Expenditures	236,363,600	(105,182,000)	369,155,500	(188,642,800)	

Note: N = 11.

Meanwhile, the need remains to retain many traditional disciplines as well. Similarly, the amount of remedial coursework has grown to meet the needs of a changing student body. Approximately 78 percent of all colleges and universities offer some type of remedial courses. While it is hard to place a price tag on the cost of remediation, the National Commission on the Cost of Higher Education notes that the costs for such classes in just one state (California) exceed $9 million annually (1998: 10).

One instructional expense that often arises in the minds of taxpayers and public officials alike is the cost of faculty. Since faculty salaries and fringe benefits are included under the category of instruction in the IPEDS data and since we see consistent evidence that this category of spending has decreased

Table 3.8
Mean and Proportional Institutional Expenditures, Carnegie 13 Private Institutions

	1988/89		1994/95		
	M	(SD)	*M*	(SD)	% Change
Instruction	29,677,120	(16,559,840)	43,213,630	(24,990,150)	
	33.8%	(8.8)	32.8%	(7.4)	-1.0
Research	4,025,684	(3,104,981)	5,596,200	(4,456,039)	
	5.0%	(4.2)	4.9%	(4.3)	-0.1
Public Service	1,354,897	(1,070,681)	2,099,148	(3,272,394)	
	1.4%	(1.2)	1.4%	(2.5)	0
Academic Support	7,159,392	(4,974,219)	10,184,320	(7,402,617)	
	8.2%	(3.3)	7.7%	(3.0)	-0.5
Student Services	4,579,999	(2,947,578)	6,848,234	(3,914,189)	
	4.9%	(1.8)	5.4%	(2.0)	+0.5
Institutional Support	11,419,870	(7,190,678)	16,743,980	(11,396,890)	
	14.1%	(6.0)	12.6%	(3.3)	-1.5
Physical Plant	5,935,252	(4,217,396)	9,028,651	(5,711,761)	
	6.5%	(2.7)	6.6%	(2.5)	+0.1
Scholarships/Fellowships	9,458,213	(6,090,107)	18,829,320	(13,116,430)	
	10.9%	(4.3)	13.6%	(5.3)	+2.7
Auxiliary Enterprises	10,254,610	(10,942,560)	13,278,150	(16,034,070)	
	9.3%	(6.5)	8.3%	(5.7)	-1.0
Total Expenditures	99,421,100	(86,252,800)	148,794,100	(130,674,700)	

Note: N = 23. Data missing for Florida Institute of Technology (1988–1989).

in recent years among the majority of Carnegie categories (Carnegie 13 public institutions are the distinct exception here), it appears that faculty salaries have not been a major contributor to cost increases over the period we have examined. This impression is confirmed in the report of the National Commission on the Cost of Higher Education. The commission found that faculty salaries have merely kept pace with inflation among private institutions and have actually decreased in real terms for faculty at public institutions. One reason for this cost containment has been the greater willingness of colleges to rely on part-time instructors. Currently, the percentage of full-time instructional faculty and staff at all institutions is 58 percent, down from 67 percent

Table 3.9
**Mean and Proportional Institutional Expenditures, Carnegie 14 Private
Institutions**

	1988/89		1994/95		
	M	(SD)	M	(SD)	% Change
Instruction	28,372,530	(18,607,740)	46,030,880	(42,519,670)	
	30.8%	(6.9)	31.3%	(8.1)	+0.5
Research	5,745,889	(8,692,899)	9,452,171	(15,700,390)	
	4.8%	(4.3)	6.2%	(5.6)	+1.4
Public Service	1,526,099	(1,271,178)	1,905,412	(2,093,064)	
	1.8%	(1.6)	1.9%	(1.2)	+0.1
Academic Support	6,963,738	(5,062,563)	9,995,587	(5,612,788)	
	7.8%	(3.8)	7.4%	(3.3)	-0.4
Student Services	4,805,394	(3,880,251)	7,843,705	(5,543,323)	
	5.3%	(2.3)	6.1%	(2.6)	+0.8
Institutional Support	10,308,200	(5,236,432)	15,115,730	(9,050,123)	
	12.4%	(5.4)	11.0%	(3.7)	-1.4
Physical Plant	6,031,546	(3,581,943)	8,464,916	(6,029,642)	
	6.6%	(2.8)	6.0%	(2.1)	-0.6
Scholarships/Fellowships	9,064,558	(3,957,057)	17,576,030	(8,589,641)	
	11.3%	(4.2)	14.6%	(5.8)	+3.3
Auxiliary Enterprises	9,961,828	(7,342,826)	13,112,680	(10,207,590)	
	11.1%	(5.5)	9.5%	(5.1)	-1.6
Total Expenditures	96,163,360	(59,914,860)	143,859,100	(93,225,780)	

Note: N = 22.

in 1987, while the proportion of part-time employees has increased from 33
percent to 42 percent over the same period (NCCHE, 1998: 252). The commission also found a decline in the percentage of employed faculty with tenure (from 58% in 1987 to 54% in 1992) and a commensurate increase in
classroom workload as measured by both student-contact hours and mean
number of hours spent in the classroom.

Another way of measuring the impact of faculty costs on higher education
is to examine the proportion of overall expenditures dedicated to faculty salaries and fringe benefits. An analysis of the data indicates that faculty salaries
and non-Social Security retirement benefits (for nine–ten month full-time fac-

ulty) constitute a surprisingly small percentage of total expenditures, even at Carnegie 13 public institutions, which was the category that experienced the highest increase in instructional costs over the period examined. For the twenty-two of twenty-eight institutions that reported data, the mean proportion of the total budget allocated for both purposes was 17.5 percent in 1994–1995 with a standard deviation of 3.9.

Scholarships

The category of scholarships–fellowships includes some external federal funds (e.g., Pell Grants) but, more importantly for the present analysis, it includes institutional funds in the form of tuition and fee waivers and reductions in price that represent a real increase in the cost of doing business. The impact of federal and state student aid on the cost of delivering education continues to undergo spirited debate.[6] For present purposes, we will concentrate on the impact of intrainstitutional sources of aid on tuition and price.

One clear finding from the accompanying tables is that the costs of institutional aid or scholarships has been rising at a rapid rate, particularly at private institutions. According to the College Board, institutional aid increased by about 111 percent during the period from 1987–1988 to 1997–1998 to about $11 billion (College Entrance Examination Board, 1998: 16). During this same period, inflation-adjusted tuition increased by 34 percent at private four-year colleges and by 46 percent at public four-year institutions. The relationship between aid and tuition is not coincidental since tuition is a major source of revenue for institutional aid. Institutional scholarships are most often paid for by discounting tuition for the recipient and recouping these costs by increasing tuition for nonrecipients.

The use of such aid has traditionally been fueled by the laudatory goal of funneling resources to those who can benefit most but least afford the price of attending college. In actuality, this goal seems only partially fulfilled. While low-income students do receive more aid on average than higher income students, the evidence suggests that students at *all* income levels receive some benefits (see Table 3.10).

Before we can confidently conclude that current practices in the award of institutional aid drive up the cost of tuition, many other factors (including federal grants-in-aid and the use of student loans, which are necessary add-ons for many low-income students) must be considered. Still, the National Commission on the Cost of Higher Education found enough evidence to conclude that this was a real possibility (NCCHE, 1998: 282).

Considering the purported aim of institutional aid and the extent to which such aid has increased in the recent past, one more question may legitimately be raised: How successful has the use of such aid been in encouraging low-income students to seek the benefits of higher education? Available data seem

Table 3.10
Average Institutional Grant by Type of Institution, Dependency, and Income Level in Constant Dollars (1987 to 1996)

	Public Four-Year Colleges		Private Four-Year Colleges	
	1987	1996	1987	1996
Dependent Students[1]				
Low Income	$364	$728	$2,483	$4,141
Middle Income	331	506	2,393	4,396
Upper-Middle Income	281	345	2,051	3,624
Upper Income	151	255	1,044	1,895
Independent Students[2]				
Low Income	381	363	1,610	1,719
Middle Income	341	285	1,323	1,309
Upper Income	260	122	1,000	721

Source: National Commision on the Cost of Higher Education, 1998. *Straight Talk about College Costs and Prices*. Phoenix: Oryx Press, 286.

[1]Income level for dependent students (1996 dollars): low = less than $40,000; middle = $40,000 to $59,999; upper-middle = $60,000 to $79,999; and upper = greater than $80,000.

[2]Income level for independent students (1996 dollars): low = less than $10,000; middle = $10,000 to $24,999; upper = greater than $25,000.

to suggest that the increased availability of institutional aid has been accompanied by a rise in the number of students from the lowest-income quartile attending our nation's colleges. But the *rate of increase* is no better for this group than for groups from higher-income quartiles, and the overall percentage of college attendees among the lowest quartile is stalled at around 50 percent compared to 85 percent of attendees coming from the highest quartile (see Figure 3.1). Clearly, educators and policy makers need to ask serious questions about the goals and current practices of awarding institutional aid and about its potential impact on ever-increasing tuition costs.

Research

Our analysis demonstrates how research costs in recent years have increased, most notably among public institutions. In some cases, the increase was substantial. For example, the percentage of expenditures allocated to research at Carnegie 14 public institutions rose by 2.1 percent from 1988–1989 to 1994–1995. Such increases may be justified given the exponential increases in knowl-

Figure 3.1
College Participation Rates by Family Income Quartile, Unmarried 18- to 24-Year-Old High School Graduates, 1970 to 1996

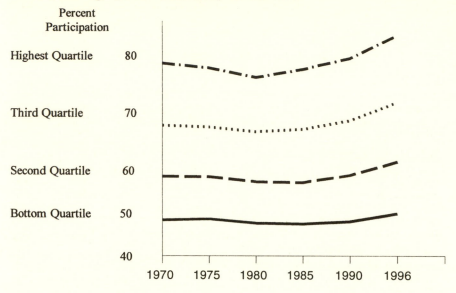

Source: Adapted from College Entrance Examination Board, *Trends in College Pricing* (Washington, D.C.: The College Board, 1998), 17.

edge emanating from university communities and the apparently insatiable appetite of our society for medical and technological innovation. Yet, the rate of increased spending on research poses a legitimate concern and raises questions about the relationship between research costs and tuition increases.

There is some evidence to suggest that increased spending on research does contribute to the escalation of higher-education costs and prices (Reynolds, 1998; Coopers & Lybrand, 1997). These researchers suggest that as institutions gear up for increased research funds, they must redirect resources away from instruction. This in turn limits student entry and forces a rationing of tuition and fees by increasing the prices for those who can afford to pay. One researcher goes even further, suggesting that research-imposed enrollment restrictions at more prestigious institutions forces increased competition for entry to lesser state colleges which, consequently, are able to increase their fees as well (Reynolds, 1998: 112). The cost-increasing effects of federal research grants are thought to be particularly pernicious at public institutions, which have enjoyed a large advantage in the award of grant money over their private counterparts: "[B]etween the 1989–90 and 1994–95 school years, federal grants and contracts per FTE student increased by 37.6% for public four year institutions, compared with 13.2% for private four year institutions" (Reynolds, 1998: 111).

The cost-increasing impact of federal research funds on higher education is not universally accepted, however. The National Commission on the Cost of Higher Education steered clear of endorsing such accounts. Instead, members called for further study as well as for institutional evaluation of the effects of federal policies at individual campuses. While the latter approach may well yield self-serving conclusions, there can be little objection to further academic study. In fact, considerations of the value and cost of federally sponsored research should be a major component of the national dialogue about higher education that we believe needs to take place.

Academic Support

A number of expenditures contribute to the academic mission of the academy. These expenditures include spending on libraries, museums, personnel and curriculum development, academic computing support, and academic administration. Our sample shows modest increases for these academic support areas in three of the four Carnegie public institutional categories we examined, but a decrease among three of the four private Carnegie categories. This is somewhat remarkable given the growth in the base of knowledge with which libraries must keep current and in the use of academic computing. Only one category, Carnegie 12 private institutions, experienced more than a one percent growth in this expenditure category from 1988–1989 to 1994–1995. Of course, the problem with the expenditure category of "academic support" is that it aggregates a variety of somewhat different types of spending. To get a better idea of what has happened in college spending, we must disaggregate some of these components. We will examine only three of the more significant subcomponents: libraries, administration, and technology.

Table 3.1 clearly illustrates that, nationally, spending on libraries, a central component of the university's mission, has suffered a net decline in percent of overall expenditures across the board. Given the exponential growth in knowledge, the increase in the number and cost of professional journals, and increased academic specialization, this trend seems particularly noteworthy. This is a case where technology may have contributed to cost containment. The Internet, interlibrary loan programs, computerization of holdings, and better tracking of resources make it possible for libraries to do more with less. This trend is likely to continue.

According to the National Survey of Information Technology in Higher Education (NCCHE, 1998: 251), technological use and replacement rates have escalated at all college campuses, and a large number of institutions (20.4%) report that technology costs are a major concern. Yet, less than a third of institutions reported having a working financial plan for financing information technology, and a large majority (70.1%) continue to fund most of their technology needs with one-time budget allocations or special appropriations. A growing number of institutions are charging mandatory user fees to finance campus technology. In 1997, these fees ranged from a low of $55 per student on average at community colleges to $140 per student on average at public universities. Most notable, however for our purposes, is the fact that there is no one category of expenditures that captures the true cost of information technology for higher-education institutions. Some costs (e.g., computer hardware and software) are obvious. Others, however (e.g., space, time, and personnel) are either difficult to quantify or spread across several funding categories. On the basis of available information, the National Commission on the Cost of Higher Education concluded that technology costs have *possibly* contributed to increased tuition, although they call for further study to make explicit exactly how much colleges and universities are spending in this area (NCCHE, 1998: 266).

There is general agreement that the escalation of administrative expenditures has contributed to tuition increases, though the growth has been sporadic. For the period of 1980 to 1987, even after adjusting for inflation, administrative costs at private universities increased by 38 percent, at public universities by 23 percent, and at private four-year institutions by 34 percent. Public four-year institutions kept their administrative increases to just below 15 percent during this period (see Table 3.11).

Between 1987 and 1995, administrative costs increased more slowly even though salaries for a wide range of administrators rose above the inflation rate, averaging between 5 and 6 percent per year. After 1994, chief executives and business officers maintained this higher rate of compensation while salaries for lower-level administrators merely kept pace with inflation (see Table 3.12).

University officials often point to increased government regulation as the reason for increased administrative costs. While there are no firm data on this claim, the National Commission on the Cost of Higher Education pointed to studies of the cost of compliance with provisions of the Americans with Disabilities Act (ADA) as anecdotal support for this position. Still, how much of the reported $97 million in costs of compliance at universities nationwide can be attributed to administration is questionable since much of the compliance involved renovation and construction costs. Similarly, regulatory costs like those related to complying with social security regulations may involve cash costs but administrative costs are not appreciable. Still, research universities with large investments in scientific labs may incur substantial administrative costs as they struggle to comply with environmental regulations (NCCHE, 1998: 83, 146–148, 287–293).

For the expenditure category of academic support, our conclusions must be tentative. Library costs have clearly declined, administrative costs have stabilized after a period of growth, and costs associated with technology, while substantial, are insufficiently understood to draw any firm conclusions.

Table 3.11
Administration Costs per FTE, Selected Years (1997 Constant Dollars)

	Private Universities	Public Universities	Private Four-Year Colleges	Public Four-Year Colleges
1980	$3,490	$2,032	$2,543	$2,076
1987	4,809	2,494	3,410	2,380
1995	5,227	2,687	3,507	2,601

Source: Compiled by authors using data from U.S. Department of Education, *Integrated Postsecondary Education Data System*: Glossary. Washington D.C.: U.S. Government Printing Office, 1995.

Table 3.12
Change in Median Salaries of Selected Administrators, Selected Years (1996 Constant Dollars)

	1988-89	1993-94	1996-97
Chief Executive (Single Institution)	$106,103	$111,079	$119,219
Dean of Arts and Sciences	82,230	86,644	83,548
Chief Business Officer	77,173	82,109	85,756
Director of Admissions	52,388	54,291	52,326
Director of Alumni Affairs	41,221	41,912	41,743

Source: National Commision on the Cost of Higher Education, 1998. *Straight Talk about College Costs and Prices*. Phoenix: Oryx Press, 251.

Student Services

Student services include funds expended for activities contributing to students' emotional, physical, cultural, and social development outside the classroom. There has been some research indicating that such services can significantly contribute to the intellectual development of students (see Astin, 1993).

Our sample yielded an increase in student services spending in three out of the four public categories but in only two of four private categories. This compares to stable spending or modest increases among all higher education institutions (Table 3.1) with the exception of private four-year colleges, which experienced greater than 1 percent growth since 1977. A variety of local ecological factors not examined here may be responsible for increases where they occur. This seems particularly likely where institutions are struggling to attract students and to maintain stable enrollments in the face of declining prospects. Anecdotal accounts (Matthews, 1997) are available that describe the escalation of amenities that may be accompanying the competition for students. Colleges are adding a number of culinary, physical fitness, and entertainment options that may contribute to rising costs. Some researchers believe that the use of federal loans and grants to support not merely tuition and books but the costs of room and board as well may be driving costs upward as these funds subsidize student lifestyle choices (Hauptman and Krop, 1998: 71).

Public Service

The cost of providing public service increased in three of the four public sector categories in our sample and at only one of the four private sector categories, though the large standard deviations demonstrate that there is a great deal of variance in spending within each category. This compares with overall figures (Table 3.1) in which public service increased across the board but most sharply at private institutions. How do we make sense of these scattered results?

Public services include funds budgeted for activities established primarily to provide noninstructional services beneficial to groups external to the institution. Examples include community seminars and service projects as well as cooperative extension services. Our findings eschew facile generalizations. It appears that some institutions believe this is a valuable expenditure while others place less priority on this category of spending. Again, local ecological factors like size of community, availability of nonuniversity based services, degree of urbanization, size of the campus, and enrollment trends all play a part in explaining differences in spending patterns, but such considerations are beyond the scope of the present chapter.

Institutional Support, the Physical Plant, and Auxiliary Enterprises

None of these items have contributed significantly to cost increases over the period examined. Nevertheless, differences do surface among various institutional categories.

Institutional support includes funds for executive planning, legal and fiscal operations, public relations, and development. Expenditures in these categories fell modestly in three of the four Carnegie public categories we examined. For private institutions, schools in all categories experienced a decline, two by slight margins ($\leq 0.2\%$) but the remaining two fell sharply ($\geq 1.4\%$).

Changes in expenditures for the physical plant appeared modest both in our sample and among all four-year institutions nationwide (Table 3.1). This category includes expenditures for service and maintenance related to campus grounds and facilities. In only two cases in our sample (Carnegie 12 and 14 public institutions) were the changes greater than 1 percent and both were negative. Reduced costs for fuel and reductions in maintenance are probable reasons for the decline. Of course, both the need for and type of maintenance will vary widely depending on the type and the age of the institution in question.

Auxiliary enterprises include self-supporting operations that furnish services to the campus community (e.g., residence halls, college bookstores, food services, and barber shops). These expenditures increased modestly for only two categories in our sample (Carnegie 11 public and Carnegie 12 private), while declining at institutions in the other categories examined. Reductions at Carnegie 13 and 14 private institutions were greater than 1 percent. Again, local needs and populations probably explain such differences.

Of related importance to both physical plant and auxiliary expenditures, however, is deferred maintenance and new construction. The National Commission on the Cost of Higher Education reports an increase in accumulated deferred maintenance that may soon begin driving these costs upward. This is particularly true at research universities where science facilities await upgrading or where new facilities must be added. The commission concludes that "these costs will continue to exert pressure on institutions to either raise tuitions or revenue from sources other than tuition" (1998: 266).

CONCLUSION

Higher education will no doubt become a more valuable commodity in the twenty-first century. As an engine of technological change and economic development, a laboratory for workplace training, and a repository of general knowledge, American higher education remains the envy of the world. Yet, escalating costs are moving the world of the academy beyond the grasp of those who have most need for it, and the prospects for cost containment in the new millennium are not bright. If the academy is to prosper, we must commence a new dialogue about the promises and problems facing higher education as we move into the twenty-first century. We must reassess the goals and mission of higher education and then prioritize them. It is not a discussion that can be confined to members of the academic community alone, since higher education involves the expenditures of large amounts of public resources and since it affects the opportunities of many who have not thus far been given sufficient access to its decision structure. We include here a handful of discussion items gleaned from our study that must be addressed in the coming dialogue that we hope will develop.

First, as most recent studies of the cost of higher education have concluded, there is a need for better information about college costs. Current reporting procedures are too slow and cumbersome for timely discussion of policy options. Accounting techniques should be simplified and yet expanded so that more data are available about specific expenditures in a form that is readily understandable. In addition, current data are somewhat incomplete since many institutions do not fully account for their expenditures despite their obligation to do so as recipients of federal aid. Enforcement of reporting should be strengthened.

Some solution must be found for students who cannot afford the cost of higher education without driving the general cost for all students upward. As we have seen, internal scholarships and price discounts have been a significant contributing factor to spiraling higher-education costs.

Research and public service are also cost drivers, but these remain significant contributions that the academy makes to society at large. Greater research support from the private sector, which often reaps the harvest of university research, must be forthcoming.

Administrative leaders must find new ways to do more with less. While technological advances may help in this regard in some areas of operation—as in the case of lowered library costs—care must be taken not to solve all problems with a technological fix (see, for example, the chapter by Cárdenas in this volume). The fact is that technology will continue to exert upward pressure on college costs unless policy makers and educators make judicious choices about how and when to employ technological innovation. Similarly, care in planning and appropriating for new physical facilities, efficiencies in operational functions and compliance with regulations, and consolidation of administrative functions all await the hand of the creative administrator.

Finally, higher education must remain true to the humanistic roots that have taken it as far as it has come. One of the more significant features of institutional funding in recent years has been the precipitous decline in funding for instruction. Yet, classroom instruction—characterized by some as inefficient and clumsy in this era of high technology—must be funded at a level that recognizes that it remains the central mission of higher education and that there is simply no adequate substitute for personal and small-group intellectual exchange. These remain some of the more significant challenges for all of those interested in the cause of higher education in the twenty-first century, whether inside or outside the academy.

APPENDIX A

Variable Descriptions

1. *Current Funds Expenditures and Transfers*: Costs incurred for goods and services used for the purpose of operating the institution. This includes the acquisitions cost of capital assets, such as equipment and library books, to the extent that current funds are budgeted for and used by operating departments for such purposes. This includes the following: instruction, research, public service, academic support, student services, institutional support, operation and maintenance of the physical plant, scholarships and fellowships, auxiliary enterprises, hospitals, and independent operations. Auxiliary expenditures are essentially for self-supporting operations of the institution that exist to provide a service to faculty, students, or staff, that charge a fee that is directly related to, although not neces-

sarily equivalent to, the cost of the service. Examples include college stores, student-health services, residence halls, and food services. Hospital expenditures are associated with operational costs, including nursing expenses, other professional services, general services, administrative services, fiscal services, and charges for physical-plant operations. Independent expenditures are funds utilized for operations that are independent of or unrelated to the primary missions of the institution (i.e., instruction, research, and public service), although they may contribute indirectly to the enhancement of these programs. This category is typically limited to expenditures of a major federally funded research-and-development center.

2. *Instruction*: This includes expenditures of the colleges, schools, departments, and other instructional divisions of the institution and expenditures for departmental research and public service that are not separately budgeted. This figure includes expenditures for credit and noncredit activities and excludes expenditures for academic administration where the primary function is administration (e.g., academic deans). It also includes general academic instruction, occupational and vocational instruction, special-session instruction, community education, preparatory and adult basic education, and remedial and tutorial instruction conducted by the teaching faculty for the institutions's students.

3. *Research*: This category includes funds expended for activities specifically organized to produce research outcomes and commissioned by an agency either external to the institution or separately budgeted by a unit within the institution.

4. *Public Service*: This entails funds budgeted specifically for public service and expended for activities designed to provide noninstructional services that are beneficial to groups external to the institution. Examples include seminars and projects provided to the community and expenditures for community services and cooperative extension services.

5. *Academic Support*: This includes expenditures for the support services that are an integral part of the institution's primary mission of instruction, research, and public service. Included in this category are expenditures for libraries, museums, audio–visual services, academic-computing support, ancillary support, academic administration, personnel development, and course and curriculum development. It also includes expenditures for veterinary and dental clinics if their primary purpose is to support the institutional program.

6. *Student Services*: This category includes expenditures for admissions, registrar activities, and activities whose primary purpose is to contribute to students' emotional and physical well-being and to their intellectual, cultural, and social development outside the context of the formal instructional program. Examples include career guidance, counseling, financial-aid administration, and student-health services.

7. *Institutional Support*: Expenditures for day-to-day operational support of the institution are included, such as expenditures for general administrative services, executive direction and planning, public relations and development, and legal and fiscal operations. This category does not include expenditures for physical-plant operations.

8. *Physical Plant*: This entails the operation and maintenance of the physical plant and includes expenditures for operations established to provide service and main-

tenance related to campus grounds and facilities used for educational and general purposes.

9. *Scholarships and Fellowships*: These are expenditures made in the form of outright grants-in-aid, tuition and fee waivers, prizes, and stipends to students enrolled in undergraduate or graduate coursework. Pell Grants are included in this category. College work–study expenses and remissions that are granted because of faculty or staff status are not included.

10. *Mandatory Transfers*: These include transfers that must be made to fulfill a binding legal obligation of the institution, and include debt-service provisions relating to academic and administrative buildings, including funds set aside for debt retirement and interest, required provisions for renewal and replacements to the extent not financed from other sources, and the institutional matching portion for Perkins Loans, when the source of funds is current revenue.

11. *Nonmandatory Transfers*: These include transfers from current funds to other fund groups made at the executive discretion of the governing board to serve a variety of objectives (e.g., additions to loan funds, funds functioning as endowment, general or specific plant additions, voluntary renewals and replacement of plant, and prepayments on debt principal).

12. *Auxiliary Enterprises*: Expenditures for essentially self-supporting operations of the institution that exist to furnish a service to students, faculty, or staff are included in this category. A fee is charged that is directly related to, although not necessarily equal to, the cost of the service (e.g., residence halls, food services, student-health services, college stores, and barber shops).

13. *Hospitals*: Expenditures associated with the operation of a hospital are included in this category (e.g., nursing services, other professional services, general services, administrative services, fiscal services, and charges for physical-plant operations).

14. *Independent Operations*: These are funds expended for operations that are independent of or unrelated to the primary missions of the institution (e.g., instruction, research, and public service), although they may contribute indirectly to the enhancement of these programs. This category is generally limited to expenditures of a major federally funded research and development center (U.S. Department of Education, 1998a, *Integrated Postsecondary Education Data System–1995* [CD–Rom Version]. Washington, D.C.: National Center for Education Statistics Office of Educational Research and Improvement).

APPENDIX B

Carnegie Foundation Classification Codes

The Carnegie classification system dates back to 1970 and was created by the Carnegie Foundation for the Advancement of Teaching. For the IPEDS data set, codes were not available prior to 1994. Thus, institutions in this analysis are classified in conformance with the 1994 categorizations. This classification design currently includes about 3,600 universities and colleges in the United States that are degree granting and accredited by an agency recognized by the U.S. Secretary of Education. There are now eleven categories. This study focuses on doctoral-granting institutions only (there are four for both public and private institutions). The classification schemes are based largely on academic mission and are not intended to measure quality. Institutions are classified according to the following: highest level of degree offering, the number of degrees conferred by discipline, and the amount of federal support for research received by the institution. The four doctoral categories are as follows:

11–Research Universities I: These institutions award fifty or more doctoral degrees annually, offer a full range of baccalaureate programs, and receive $40 million or more annually in federal support.

12–Research Universities II: These institutions award fifty or more doctoral degrees annually, offer a full range of baccalaureate programs, and receive between $15.5 and $40 million annually in federal support.

13–Doctoral Universities I: These institutions award forty or more doctoral degrees annually in five or more disciplines and offer a full range of baccalaureate programs.

14–Doctoral Universities II: These institutions award at least ten doctoral degrees annually (in three or more disciplines), or twenty or more doctoral degrees in one or more disciplines and offer a full range of baccalaureate programs (U.S. Department of Education, 1998a, *Integrated Postsecondary Education Data System–1995* [CD–Rom Version]. Washington, D.C.: National Center for Education Statistics Office of Educational Research and Improvement).

APPENDIX C

Carnegie Classified Doctoral Institutions

Public Institutions

Carnegie 11 (N = 59): University of Alabama–Birmingham; Arizona State University; University of Arizona; University of California–Berkeley; University of California–Davis; University of California–Irvine; University of California–Los Angeles; University of California–San Diego; University of California–San Francisco; University of California–Santa Barbara; University of Colorado–Boulder; Colorado State University; University of Connecticut; Florida State University; University of Florida; Georgia Institute of Technology; University of Georgia; University of Hawaii–Manoa; University of Illinois–Chicago; University of Illinois–Urbana; Indiana University; Iowa State University; University of Iowa; University of Kansas; University of Kentucky; Louisiana State University; University of Maryland–College Park; University of Massachusetts–Amherst; University of Michigan; Michigan State University; Wayne State University; University of Minnesota; University of Missouri–Columbia; University of Nebraska–Lincoln; Rutgers University–New Brunswick; University of New Mexico; New Mexico State University; State University of New York at Buffalo; State University of New York at Stony Brook; University of North Carolina–Chapel Hill; North Carolina State University; University of Cincinnati; Ohio State University; Oregon State University; Pennsylvania State University; University of Pittsburgh; Temple University; University of Tennessee; Texas A&M University; University of Texas–Austin; Utah State University; University of Utah; Virginia Polytechnic & State University; Virginia Commonwealth University; University of Virginia; University of Washington; West Virginia University; University of Wisconsin–Madison; and Purdue University.

Carnegie 12 (N = 26): Auburn University; University of Arkansas–Fayetteville; University of California–Riverside; University of California–Santa Cruz; University of Delaware; University of South Florida; University of Idaho; Southern Illinois University–Carbondale; Kansas State University; University of Mississippi; Mississippi State University; State University of New York at Albany; Kent State University; Ohio University; Oklahoma State University; University of Oklahoma; University of Oregon; University of Rhode Island; Clemson University; University of South Carolina; University of Houston–University Park; Texas Tech University; University of Vermont; Washington State University; University of Wisconsin–Milwaukee; and University of Wyoming.

Carnegie 13 (N = 28): University of Alabama–Tuscaloosa; Northern Arizona University; University of Northern Colorado; Georgia State University; Illinois State University; Northern Illinois University; Ball State University; University of Louisville; Western Michigan University; University of Southern Mississippi; University of Missouri–Kansas City; University of Missouri–Rolla; City University of New York Graduate School; State University of New York at Binghamton; University of North Carolina–Greensboro; University of Akron; Bowling Green State University; Miami University; University of Toledo; Indiana University of Pennsylvania; University of Memphis; East Texas State University; University of North Texas; University of Texas–Arlington; University of Texas–Dallas; Texas Women's University; College of William and Mary; and Old Dominion University.

Carnegie 14 (N = 38): University of Alabama–Huntsville; University of Alaska–Fairbanks; San Diego State University; University of Colorado–Denver; Colorado School of Mines; University of Central Florida; Florida Atlantic University; Florida International University; Idaho State University; Indiana University–Purdue University Indianapolis; Indiana State University; Wichita State University; Louisiana Tech University; University of New Orleans; University of Southwestern Louisiana; University of Maine; University of Maryland–Baltimore County; University of Massachusetts–Lowell; Michigan Technological University; University of Missouri–St. Louis; Montana State University; University of Montana; University of Nevada–Reno; University of New Hampshire; New Jersey Institute of Technology; Rutgers University–Newark; State University of New York College of Environmental Science; University of North Dakota; North Dakota State University; Cleveland State University; Wright State University; Portland State University; University of South Dakota; Middle Tennessee State University; Tennessee State University; Texas Southern University; George Mason University; and University of Puerto Rico–Rio Piedras Campus.

Private Institutions

Carnegie 11 (N = 29): California Institute of Technology; University of Southern California; Yale University; Georgetown University; Howard University; University of Miami; Emory University; University of Chicago; Northwestern University; Johns Hopkins University; Boston University; Harvard University; Massachusetts Institute of Technology; Tufts University; Washington University; Princeton University; Columbia University; Cornell University–Endowed Colleges; New York University; University of Rochester; Rockefeller University; Yeshiva University; Duke University; Case Western Reserve University; Carnegie Mellon University; University of Pennsylvania; Brown University; Vanderbilt University; and Stanford University.

Carnegie 12 (N = 11): George Washington University; University of Notre Dame; Tulane University; Brandeis University; Northeastern University; St. Louis University; Rensselaer Polytechnic Institute; Syracuse University; Lehigh University; Rice University; and Brigham Young University.

Carnegie 13 (N = 23): Claremont Graduate School; U.S. International University; University of Denver; American University; Catholic University of America; Florida Institute of Technology; Nova Southeastern University; Clark Atlanta University; Illinois Institute of Technology; Loyola University of Chicago; Boston College; Andrews University; Adelphi University; Fordham University; Hofstra University; New School for Social Research; Polytechnic University; St. John's University; Teachers College at Columbia University; The Union Institute; Drexel University; Southern Methodist University; and Marquette University.

Carnegie 14 (N = 22): Biola University; University of Laverne; Loma Linda University; University of the Pacific; Pepperdine University; University of San Diego; University of San Francisco; DePaul University; Clark University; Worcester Polytechnic Institute; University of Detroit; Dartmouth College; Seton Hall University; Stevens Institute of Technology; Clarkson University; Pace University; Wake Forest University; University of Tulsa; Duquesne University; Allegheny University of the Health Sciences; Baylor University; and Texas Christian University. (U.S. Department of Education, 1998b, *Integrated Postsecondary Education Data System– 1995* [CD–Rom Version]. Washington, D.C.: National Center for Education Statistics Office of Educational Research and Improvement).

NOTES

1. The most recent survey of college prices shows that between the 1997–1998 and 1998–1999 academic years, average tuition for public two- and four-year institutions and for private two-year schools increased at a rate of 4 percent, approximately double the rate of inflation as measured by the Consumer Price Index (CPI). Tuition at private four-year schools increased an average of 5 percent (College Entrance Examination Board, 1998).

2. There was some moderation of college prices between 1993 and 1996. When all forms of financial aid are subtracted from the total price of attending college, there was no significant increase in "net" price over this three year period (NCCHE,

1998:160). Nevertheless, the impact of financial aid on sticker price is complex, and there is some evidence that it may actually drive up overall costs. We will return to a discussion of financial aid in our examination of institutional support.

3. Following the pioneering word of Gordon Winston, we will use the term "price" to indicate the amount paid by students and their families. Cost refers to the overall financial resources needed to educate each pupil. Because colleges and universities subsidize education by the use of scholarships, grants, tax revenue (in the case of public institutions), endowment resources, and other funds, there is a sizeable difference between what the student pays (price) and the final cost of education for her/him (see for example, Winston, 1998).

4. While internal institutional scholarships are revenue for some students, they are a cost for others who pay full price. For accounting purposes, they are traditionally treated as an expenditure since they represent a cost of doing business.

5. Mandatory expenditures are those that must be made to fulfill binding contracts. For the most part, they represent an interest expense on debt.

6. See for example, NCCHE, 1998: 296–302, and a discussion by Alan Reynolds (The Real Cost of Higher Education, Who Should Pay It and How?) in the same volume, 103–116.

BIBLIOGRAPHY

Astin, Alexander W. 1993. *What Matters in College?* San Francisco: Jossey-Bass.

Carnegie Foundation. 1998. *Enrollment in Institutions of Higher Education and Number of Institutions, by Type and Control, 1994*. (http://www.carnegiefoundation.org/cihe/table4.htm).

College Entrance Examination Board. 1998. *Trends in College Pricing*. Washington, D.C.: The College Board.

Coopers & Lybrand. 1997. *The Impact of Federal Student Assistance on College Tuition Levels*. Washington, D.C.: Coopers & Lybrand.

Council for Aid to Education. 1997. *Breaking the Social Contract: The Fiscal Crisis in Higher Education*. Santa Monica: Rand Corporation.

Getz, Malcolm, and John J. Siegfried. 1991. Costs and Productivity in American Colleges and Universities. In *Economic Challenges in Higher Education*, ed. Charles T. Clotfelter, Ronald G. Ehrenberg, Malcolm Getz, and John J. Siegfried. Chicago: University of Chicago Press, 261–392.

Hauptman, Arthur M., and Cathy Krop. 1998. Federal Student Aid and the Growth in College Costs and Tuitions: Examining the Relationship. In *Straight Talk about College Costs and Prices*, ed. National Commission on the Cost of Higher Education. Phoenix: Oryx Press, 70–83.

Hauptman, Arthur M., and J. Merisotis. 1990. *The College Tuition Spiral* Princeton, N.J.: American Council on Education and the College Board.

Lindbloom, Charles. 1959. The Science of Muddling Through. *Public Administration Review* 19, 79–88.

Matthews, Anne. 1997. *Bright College Years: Inside the American Campus Today*. New York: Simon & Schuster.

National Commission on the Cost of Higher Education. 1998. *Straight Talk about College Costs and Prices*. Phoenix: Oryx Press.

Reynolds, Alan. 1998. The Real Cost of Higher Education: Who Should Pay It and How? In *Straight Talk about College Costs and Prices*. ed. National Commission on the Cost of Higher Education. Phoenix: Oryx Press, 103–116.

Snyder, Thomas P., and Eva C. Galambos. 1988. *Higher Education Administrative Costs: Continuing the Study*. Washington, D.C.: U.S. Department of Education, Office of Educational Research and Improvement.

The New York Times. 1997. Why College Isn't for Everyone. August 31, 4:1.

U.S. Department of Education. 1998a. *Integrated Postsecondary Education Data System—1995* (CD–ROM version). Washington, D.C.: U.S. National Center for Education Statistics, Office of Educational Research and Improvement.

———. 1998b. *Preliminary Report on the Condition of Education 1998*. http://nces.ed.gov/pubs98/condition98/index.html.

———. 1997a. *The Condition of Education 1997*. Washington, D.C.: U.S. Government Printing Office.

———. 1997b. *The Condition of Education 1997: Supplemental and Standard Error Tables*. Washington, D.C.: U.S. Government Printing Office.

———. 1997c. *Integrated Postsecondary Education Data System—1994* (CD–ROM version). Washington, D.C.: U.S. National Center for Education Statistics, Office of Educational Research and Improvement.

———. 1995. *Integrated Postsecondary Education Data System: Glossary*. Washington, D.C.: U.S. Government Printing Office.

Winston, Gordon C. 1998. College Costs: Subsidies, Intuition, and Policy. In *Straight Talk about College Costs and Prices*, ed. National Commission on the Cost of Higher Education. Phoenix: Oryx Press, 117–127.

4

The Higher Education Policy Arena: The Rise and Fall of a Community

Michael D. Parsons

The question of power and influence in the higher-education policy arena has received considerable scholarly attention over the past twenty years (Cook, 1998; Finn, 1980; Hearn, 1993; Gladieux and Wolanin, 1976; Parsons, 1997). Policy scholars have been troubled by the apparent contradictions in their findings. On the one hand, they find that the Washington-based higher-education associations are not powerful, while on the other hand they find that the associations are highly effective in achieving their policy goals. The source of this paradox resides in the methodological approach to power used by higher-education policy scholars (Parsons, forthcoming). Policy analysts and researchers start with a preconceived notion of power: for example, "A has power over B to the extent that he can get B to do something that B would not otherwise do" (Dahl, 1957: 202–203). When the higher-education associations fail to conform to the preconceived definition of power, policy scholars conclude that the associations are weak and powerless. This approach has done little to advance our understanding of power and politics in the higher-education policy arena.

The purpose of this chapter is to examine the influence of the Washington-based higher-education associations. In the first section, the concept of foundations of power is introduced as a framework for policy analysis. The development of a communication community in the higher-education policy arena is discussed in the section that follows. In the third section, the events that caused the fracture and dissolution of the community are examined. The essay concludes with a discussion of the ability of the higher-education associations to influence federal higher-education policy as the millennium approaches.

FOUNDATIONS OF POWER

The foundations of power concept calls on earlier concepts of power developed in communicative action theories, but goes beyond the work of Arendt (1968, 1969, 1986), Dewey (1988), Habermas (1979, 1984, 1986, 1987) and others to search for the foundations of power. These foundations, suggested by the historical and social context of the higher-education policy arena, interact to give form, shape, and meaning to power. Power in the arena rests on three broad foundations and takes the form of problem solving. The institutional foundation of power is formed by society's defining institutions and structures. These visible structures of power are the products of decisions made in earlier policy arenas. These monuments to past power form the relatively fixed obligatory passage points of power in the present. While they do not generate power in the present, problems must be addressed within these structures. Institutions become important when occupied and manipulated by humans who are addressing problems.

Without human occupants, the institutional structures are mere monuments to the past. The social foundation of power consists of the rules governing the relationships between policy actors and programs in a policy arena. In addition to the formal rules and relationships, it includes the personal relationships that develop between policy actors apart from any formal relationships created by the rules of the game. Over time, these relationships, formal and informal, become relatively fixed, but this stability should not be interpreted as permanence. Instead, what is being observed is adherence to customs, loyalties, and norms that have developed over the years and which guide the policy arena in the conduct of its affairs.

Many of the beliefs, principles, and values that guide the arena are well defined, but the community often works with a tacit understanding of its beliefs and values. At times, the values and beliefs that underlie student-aid policies are unconnected, compartmentalized, and even conflictual. The arena does not seek philosophical coherence nor does it have a mechanism for value clarification. Over the years, new programs and policies have been created to match policy actors' assumptions about problems without any concern over whether the guiding assumptions and beliefs mesh to form a coherent philosophy. This explains why supporters of seemingly contradictory policy proposals can each claim that his/her problem solution is grounded in the values of the arena and vital to its future. While the values and beliefs that guide the policy arena are not always well defined and articulated and at times are conflictual and contradictory, successful problem solving is dependent on solutions that are grounded in the beliefs and values of the higher-education policy arena.

Interaction between foundations generates power, regulates power, and provides the channels and boundaries of power in the higher-education policy arena. Successful problem solvers in the higher-education policy arena are those who build their solutions upon the foundations of power and show how the community's past and future are linked to acceptance of those solutions. Over time, institutional foundations crumble, fall, shift and are replaced as policy actors build new institutions and renovate existing ones to meet societal needs. Personal and social relationships change as new actors enter the community and new rules are created to govern the relationships of the community. Time and a changing world undermine some beliefs and values, renew others, and generate entirely new community beliefs and values as policy actors seek to make sense of a dynamic world. There are always interactions as ideas, institutions, and individuals bump, clash, conflict, and join, creating the need for problem solving.

A COMMUNITY DEVELOPS, 1965 TO 1992

The story of the birth of the higher-education policy arena actually starts in the spring of 1964 when President Lyndon Johnson began planning for his next term of office. Sensing what would soon become reality, Johnson anticipated an overwhelming victory over Republican candidate Barry Goldwater and large Democratic majorities in the 89th Congress. Not wanting to miss a historic opportunity, Johnson instructed his staff to organize a number of task forces to work on legislative proposals for immediate presentation to the new Congress. The President wanted to present Congress with a massive social reform program and enabling legislation when it met in January, 1965 (Graham, 1984).

After having witnessed the Kennedy policy defeats firsthand, Johnson created small, secret task forces oriented toward policy formation (Graham, 1984). Each task force was comprised of practitioners, intellectuals, a White House liaison, and an executive secretary who usually came from the Bureau of the Budget. Altogether, some 135 task forces were formed to help plan the legislative and policy proposals of the Great Society. This device not only allowed the planning of policy initiatives without the hindrance of public criticism, but it also guaranteed tight executive control over policy formulation. Congress would have input, but it would come after the administration had formed the policy, thus forcing Congress to respond according to Johnson's terms.

The legislative task force on education was chaired by John W. Gardner, then president of the Carnegie Corporation, William B. Cannon of the Bureau of the Budget served as executive secretary, and Richard Goodwin acted as White House liaison (Graham, 1984). Task force members included, among others, Clark Kerr, Francis Keppel, David Riesman, Ralph W. Tyler, Stephen J. Wright, and Jerrold R. Zacharias. Their mission was "to think in bold new terms and strike out in new directions" (Graham, 1984: 57). By November 10, 1964, the task force was to have its action report ready for the White House. Johnson's plan was to hit Congress with a full package of legislative proposals, rush the bills through committee, and then force a floor vote before he lost his election momentum (Thomas, 1975).

The success of this strategy is well documented. Through skillful use of his election mandate and well-honed legislative skills, Johnson was able to move the Elementary and Secondary Education Act (ESEA) through Congress in less than three months. The ESEA's "five substantive titles managed to fashion artful compromises that dodged the thorny problems of religion and federal control" (Thomas, 1975: 29). The compromises successfully directed the legislation between what Senator Lister Hill had once called "the Scylla of race and the Charybdis of religion" (quoted in Sundquist, 1968: 176). On April 11, 1965, Johnson signed ESEA in the one-room schoolhouse in Texas that he had attended as a child. With his signature, education moved from the policy periphery to center stage and from being an instrument of policy to being an object of policy.

The intent of the legislation and the composition of its constituency are reflected in the Higher Education Act's (the HEA) eight titles. Title I attempted to expand the land-grant extension concept to urban universities. This was included as a concession to the American Council on Education and to the U.S. Office of Education (USOE) (Graham, 1984). The urban riots of the early 1960s also gave an impetus to the urban land-grant concept. Title II provided money to expand college and university libraries and to train librarians. This was supported by the USOE, the American Library Association, and the Association of Research Libraries as a necessary program to meet the demands of a rapidly expanding college population (Graham, 1985; Keppel, 1987). Title III was designed to aid historically black colleges, but was "drafted in terms that veiled the basic intent of supporting primarily black institutions" (Keppel, 1987: 53). While it was presented as an aid to developing colleges, Representatives Edith Green, Keppel, and Zacharias lobbied for Title III with the clear understanding that it was intended to assist historically black institutions (Graham, 1984; Keppel, 1987). Title IV, with its four-part package of financial aid, is the heart of the HEA. The Democrats were finally able to gain student scholarships in the form of Educational Opportunity Grants to institutions. To forestall support for tuition tax credits and to undermine Republican opposition, a guaranteed student-loan program for the middle class was included (Graham, 1984). College work–study and an extension of the National Defense Education Act (NDEA) loan program completed the aid programs. Title V established the National Teachers Corps. The corps was to provide teachers to poverty-stricken areas of the United States (Thomas, 1975). Title VI created a program of financial assistance for improving undergraduate instruction. Finally, Title VII amended the Higher Education Facilities Act while Title VIII contained the law's general provisions.

If the passage of the HEA was anticlimactic, its impact was certainly dramatic. For the first time in history, Congress had passed a general aid-to-higher-education bill. The national defense link that was so vital to the NDEA was not important in the passage of the HEA. While the goals of social equality and equal educational opportunity were important aims of the new legislation, the HEA marked the beginning of higher education's emergence as an independent policy issue supported by its own policy arena. It tied together a diverse group of constituents—higher-education associations, teacher unions, historically black institutions, urban institutions, librarians, and civil-rights groups—that would fight to defend the HEA and to expand "their" programs in the years ahead. The diverse composition of the evolving policy arena was consistent with Johnson's belief that the creation of a program was more important than the size and scope of a program. Once created, programs take on a life of their own and are very difficult to eliminate.

With the HEA, Johnson had not only created a legislative program, but had laid the foundation for the development of a higher-education policy arena. Over the next twenty-seven years, the HEA would be reauthorized six times. From these common experiences a communication community developed. One of the prerequisites of a communication community is a common language that can be used and understood by all of the community. In the beginning, it did not have a common language, but today terms such as ability to benefit, congressional methodology, direct lending, GSL, loan-grant imbalance, needs analysis, Pell Grant, Sallie Mae, TRIO, and dozens of other terms need no explanation or definition for community members.

Language by itself is not enough to foster fully understood communications. The community also needed widely understood signs and symbols to convey shared meanings. The hearings associated with each reauthorization were an opportunity to display the signs and symbols of the community. Jerold Roschwalb of the National Association of State Universities and Land-Grant Colleges tells the story of how Representative William D. Ford used the hearings for just such a purpose. According to Roschwalb,

Ford had the greatest hearing ever done in education out at Oberlin. . . . after two or three people, the President of the campus spoke, he said that we have to take a few minutes break to set up for the next hearing, which sounded bizarre to start with, and a bunch of heavy, big guys, campus football types, wheeled in a Steinway, right smack in the middle of the hearing room. And then a young man was called up, from the Cleveland ghetto, scared, very unsure of himself, and he was introduced . . . as his testimony, he was going to perform the testimony, the kid sat down and played the Polonaise, Chopin Polonaise, brilliantly. And the usual . . . he spoke for just a couple of minutes, he was asked questions. He has no money, his family has no money, he's there because he's got a Pell grant, he's got his work-study, he's got his loan, he's got the university putting up a lot of money for him, and that was the best piece of testimony about student aid ever. And if you want to see it, the notes are in the book. (National Association of State Universities and Land-Grant Colleges, 1991)

In addition, community members need to interact in cooperative activities because "the pulls and responses of different groups reinforce one another and their values accord" (Dewey, 1988: 148). The various reauthorizations and associated activities provided scores of opportunities for cooperative activities between 1965 and 1992. The shared activities also produce emotional, intellectual, and moral bonds that help bind the community. These prerequisites for a communication community, and the extent to which they are met, produce a community that is capable of transforming the power of domination into the power of problem solving.

In addition to its focus on problem solving, the policy arena was characterized by low internal complexity, high functional autonomy, strong unity within types of participants, and cooperation among different participants. A small group of policy actors worked together on virtually every reauthorization. The White House was primarily a nonactor after 1965, leaving the field to the congressional committees and the higher-education associations. In the House, Representative Ford had been an active participant starting with the Great Society programs. He was joined by long-term Republican members such as Representatives E. Thomas Coleman and William F. Goodling, who valued educational opportunity for students above party politics.

In the Senate, Edward Kennedy and Claiborne Pell had been there from the first days of the HEA. Pell guided the 1972 reauthorization that created the framework for the major student aid programs. He was so highly thought of by his colleagues that they gave his name to the largest student grant program: the Pell Grant. As in the House, Republican Senators such as Nancy Kassebaum and James Jeffords worked more closely with committee members than with their own party to fashion higher-education legislation. Vermont Republican Senator Robert Stafford was so respected by his fellow senators that they gave his name to the student-loan program.

Congressional staff members also played an important role in the community. Thomas R. Wolanin, who worked for Ford, was known in Congress for his detailed knowledge of the HEA and in academe for his writing on higher-education policy issues. David V. Evans started working for Pell in 1978. Given the broad jurisdiction of Senate committees, Evans shared the higher-education workload with Sarah A. Flanagan who had been with the subcommittee since 1987. Terry W. Hartle was a key aide to Senator Kennedy on higher education issues. Hartle, a former policy analyst with the American Enterprise Institute, had also written on federal student aid programs.

While there are a large number of higher-education associations, only a few are recognized as active policy actors. The major higher education associations are housed in the National Center for Higher Education at One Dupont Circle in Washington, D.C., and the address has become a shorthand way to refer to higher-education associations. Of the twenty plus associations that reside at One Dupont, only the American Association of Community and Junior Colleges (AACJC), the American Association of State Colleges and Universities (AASCU), the American Council on Education, the Association of American Universities (AAU), and the National Association of State Universities and Land-Grant Colleges (NASULGC) have been consistently active policy actors in the higher-education policy arena. The American Council on Education (ACE), an umbrella organization, has often attempted to forge consensus positions on policy issues, getting as many associations as possible to speak with one voice on the issue before attempting to influence Congress or the president. The other five associations, all of which are institutional associations, have then provided the expertise on the issues that most impact their member institutions.

The higher-education associations that work with the committees to shape higher education legislation benefit from an extensive circulation and flow of personnel within the policy arena. For example, Beth B. Buehlmann, William A. Blakey, John Dean, Rose DiNapoli, Jean S. Frohlicker, Richard T. Jerue, Patty Sullivan, Lawrence S. Zaglaniczny, and other professional staff have remained in the community for many years but have moved between positions within the community. While the leaders of the associations and committees change, the staff remains, providing an institutional memory. This movement has contributed to the maturation of the communication community as policy actors have gained shared experiences and multiple perspectives.

Over a nearly thirty-year period, the higher-education policy arena evolved into a communication community devoted to problem solving. Higher-education associations were powerful policy actors because of their ability to work with other policy actors to solve student aid and other higher-education policy problems. Problem solving rested on an axiomatic system of beliefs, institutional relationships, and personal relationships which guided the higher-education policy arena in the construction and design of student-aid programs. Problems were frequently addressed on the basis of a recommendation from a policy actor with whom other policy actors shared personal relationships. The reason for following the recommendation is explained by policy actors in terms of knowledge, longevity, respect, trust, and other characteristics that define personal relationships. Institutions are defended because they are the institutions that policy actors know. Programs are created and defended on the basis of what a member believes to be right.

THE COMMUNITY FRACTURES, 1992 TO 1998

No one would have guessed that the foundations of power would shift so quickly and so dramatically in the years immediately following the 1992 HEA reauthorization. Two events produced changes in the higher-education policy arena that were far different from what could have been predicted at the conclusion of the 1992 reauthorization. The first event was the election of Bill Clinton as president. The newly elected Democratic president came to the White House intent on keeping a campaign promise to create a national-service program that would allow students to exchange community service for student aid and on replacing existing student-loan programs with an income contingent, direct loan program with Internal Revenue Service (IRS) collection. For Bill Clinton, the national-service and direct-lending programs would make history and leave a legacy in the way that the Peace Corps had for his boyhood hero, President John F. Kennedy.

The second event was the 1994 midterm election. The midterm elections gave the Republican party a majority in the House and Senate for the first time since 1955. Congressional leaders who had worked to expand the student-aid program since the days of the Johnson administration were replaced by leaders intent on repealing the Clinton student-aid agenda and reopening the contested principles and assumptions that had guided the policy arena for almost thirty years. More than simply repealing the Clinton agenda, the new Republican majority with its "Contract with America" wanted to make its place in history and leave a legacy by eliminating the last vestiges of the Great Society.

The Clinton Agenda

"Opportunity for all, means giving every young American the chance to borrow the money to go to college and pay it back. Pay it back as a percentage of income over several years, or with years of national service here at home—a domestic G.I. Bill" (Clinton, quoted in Waldman, 1995a: 34). With those words, presidential candidate Bill Clinton presented his plan to widen access to higher education, reform the GSL program, and fight cynicism with the idealism of volunteerism. The campaign promise would become AmeriCorps, a centerpiece of Clinton's domestic policy agenda, a program that he believed would be his legacy to future generations (Gerstenzang, 1995).

Candidate Clinton had promised national service, direct lending, and IRS collection of student loans. President Clinton moved quickly to turn the promises into programs. In the spring of 1993 the decision was made to split the promise into its component parts (Kennedy, 1994). The administration would present national service as an amendment to the National Service Act of 1990 and the Domestic Volunteer Act of 1973 (Segal, 1994). Direct lending took the form of the Student Loan Reform Act of 1993, which was incorporated into the Omnibus Budget Reconciliation Act (Ford, 1994).

For Kennedy, it was a labor of love that built on his earlier legislative work and reflected his family's long commitment to service. Secretary of Education Richard Riley and Deputy Secretary Madeleine Kunin (1994) were given responsibility for the direct lending legislation. Ford (1994) agreed to be the bill's sponsor and floor manager in the House. For Ford it was one last chance to leave an education legacy after being frustrated by the Reagan and Bush administrations, as well as by his own Democratic leadership during the 1992 reauthorization. In Clinton, Ford saw an education partner whose ambitions were as great as his own.

The administration had moved quickly on its campaign promise and seemed poised to deliver the legislation. The congressional sponsors controlled important obligatory passage points in the House and Senate. The staff behind the two bills were more than able with a history of legislative success. National service was an idea that resonated with the public and with members of Congress. The administration's service proposal could build on legislation and programs that had been previously approved by Congress. In contrast, the GSL programs had been the subject of increasing criticism in recent years. The banks, secondary markets, and guarantee agencies that earned considerable profits off the student-loan programs found it harder and harder to justify their role in the system. These criticisms and questions had helped start the move away from the complex GSL system with the creation of a pilot direct-loan program in the 1992 HEA.

In May 1993, Kennedy (1994) and 19 cosponsors introduced the administration's national-service bill. True to the history of bipartisan support for education issues, Kennedy's cosponsors included four Republican senators. While separate from the direct-loan bill, the two were clearly companion pieces of legislation intended to form a complete vision when joined together. The national-service bill was reported to the full Senate from the Labor and Human Resources Committee by a vote of 14 to 3 on June 16, 1993 (Kennedy, 1994).

Conspicuous by her absence from the majority vote was the ranking Republican member of the committee, Nancy Kassebaum. Historically, education legislation in the Senate Labor and Human Resources Committee has enjoyed bipartisan support. Kassebaum supported the idea claiming that "the concept of community-based volunteerism is the most important aspect of service" (1994: 35), but questioned the legislation designed to move the concept into reality. Earlier, Kassebaum had urged the Administration to split the national service program into two pieces of legislation. Now that she had seen the piece devoted to national service, Kassebaum was concerned about the rate of expansion and projected costs, its bureaucratic structure, the lack of state and local autonomy, and the use of scarce higher education dollars for a new program while the Pell Grant program continued to be seriously underfunded (1994).

Ironically, higher-education associations privately shared some of Kassebaum's concern about the use of scarce education dollars being diverted to a new program while existing programs were wanting for funds. The Budget Enforcement Act of 1990 (BEA) would force the programs to compete with one another for a limited number of dollars. As proposed, the program would accelerate the move away from grants and toward loans. This would be true regardless of whether students participated in the national-service program. The direct-loan program would enjoy entitlement status, and thus any qualified student would be entitled to a loan. Loan volumes would explode just as they had exploded under the Middle Income Student Assistance Act (MISAA) in 1978. In contrast, qualified students receive a Pell Grant, if, and only if, Congress provides funds for the program. Barmak Nassirian, AASCU's director of federal relations, claimed that "this whole national service thing is a bunch of ideological garbage. Combine it with income-contingent loans and its a real piece of shit" (quoted in Waldman, 1995a: 61). Nassirian's view may have expressed rather bluntly the feelings of the higher-education associations' toward direct lending, but it did not matter because Clinton was the first president in more than twelve years to offer higher education anything new. The higher-education associations could oppose their new friend, the president of the United States, or they could get on board with his program. Without any real alternative, they elected to support Clinton's agenda.

As a senator, Kassebaum had other alternatives available. On July 1, she introduced S.1212, the National Service and Community Volunteers Act of 1993, as an alternative to the administration's bill. She also went to work preparing a series of amendments to be offered during the floor debate on the administration's bill. During the floor debate, Kassebaum's amendments were defeated, but helped focus opposition to the administration's bill. After a series of defeated amendments, the Republicans had identified enough votes to sustain a filibuster. Once it became clear that the Democrats could not break the filibuster, Kennedy moved to satisfy opposition to the bill. On July 28, the Kennedy–Durenberger–Wofford bill was introduced as a substitute for the administration bill (Kennedy, 1994). On August 3, the Senate passed the bill on a vote of 58 to 41 with only 7 Republicans joining 51 Democrats. The bill now headed towards conference where the House bill had been waiting since July 28.

The House version of national service was controlled by Ford. Although Democrats enjoyed a majority in the House, the administration worked with Ford to build a broad base of support for the bill. Working with Republicans Christopher Shays of Connecticut, a former Peace Corps volunteer, and Steve Gunderson of Wisconsin, a moderate Republican, the administration sought to create bipartisan support that would cut the ground out from under the opposition before it could start a campaign against the national service bill. Shays and Gunderson responded with a "Dear Colleague" letter that claimed national service as nothing less than a Republican idea (Waldman, 1995a). As the bill's prime sponsor and floor manager, Ford's strategy was to sign on so many cosponsors that passage of the bill would seem inevitable when it was formally introduced.

Opposing the bill represented a difficult choice for would-be opponents. The idea of national service was a bit like campaigns against waste and fraud. If one dared to claim that such a campaign was ill designed, then one might appear to be a defender of waste and fraud. If the associations opposed national service, especially with Ford lining up so many cosponsors, then they ran the risk of looking like an opponent of access to college, service to meet unmet community needs, and in favor of helping greedy banks make money at the expense of needy students. ACE found itself at odds with Ford when it offered a letter of support for the means-testing amendment in the House. When Ford saw the letter, he exploded, telling his staff to "tell Terry Hartle never to darken my goddamn doorway again" (quoted in Waldman, 1995a: 196). Ford demanded and received a new letter from ACE which supported the national service bill in its entirety (Waldman, 1995a). Finally, IRS collection was quietly dropped to avoid conflict with the Ways and Means committee.

While Ford was able to handle these and other challenges to the bill, he was unable to bring Representative Bill Goodling, the ranking Republican on the House Education and Labor Committee, on board in support of the bill. Goodling (1994) had opposed direct lending during the 1992 reauthorization, and his relationship with Ford had been bruised during the reauthorization process. One year later, he was no more enamored with a national-service program that would be linked to a direct-lending program designed to accomplish what its supporters had failed to achieve during the 1992 reauthorization. Goodling publicly expressed what some of the higher-education associations had been saying in private: National service coupled with direct lending would take education dollars from the many to give to the few. Without dollars to fund current programs at their authorized levels, Goodling found it difficult to support a new program that would compete for the same limited funds, thus leaving existing programs poorer still.

Goodling had serious questions about the bill, but was also concerned that Ford had moved away from the bipartisan tradition associated with education legislation. This movement had started during the 1992 reauthorization and continued under the Clinton administration. Ford did not need Republican votes in the House the way Kennedy did in the Senate. Without a need for these votes, the committee was starting to take on the more partisan atmosphere of the larger House. Goodling's anger and hostility over not being treated as a full partner finally erupted during the House–Senate conference on national service. In response to a remark by Ford about his being a good friend, Goodling retorted "Oh! it was fun when I was *needed*. Some kind of friendship" (emphasis in original, quoted in Waldman, 1995a: 232). Bill Goodling, the ranking Republican on the committee, would not support his old friend Bill Ford on the national-service bill nor would he get on board for the upcoming direct-lending bill. Ford delivered the bill 270 to 156 without Goodling's support and over his opposition.

The conference committee proved to be a relatively tame affair with less than twelve hours being spent on reconciling the differences between the House and Senate versions of the national service bills (Kassebaum, 1994). The conference committee met briefly on August 5 to approve the bill and the House passed it on August 6 (Kennedy, 1994). The calendar in the Senate forced a delay until after the August recess, but the bill was passed on September 8 and sent to the president. Clinton signed the National and Community Trust Act on September 21, 1993 on the White House lawn in front of youth corps members from around the nation (Segal, 1994). The administration had moved national service from a campaign idea to legislation in less than nine months.

National Service

National service was relatively unimportant compared to the struggle that would take place over the administration's direct-lending proposal. National service was about principles, but direct lending was about money. Commercial banks enjoyed more than $1 billion in profits from their student-loan portfolios each year, a profit that is nearly 100 percent guaranteed by the federal government (Bluestone and Comcowich, 1992). Sallie Mae, with some $46 billion in total assets, reported some $394 million in profits in 1993, making the federally created organization one of the 100 largest U.S. corporations (Konigsberg, 1993). National service would create new revenue opportunities while direct lending would end a revenue source that produced billions of dollars in government-guaranteed profits for the Guaranteed Student Loan industry. Sallie Mae, the banks, the state and private guarantee agencies, the secondary loan markets, the loan servicers, and the collection agencies could not be expected to quietly relinquish their interests.

Defeating the direct-lending proposal would not be an easy task. In Congress and in the larger policy arena, there was a strong feeling that the lenders and guarantee agencies were making money at the expense of needy students, were not performing as intended, and were unfairly sheltered from real risk by the federal guarantee of loans and profit rates. Public-policy concerns over high default rates had not been assuaged. The budget agreement and credit reform continued to favor direct lending over the GSL program. Democrats still controlled the obligatory passage points in the Congress and were now joined by a president and a secretary of education who were committed to direct lending. In sum, the changes that had occurred since 1992 advantaged the proponents of direct lending and disadvantaged its opponents.

If the industry was to have any success, then it would have to look for help in the House or Senate rather than in the court of public opinion. In the House, Ford seemed to remain firmly in control of and devoted to the president's proposal. The direct lending bill was easily included in the Omnibus Budget Reconciliation Bill. More important than its inclusion was the way the bill was scored by the Congressional Budget Office. Thanks to credit reform, the direct lending bill was scored as a budget savings item. Under the BEA, this meant that any critic of the proposal would have to substitute a proposal with savings equal to the $4 billion plus direct lending savings. The same rules that had prevented Ford and others from realizing a Pell Grant entitlement during the 1992 HEA reauthorization were now protecting the direct-lending proposal.

With the House seemingly out of reach, the Senate represented the last opportunity for opponents of direct lending to derail the administration's proposal. As in the House, the Senate version of direct lending was to be included in the budget resolution. It looked as if the proposal would pass quietly through the Senate until Kassebaum focused attention on the proposal with the introduction of an amendment to alter the bill (Kunin, 1994). As with national service, she had doubts about the federal government's ability to administer the program. Kassebaum also worried because "it's an enormous change. I'm only pausing because if it can be shown to be successful, then no, I wouldn't have a problem" (quoted in Zuckman, 1993b: 1153). The purpose of the Kassebaum proposal was to scale down the direct-lending program and to recapture the lost savings from other domestic programs.

Kassebaum was not alone in questioning the wisdom of substituting direct lending for the current GSL program. Pell also voiced "concerns over the ability of the department and many institutions to administer a direct lending program" (quoted in Zuckman, 1993b: 1153). Jeffords supported direct lending but was also uneasy about dismantling the GSL program without first testing the reliability and validity of a direct lending program. The Kassebaum amendment failed by a vote of 51 to 47, but it revealed the weakness of the administration's position in the Senate with five Democratic Senators voting against their president (Kunin, 1994).

The Kassebaum amendment had failed in large part because it would have required real cuts in existing education programs to replace the paper savings created by the Congressional Budget Office (CBO) scoring of direct lending. The administration had prevailed on the amendment, but a final victory looked less certain. Kennedy was willing to support the administration's version of direct lending, but he did not want to roll his old friend Pell and he would need Kassebaum and Jeffords's support. Something less than a complete replacement of the GSL program would have to be offered as a compromise.

Uncertainty about the legislation in the Senate created an opportunity for the GSL industry to redefine the problem and to offer a new solution. John Dean, speaking for the Consumer Banking Association (CBA), had attempted to redefine the relationship between national service and direct lending, but the point was lost in media reports. The point that Dean had attempted to make was that national service could go forward without direct lending (Jaschik, 1993). Students who participated in a qualified service program could be given a certificate or voucher for a loan that would be repaid by the federal government. The existing GSL industry could make and service the loans, thus eliminating the need for a new loan program.

Unable to gain support for decoupling the two programs, the GSL industry played upon questions about the Education Department's ability to administer a massive direct-lending program. Failure would mean that students who depended on loans would be denied access to higher education. Colleges that depended on students having loans would be facing financial crisis. Once the banks left the program, it would be impossible for them to return on short notice, thus higher education would be facing a catastrophe. Rather than risk this disaster, the GSL industry proposed a phase-in of direct lending while maintaining the current system as a safety net. An additional advantage of this approach would be the opportunity to test the two systems in a direct competition.

Pushing this approach, the GSL industry worked hard to fashion an alternative with "unusual direct assistance from a member of Congress" (Jaschik, 1993), Representative Bart Gordon. Gordon, with the help of Representatives Earl Pomeroy and Goodling, worked with the industry, including "actively participating in meetings with banks, guaranty agencies, secondary markets, and Sallie Mae" (Jaschik, 1993). The industry also worked with the staffs of Jeffords, Kassebaum, and Pell to develop an alternative to direct lending in the Senate. Despite these efforts, an industry consensus was not forthcoming, "largely because of Sallie Mae's refusal to accept any package containing a user fee on its holdings or new financing" (Jaschik, 1993: A28).

To everyone's surprise, the alternative to the administration's proposal came not from the GSL industry or Kassebaum, but from Pell (Waldman, 1995b). The Pell proposal called for a phase-in of direct lending until 30 percent of schools were under the program. At that point, a commission would review the program, and Congress would vote on continued expansion. To recapture money lost by the scaled-down program, Pell's proposal reduced fees to banks. The proposal appealed to those with concerns about direct lending while still allowing them to move the president's plan forward. The proposal formed the basis of a compromise between Kennedy, Pell, Kassebaum, and Jeffords. As approved by the committee, the new bill called for 5 percent of schools to participate in 1994–1995 increasing to a maximum of 50 percent in 1997–1998 (*The Wall Street Journal*, 1993). At that time, a bipartisan commission would review the program and make recommendations to the Congress. Finally, fees to banks would be sliced.

The Senate bill's passage set the stage for an interesting conference committee. Participants such as Ford, Kennedy, and Pell, normally allies, found themselves on opposite sides of the issue. The key players in the conference committee were Ford and Kennedy. Ford was committed to making 100 percent direct lending a reality. Kennedy supported Clinton's plan but did not have the votes in the Senate to pass a complete direct-lending plan. As a result, the conference committee meetings were "combative, frustrating, tedious" (Zook, 1995a: A25), and intense as the members met several times over the week and four times on the last day of the conference (Zuckman, 1993a). The final language on direct lending looked more like the Senate proposal than the House proposal, but it was hardly cause for celebration by the GSL industry. With the passage of direct lending, Clinton had successfully implemented most of his student-aid reform agenda during his first year in office.

The Republican Revolution

In September of 1994, Republican members of Congress and Republican congressional candidates gathered on the steps of the Capitol to offer a promise and present a contract to the American people. If the electorate voted the Republican Party into a numeric majority in the House, then the leadership would bring to a vote the items that formed its "Contract with America." The intent of the contract was nothing less than a revolution aimed at dismantling the social structures of the New Deal and Great Society and the regulatory structures created by the Nixon administration. In November, the voters responded by giving Republicans a majority on Capitol Hill for the first time in forty years.

The architect of the Contract with America, Newt Gingrich, was elected Speaker of the House. The new leaders of the 104th Congress moved quickly to translate campaign promises into legislation. The new leadership also acted to reorganize committees, hire new staff, and award committee and subcommittee chairs. The new Congress looked very different from the 103d Congress, which had so recently enacted national service and direct lending for an eager President Clinton, and from the 102d Congress which had sent the HEA reauthorization to a reluctant President Bush.

Among the changes enacted by the new Republican leadership was the renaming and reorganizing of the House Committee on Education and Labor. The committee was renamed the Committee on Economic and Educational Opportunities. After years of toiling in the minority, the 67-year-old Bill Goodling finally took the committee chair. He quickly acted on the Republican promise to reduce the size of government by consolidating the subcommittees and reducing the size of the staff by one-third (Stanfield, 1995).

The new tone and direction may have made some senior Republicans and staff uneasy, but it fit well with Goodling's desire to revisit direct lending and national service (Sanchez, 1995; Stanfield, 1995). It also fit well with the political philosophy of Victor F. Klatt, the committee's education coordinator, who was described as "fervently conservative" (Stanfield, 1995: 1487). Even if the change had not suited Goodling, a political moderate, and the senior staff, they were receiving their orders from Speaker Gingrich, and he was calling for "a double-time march to the right" (Stanfield, 1995: 1487). The entire policy arena was open to reconsideration and change.

The chair of the Subcommittee on Postsecondary Education, Training, and Lifelong Learning, another new name, was Howard P. "Buck " McKeon, a second-term member from California. McKeon was neither reluctant nor hesitant to admit that he did not know enough about the key higher-education issues to discuss those issues in an interview with *The Chronicle of Higher Education* (Zook, 1995b). When asked, McKeon "said he had no opinion on the role of the new State Postsecondary Review Entities, the proposed privatization of the Student Loan Marketing Association, or whether the federal government should continue to focus its higher education efforts on insuring student access to colleges" (Zook, 1995b: A33). If Republicans were to review, consolidate, and reduce the role of government in education, then much of the effort would have to flow through McKeon's subcommittee.

The Senate had also changed, but the changes were less dramatic than those in the House. The Senate had moved from Democratic to Republican control and back again in recent years, thus it was not the same historic shift that took place in the House. Republican members of the Senate had experience as both the majority and the minority party, while the House Republicans had experience only as members of the minority. In addition, Senate members and candidates had not been part of the Contract with America. Finally, the Senate had a better record of bipartisanship on education issues. This was especially true when Pell and Stafford had moved between the roles of subcommittee chair and ranking minority member.

While the changes in the Senate may not have been as dramatic, they should not be understated. The Committee on Labor and Human Resources was now chaired by Kassebaum. She was the first woman in Senate history to hold such an important position. Absent from the new committee were key members such as Bingaman, Durenberger, Hatch, Metzenbaum, and Wofford. When it reached the Senate, the Republican Revolution in education would have to come through Kassebaum's committee, where much of it would be referred to the Subcommittee on Education, Arts, and Humanities.

Setting the Agenda

In the first heady days of the 104th Congress, the flurry of activity surrounding the Republican ascendancy seemed to obscure the focus of their agenda for change. At first, the agenda seemed to focus on cosmetic and symbolic changes (e.g., changing the names of committees and reducing the size of committee staffs). Observers might have been confused but the Republican leadership in the Congress was certain of the agenda it was setting. A major part of that agenda was focused on reducing the size of the federal government's budget and its role in American life. That meant examining each federal program to determine whether the responsibility should be continued by the federal government, left to the state and local governments, or turned over to the private sector. It also meant reducing the level of domestic spending. Spending on higher education would have to be reduced as part of higher education's contribution towards the reduction of the federal budget.

The agenda was also driven by an almost "reflexively negative" (McCarthy, 1995: A13) Republican response to any Clinton administration success. This placed AmeriCorps and direct lending high on the agenda for elimination. Ironically, in the case of AmeriCorps, this put the Republican leadership at odds with a number of its business allies. Corporations as diverse as Anheuser-Busch, General Electric, Nike, and Shell viewed AmeriCorps as a positive factor in reviving the economic and social life of communities (McCarthy, 1995). Corporate leaders not only praised AmeriCorps, but also supported it with equipment and supplies, money, and volunteers. Eric Chapman, CEO of U.S. Health Corporation and a loyal Republican, commented that "it's tragic to cut these programs. Why shoot a bunch of innocent kids to get at the president?" (quoted in McCarthy, 1995: A13).

Part of what *The New York Times* called "political animus carried to an extreme" (1995: A24) reflected a sincere difference in political philosophy between Clinton and the new Republican leadership. Even accounting for the difference in views over the proper role of the federal government, AmeriCorps was a target for elimination largely because Clinton claimed it as an accomplishment. Shays summarized the Republican attitude stating, "We have a wounded President. AmeriCorps is something the President deserves to be proud of, but it's a target for those people who don't even want to give him that" (quoted in Manegold, 1995: A25).

The debate over the future of AmeriCorps and direct lending was marked by sharp ideological divisions that were uncharacteristic for the higher-education policy arena. The divisions grew sharper as 1995 progressed, with Republicans repeatedly stating their intent to reduce student aid, eliminate various higher-education programs, and eliminate AmeriCorps and direct lending. Clinton repeatedly stated his intent to defend the centerpieces of his domestic policy agenda with all the resources of his office, including the veto. The two sides offered no ground for compromise.

The summer of 1995 was spent debating the budget numbers and political philosophy, but the debate did nothing to alter the fact that the Republicans controlled a majority of votes in the House and the Senate. The chairs of the key committees had opposed national service and direct lending when they were in the minority and had not changed views with the move to the majority. College officials such as Edmond Vignoul of the University of Oregon could claim that "direct lending is the finest thing to hit financial aid in the 29 years that I've been in it" (quoted in Burd, 1995a: A30), but his claim and pleas from colleges and students to keep the direct-lending program alive fell on deaf ears. The agenda was set.

By the fall of 1995, leaders in the House and Senate had agreed on a series of changes to the HEA programs and budgets. The net impact of the changes was less than college students and officials had feared, in large part because of the intense lobbying of school and student representatives. The 0.85 percent tax per college on student-loan volume, the elimination of the six-month loan waiver, the increase in PLUS loan interest rates, and the elimination of the direct-loan program were no longer part of the budget bill (Burd, 1995b). Still, the direct lending program was capped at 10 percent of total student-loan volume (Burd, 1995a). The cap would force the Education Department to eliminate almost seventy-five percent of the institutions participating in the direct lending program.

The House and Senate leaders were less kind to AmeriCorps. The budget bill eliminated all funding for the program (Gray, 1995). While disappointing, the decision could hardly have been a surprise to the administration. Speaker Gingrich had publicly stated that he was "totally unequivocally opposed" to a program he saw as "coerced voluntarism and gimmickry" (quoted in Wartzman, 1995: A18). Clinton promised to veto any budget bill that did not include funding for AmeriCorps, but the budget bill that was sent to the president included caps on direct lending and the complete elimination of Clinton's beloved AmeriCorps.

As promised, Clinton vetoed the budget bill. The veto was the start of a seven-month budget battle that included two federal-government shutdowns and numerous temporary-spending resolutions. The Republican leadership seemed to think that the president, weakened by the midterm elections, would fold and accept their budget. Instead, the president seemed to draw strength from the battle, increasing his resolve to stand firm with each passing month. In late April of 1996, the Republican Congress gave in to the president and public opinion. The battle which had started with such sound and fury when the Republicans had first ascended to leadership "ended with a whimper" (Rosenbaum, 1996: A1). There would be no revolution for education in 1996.

The AmeriCorps program was continued under the 1996 budget (Gray, 1996). The program received $400 million in funding for the fiscal year. While this was a $69.5 million cut from 1995 and $417 million less than the administration's request, it was far from the planned elimination. The Corporation for National Service, which runs AmeriCorps, announced the results of the budget deal with a press release under the headline "AmeriCorps Lives!" (Burd, 1996: A23).

Direct lending also survived the battle of the budget with little impact or change (Burd, 1996). Under the budget agreement, colleges retained the freedom to choose which loan programs they would enter. The 40 percent cap that the House had wanted and the 10 percent cap that had been in the earlier budget bill were gone from the final 1996 budget. Vignoul probably spoke for the majority of the higher-education community when he claimed, "this is a huge victory for higher education and for students" (quoted in Burd, 1996: A23). Not sharing in his joy were members of the GSL industry, who had probably lost their best, last chance to limit the impact of direct lending on their market share.

While Vignoul and others saw the 1996 budget battle as a victory, too much attention to the details of the budget agreement obscured the larger, more significant changes in the higher-education policy arena. The arena was in a period of flux and transition. Institutional relationships were being realigned. Social relationships were changing as new leaders emerged and long-time leaders and policy-arena participants were departing. The beliefs and values that had guided the arena for so long were being questioned from without and from within. The stability that had marked the arena for nearly three decades was crumbling.

History was made in the mid-1990s, but it was neither the legacy that Clinton had hoped to leave nor the revolution that the Republicans had hoped to lead. The real historical event was the end of the communication community that had characterized the higher-education policy arena. The meaning of power and the understanding of how to address problems in the arena had fundamentally changed in a very short period of time, after having evolved over some thirty years.

INTO THE MILLENNIUM

Looking at events in the late 1990s, observers of the higher education associations see success and significant promise in the coming millennium. As noted above, Vignoul saw "a high victory for higher education and for students." Cook's (1998) account of the same events gives credit to the Big Six for protecting and defending the student-aid programs from the Republican Congress. ACE's Terry Hartle trumpeted higher education's success in the 1998 HEA reauthorization, saying that "you have to look at the Republican voting record of support for student aid and scientific research and say that they have recognized these as important priorities" (quoted in Burd, 1998: A38). By focusing on surface events, observers have missed important changes in the foundations of power—changes that leave the Washington-based higher-education associations poorly positioned to influence federal higher-education policy as we enter the millennium.

The post-1992 success of the higher education associations is attributable more to institutional conflict than to any actions taken by the associations. National service and direct lending were neither developed nor embraced by the associations. The defense and protection of student aid in the 1995–1996 budget battle between the Clinton administration and the Republican Congress was not, as Cook (1998) claims, due to the power and influence of the associations, but due to Clinton's willingness to close the federal government rather than accept Republican cuts in AmeriCorps, direct lending, and other student-aid programs. With a different president controlling that obligatory passage point in the institutional foundation, the results could have been very different.

The memory of earlier Republican defeats at the hands of the Clinton administration helped the associations claim success in the 1998 reauthorization. Republicans, with a national election just weeks away, blinked when faced with a presidential veto. Writing about House Subcommittee Chair McKeon, conservative columnist Robert Novak claimed that rather than have "his party . . . demonized for blocking college loans as it was for threatening school lunches," McKeon and his Republican colleagues decided not "to risk involuntary retirement to private life because of students' wrath" (quoted in Burd, 1998: A39). As with earlier "victories" by the associations, success is a by-product of institutional conflict.

As the association officials look to the future, they will see it as one that will be faced without many old friends and with a host of new rivals seeking to influence higher-education policy. Gone are familiar faces and friends such as Thomas Coleman, David Durenberger, David Evans, Sarah Flanagan, William D. Ford, Nancy Kassebaum, Claiborne Pell, Paul Simon, Pat Williams, and Tom Wolanin. The associations need to establish new social and personal relationships. This is vital, because the views of trusted and respected friends are one of the most important factors in policy decision making.

The associations face numerous rivals who are also seeking to become the trusted and respected friends of representatives, senators, and their staffs. Chief among these is the Rectangle Group. The Rectangle Group coordinates the activities of the Consumer Bankers Association, the National Council of Higher Education Loan Programs (NCHELP), the Student Loan Alliance, Sallie Mae, and other associations and individuals involved in the student-loan business. Student loans will provide nearly $35 billion in aid to students in 1998–1999, or 76 percent of federal student aid. The higher-education associations have studiously avoided involvement with the Rectangle Group, CCA, trade unions, and other organizations that would seem to be natural allies.

With the changes in the institutional and social foundations have come changes in the beliefs and values foundation. Steadily, and almost imperceptibly, the belief that higher education is a public good has shifted to the belief that higher education is a private good. The change can be seen in the shift from grants to loans as the primary vehicle for the delivery of student aid. The change was reflected in the Republican Congress's effort to end AmeriCorps and national service, restrict the eligibility for Pell Grants, and shift the responsibility for the cost of higher education to students and their families. Higher education is now seen as a consumer product rather than a social good whose benefits are publicly shared.

Without higher education's status as a social good, the associations become just one more special-interest group seeking a public handout for its own private benefit. As such, the associations find themselves in competition with other interest groups seeking a portion of the federal budget. In addition, the associations find themselves in competition with other segments of the higher-education policy arena. The arena of the late 1990s is characterized not by community and unity but by fragmented, specialized associations each seeking to protect and expand their share of the budget.

The shift in beliefs and values also changes the nature of federal involvement in higher education. As the principal investor in what is viewed as primarily a private enterprise, the federal government has dramatically increased its regulation of higher education. Federal regulations now cover loan default rates, the criteria for student-aid eligibility, accreditation requirements, determination of what qualifies as an academic program, and other aspects of higher education that were once considered the special province of academics. Federal regulation and oversight of academic quality will increase as the federal government acts to protect and insure its substantial investment.

A prime example of Congress's willingness to intrude on higher education was the National Commission on the Cost of Higher Education. Republican leaders in the House, believing that tuition inflation was out of control, hoped that the report of the commission could be used as a basis for writing cost-containment language into the upcoming HEA reauthorization. Much to their surprise and disappointment, the commission found that higher education was a bargain. Commission member Martin Anderson, a stern critic of higher education, warned Congress that "regulation is exactly what the government shouldn't be doing. It's the perfect example of how the government drives up costs" (quoted in Burd, 1997: A33). Despite Anderson's warning, higher education can expect more, not less, regulation in the future.

CONCLUSION

In reviewing changes in the foundations of power, no one thread seems to hold collective action together for the entire policy arena. Instead, the policy arena has fragmented into various subgroups. The various subgroups can be divided into two large categories defined by their beliefs about the proper role of government in education. The first group can be defined by its shared belief in limited government. While there is a wide range of philosophies within this group about the proper role of government, the members share a common belief that the federal government should play a limited role in education. In the area of higher education, primary responsibility should remain with the states and with individuals. Since individuals are the primary beneficiaries of higher education, they should be assisted with loans, not grants. Government does have a role to play in helping the least advantaged in society, and for the truly needy, grants should be available. This last belief may seem inconsistent with the strong belief in a restricted government role in education, but is in fact consistent with the true conservative belief that government should remove the shackles from the oppressed.

The second group is bound by its belief in an expanded government role in the lives of its citizens. This group, once the majority, has diminished in recent years. Like the limited government group, this group believes that government should play a role in assuring equal educational opportunity for economic and socially disadvantaged citizens. Unlike that group, this group believes that government has a larger, legitimate role to play in education. Higher education can and should be used to bring about social reform. Federal student-aid dollars can and should be targeted to historically disadvantaged groups. Federal funds should be spent on grants to individual students, because higher education is a public good that returns the investment to government and to society in the form of taxes, higher wages, and human capital. These and other beliefs bind this group.

Each group is strongly bounded by its belief in the proper role of government, but there is no one thread that unites the two in collective action. Even in what seems like an area of common belief, equal educational opportunity, the groups are divided by different definitions of who is disadvantaged and how they should be assisted. The differences in the arena are more ideological than at any time since the 1950s. The sharp ideological divisions increase the potential for conflict as the groups unite around and defend their beliefs.

Just as beliefs unite members in collective action within their respective groups, beliefs separate the two groups from one another, making unity across the arena difficult to achieve.

Power in this social context has devolved from problem solving to something that looks like the first face of power. To paraphrase Dahl (1957), power in the higher-education policy arena looks something like this: The limited government group has power over the expanded government group to the extent it can impose its will on the expanded government group. The limited government group is united by its beliefs, controls the key obligatory passage points in the Congress, is not bound by previous social and personal relationships, is supported by the BEA, is willing to engage in conflict to achieve its policy goals, and is limited by public opinion and the president's ability to sustain a veto.

To invoke Dahl in defining power as force and coercion is not the same as agreeing with Dahl. While his definition of power is helpful in describing the current state of affairs in the arena, his concept of power is too simple to capture the dynamics of a policy arena in transition. The foundations on which the arena rests will continue to change over the next several years, as the participants seek to move towards a stable state of policy making. The policy arena, influenced by larger society, will continue to reassess its beliefs, just as the K–12 arena has done in recent years. The social relationships of the arena will develop again as new policy actors work together and against one another. Ideological divisions in the arena, coupled with the budget, almost guarantee that the new social relationships will not replicate the previous social relationships of the arena. The arena appears to be headed towards a period of prolonged conflict.

Finally, the newly developing foundations of the policy arena will eventually crumble and fall, just as the foundations that supported the policy arena as a communication community crumbled and fell. Marked by coercion and conflict, the developing arena will not be characterized by an expansion of federal student aid. Indeed, any change, including program elimination, will be difficult to achieve because there are no common bonds that span the entire policy arena, and because the groups are willing to engage in conflict. It remains to be seen if the higher-education associations will be able to meet the challenges of the new millennium. To understand federal higher education policy making, one must understand the meaning of power in the policy arena. To understand power, one must understand the institutional, social, and beliefs foundations on which the arena rests. If the past is a prelude to the future, then the associations have shown neither the ability to respond to the challenge or to understand changes in the higher-education policy arena.

BIBLIOGRAPHY

Arendt, Hannah. 1986. Communicative Power. In *Power*, ed. Steven Lukes. New York: New York University Press, 59–74.
———. 1969. *On Violence*. New York: Harcourt, Brace & World.

———. 1968. *Between Past and Future: Eight Exercises in Political Thought.* New York: Viking Press.

Bluestone, Barry, and Jerome M. Comcowich. 1992. The Time Has Come to Establish Income-Contingent Student Loans. *The Chronicle of Higher Education*, March 18, B1, B2.

Burd, Stephen. 1998. Republicans Put a Moderate Stamp on the 1998 Higher Education Act. *The Chronicle of Higher Education*, October 16, A38–A39.

———. 1997. Federal Commission on the Cost of College Says It Isn't So Expensive after All. *The Chronicle of Higher Education*, November 28, A33.

———. 1996. A Big Win for Direct Lending. *The Chronicle of Higher Education*, May 3, A37, A45.

———. 1995a. Colleges Fight to Keep Semblance of Direct-Lending Program. *The Chronicle of Higher Education*, October 27, A30.

———. 1995b. Reprieve for Student Loans. *The Chronicle of Higher Education*, November 3, A37, A45.

Cook, Constance E. 1998. *Lobbying for Higher Education: How Colleges and Universities Influence Federal Policy.* Nashville: Vanderbilt University Press.

Dahl, Robert A. 1957. "The Concept of Power." *Behavioral Science* 2, 201–205.

Dewey, John. 1988. *The Public and its Problems.* Athens, Ohio: Swallow Press.

Finn Jr., Chester E. 1980, The Future of Education's Liberal Consensus. *Change*, 12 (September) 25–30.

Ford, William D. 1994. The Direct Student Loan Program: Acknowledging the Future. In *National Issues in Education: Community Service and Student Loans*, ed. John F. Jennings. Bloomington, Ind.: Phi Delta Kappa International, 101–113.

Gerstenzang, James. 1995. Senate Looks High and Low for Final Cuts. *Los Angeles Times*, September 27, A11.

Gladieux, Lawrence E., and Thomas R. Wolanin. 1976. *Congress and the Colleges.* Lexington, Mass.: D.C. Heath.

Goodling, Bill. 1994. Direct Student Loans: A Questionable Public Policy Decision. In *National Issues in Education: Community Service and Student Loans*, ed. John F. Jennings. Bloomington, Ind.: Phi Delta Kappa International, 115–130.

Graham, Hugh D. 1984. *The Uncertain Triumph: Federal Education Policy in the Kennedy and Johnson Years.* Chapel Hill: University of North Carolina Press.

Gray, Jerry. 1996. Both Congress and Clinton Find Cause for Cheer in the Final Budget Deal. *The New York Times*, April 26, A12.

———. 1995. Senators Refuse to Save National Service Program. *The New York Times*, September 27, D22.

Habermas, Jurgen. 1987. *Lifeworld and System: A Critique of Functionalist Reason.* Vol. 2 of *The Theory of Communicative Action.* Boston: Beacon Press.

———. 1986. Hannah Arendt's Communications Concept of Power. In *Power*, ed. Steven Lukes. New York: New York University Press, 75–93.

———. 1984. *Reason and the Rationalization of Society.* Vol. 1 of *The Theory of Communicative Action.* Boston: Beacon Press.

———. 1979. *Communication and the Evolution of Society.* Boston: Beacon Press.

Hearn, James C. 1993. The Paradox of Growth in Federal Student Aid for College Students, 1965–1990. In *Higher Education: Handbook of Theory and Research*, ed. John C. Smart. New York: Agathon Press, 94–153.

Jaschik, Scott. 1993. Popularity of Direct-Lending Proposal Blunts Banking Lobby's Assault on Capitol Hill. *The Chronicle of Higher Education*, March 10, A28.

Kassebaum, Nancy L. 1994. National Service: A Watchful Concern. In *National Issues in Education: Community Service and Student Loans*, ed. John F. Jennings. Bloomington, Ind.: Phi Delta Kappa International, 31–50.

Kennedy, Edward. 1994. Enacting the National and Community Service Trust Act of 1993. In *National Issues in Education: Community Service and Student Loans*, ed. John F. Jennings. Bloomington, Ind.: Phi Delta Kappa International, 13–29.

———. 1991. Congress Will Shape Future of Student Aid with Higher Education Act. *Roll Call*, March 18, 13, 15.

Keppel, Francis. 1987. The Higher Education Acts Contrasted, 1965–86: Has Federal Policy Come of Age? *Harvard Educational Review* 57, 49–67.

Konigsberg, Eric. 1993. Sallie Maen't. *New Republic*, July 12, 15–16.

Kunin, Madeleine M. 1994. Student Loan Reform Act of 1993. In *National Issues in Education: Community Service and Student Loans*. ed. John F. Jennings. Bloomington, Ind.: Phi Delta Kappa International, 87–99.

Manegold, Catherine S. 1995. Clinton's Favorite, AmeriCorps, Is Attacked by the Republicans. *The New York Times*, March 31, A25.

McCarthy, Colman. 1995. The Assault on AmeriCorps. *The Washington Post*, July 29, A13.

National Association of State Universities and Land-Grant Colleges. 1991. Personal interview with Jerold Roschwalb, January 10.

Parsons, Michael D. Forthcoming. The Problem of Power: Seeking a Methodological Solution. *Policy Studies Review*.

———. 1997. *Power and Politics: Federal Higher Education Policymaking in the 1990s*. Albany: State University of New York Press.

Rosenbaum, David E. 1996. Ammunition for the Fall. *The New York Times*, April 26, A1–A2.

Sanchez, Rene. 1995. Goodling Vows a Fresh Look at Education. *The Washington Post,* January 10, A15.

Segal, Eli. 1994. Toward the Reality of National Service. In *National Issues in Education: Community Service and Student Loans*, ed. John F. Jennings. Bloomington, Ind.: Phi Delta Kappa International, 3–11.

Stanfield, Rochelle L. 1995. Economic and Educational Opportunities. *National Journal*, June 17, 1487–1490.

Sundquist, John L. 1968. *Politics and Policy: The Eisenhower, Kennedy, and Johnson Years*. Washington, D.C.: The Brookings Institution.

The New York Times. 1995. Reneging on AmeriCorps. March 15, A24.

The Wall Street Journal. 1993. Senate Panel Adopts Plan for Direct Student Loans. June 11, A5.

Thomas, Norman C. 1975. *Education in National Politics*. New York: David McKay Company.

Waldman, Steven. 1995a. *The Bill: How the Adventures of Clinton's National Service Bill Reveal What Is Corrupt, Comic, Cynical and Noble about Washington*. New York: Viking Press.

———. 1995b. Sallie Mae Fights Back: The Brutal Politics of Student-Loan Reform. *Linguafranca: The Review of Academic Life,* March–April, 34–42.

Wartzman, Rick. 1995. Gingrich Differs with Clinton on Americorps. *The Wall Street Journal*, January 17, A18.

Zook, Jim. 1995a. House Votes to End National-Service Program: Clinton Vows to Veto Bill. *The Chronicle of Higher Education*, August 11, A25.

———. 1995b. Subcommittee Chairman Advocates "Limited" U.S. Role in Education. *The Chronicle of Higher Education*, February 10, A33.

Zuckman, Jill. 1993a. National Service Impasse Ends; Conference to Come. *Congressional Quarterly,* July 31, 2055–2056.

———. 1993b. Panel Favors Clinton's Plan for Direct Student Loans. *Congressional Quarterly*, May 8, 1152–1153.

5

Past and Future Pressures and Issues of Higher Education: State Perspectives

Cheryl D. Lovell

Looking to the future, forecasting trends, or predicting outcomes of any phenomenon requires an understanding of the past to appreciate the forces shaping the phenomenon of interest. What changes have influenced higher education over the last decade? Specifically, what changes have occurred in the relationship between institutions of higher education and state governments? Many of the forces mentioned in the introduction to this book and more fully discussed in other chapters have dealt with internal forces. The focus of this chapter, however, is to address the external forces impacting institutions—specifically the states. An examination of these forces of and by the states on institutions of higher learning is presented in four major sections. Issues of constitutional responsibility, recent political shifts in ideology resulting in states having more local control of federal programs, and competing state expenditures for entitlement and/or mandated programs are among the major issues shaping the state context for higher education.

Second, funding trends of the states over the last decade present a "feast or famine" or perhaps a "half empty or half full" view. More recently, as state budgets are stronger, more funding has been made available for higher-education institutions. Yet, this recent trend begs the question, Do the increases in state appropriations offset the leaner years when state budgets were not as strong? In addition to looking at state appropriations, it is also important to determine how institutions have utilized their funding by noting differences over the years in key expenditure areas such as instruction.

Third, while states do provide the largest source of operating budgets for public institutions, they are also requiring greater accountability from institutions receiving this funding. The old saying, "One who giveth can also taketh away," seems to capture the essence of this discussion on increased accountability. Institutions have had to trim budgets, reduce program offerings, and hire additional staff to meet these increasing state-based accountability measures. The mixed funding past and uncertain future which juxtapose to create increased accountability have caused many institutions to agree to and participate in "quid pro quo" relationships with their state legislatures. Many institutions have agreed to "incentive" funding programs if certain state goals are met. These quid pro quo relationships seem to be a way for states and institutions to keep the forces of tighter budgets and increased accountability from colliding. In many states, examples of more stringent accountability measures, such as increased efficiency and effectiveness and graduation policies reducing time to completion are now common reporting requirements in today's higher-education environment.

Finally, a discussion of the broader questions regarding the role of institutions of higher education with respect to the public will conclude this chapter on state perspectives of higher education. What responsibility do higher-education institutions have to their communities, and what responsibilities do state governments have in providing a quality array of higher-education opportunities? What past fortunes or mistakes will shape higher education for the new millennium? A discussion of these issues will enhance the understanding and general discourse concerning the future of higher education from the perspective of the states.

CONTEXT OF STATE ENVIRONMENTS FOR HIGHER EDUCATION

Constitutional Issues

Education (higher and K–12) is the responsibility of the states. As stated in the Tenth Amendment in the U.S. Constitution, powers not delegated or prohibited by the Constitution are powers reserved for the states (or the people). Since many at the time of the signing of the Constitution saw education closely aligned with religion or religious education, it was not seen as an appropriate activity under the jurisdiction of the new federal government. In addition, the expense of providing education was perhaps something too grave for the newly established government to support. Regardless of the reason for the new federal government not specifically accepting responsibility for education, the states were free to establish educational systems specifically tailored and designed to address the needs of their citizens.

This did not mean the new federal government ignored education. The Northwest Ordinance of 1787 is one of many examples of ongoing federal involvement (Pulliam, 1991). This provided federal land to the states for the purposes of establishing educational institutions; additional lands were given with the passage of the Morrill Act of 1862 (Brubacher and Rudy, 1976). In addition, specific purpose institutions were created with the Smith-Hugh Act, the G.I. Bill, and the National Defense Education Act. Countless other examples display the continuous interests of Congress to ensure an adequate higher-educational system in this country.

Though the legal framework for education has been with the states, there are still many examples of federal involvement with education. Michael Parsons presents a more comprehensive discussion of higher education's relationship with the federal government in Chapter 4. However, in setting the context of the state environment for higher education, it is important to recall that the federal government has four major areas of impact on higher education in direct and indirect ways: research funding, student financial aid, regulations, and tax laws (Gladieux and King, 1998). These activities of the federal government have played a major role in our higher-education system even though primary and legal responsibility for education rests with the states.

Political Shifts from Federal to State-Based Programs

Since the early 1990s, the shift in political ideology has definitely swayed views on funding for education and other programs in state houses across the country, as well as in Congress, by requiring less government and fewer taxes. These forces for reducing the federal government and budget have had direct consequences for states. Terms like "entitlements" and "discretionary" spending were formalized. In addition, a "pay as you go" mentality was established with the increased Republican representation in Washington. The result of Republican efforts to lower taxes and reduce the size of the federal government might appropriately be labeled the "devolution revolution." The focus of this new shift was to "devolve" or "to pass on" the responsibility for certain programs from the federal level to the state level. This approach seems simple enough, yet the National Conference of State Legislatures states that "it is the combination of budget reductions and program changes that add up to a considerably altered relationship between the states and the federal government" (National Conference of State Legislatures [hereinafter referred to as NCSL] INSIDE, 1996: 2).

Specifically the intention of this new budget framework was to slow down spending until a balanced budget was achieved (Congressional Budget Office, 1996). Discretionary spending was to be reduced, and the overall federal budget was to grow at a reduced pace. In order to continue programs and services formerly provided by the federal government, the states would be in charge of deciding how best to provide these programs and services. Congress's intent was to shift the responsibility for certain services to the states at a reduced level of funding (20 %) (Congressional Budget Office, 1995). States on the other hand were to receive "block grants" and have the authority to devise their own programs using federal funding. Many governors viewed

the devolution as a way to work around the cumbersome, regulatory environment in Washington, D.C. The first major program to be reformed and block
granted to the states was welfare with the passage of the Personal Responsibility and Work Opportunity Act of 1996. The passing of the welfare-reform
legislation was the beginning of a new way to do business, with states absorb-
ing the responsibility for reducing the federal budget. This devolution revolution has the potential to prejudice the state budgeting process in many ways,
with other programs also being passed on to the states.

Competing State Priorities

State governments have multiple budgeting priorities, which causes significant strain for many states, even without recent changes in how the federal government funds major programs. The infrastructure needed to provide
state services and systems requires sufficient fiscal resources to be shared
among several key services–programs. Some of the major programs to which
states typically appropriate large sums include Medicaid, corrections, welfare, K–12, and higher education. Which should receive the largest share of
the state budget is a question often debated in capitol rotundas around the
country. Topping the list for the states are the required, mandated services,
such as Medicaid and K–12 funding. Higher education is often perceived as
the budget balancer as it is not a state or federally mandated program. To
many legislatures trying to squeeze out every dollar available, it can unfortunately be viewed as a discretionary expenditure. As Figure 5.1 indicates, the
proportion of funding higher education has received over the last decade has
decreased in terms of a portion of total general fund spending, from about 15
percent in fiscal year (FY) 1987 to about 13 percent in FY1996 (NCSL, 1997).

Concomitantly, Medicaid and corrections spending from the states increased
from 8 percent in FY1987 to 15 percent in FY1996 and 5 percent in FY1987
to 7 percent in FY1996 (NCSL, 1997). The increased number of "baby
boomers" also concerns many, as increases in the number of the aged could
require even more funding for health care. Another required expenditure is
funding for K–12. This area could also require increased funding, as several
states are in lengthy court battles over their funding formulas for elementary
and secondary education (State Expenditure Report, 1997).

In addition to the real expenditures states must make, there are equally
compelling structural issues regarding statutory limits or new constitutional
provisions limiting the amount of money a state can collect in taxes as well as
how much states can spend. In fact more than half of the states have some
kind of expenditure or revenue limits (Rafool, 1996). Also, balanced budget
requirements in most states control the budgeting environments. Moreover,
political pressures for fewer taxes are inhibiting state spending. It is worth
keeping in mind that these situational political issues add another dimension
for states. The potential is great that the pressures will significantly curtail
available appropriations for higher education in the near future.

Figure 5.1
State General Fund Expenditures, by Category, to Higher Education,
FY1987 to FY1996

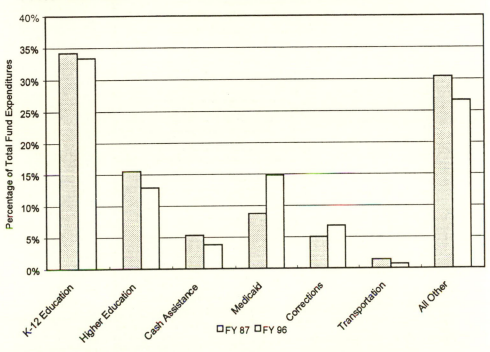

Source: National Association of State Budget Officers, 1996 Expenditure Report.

STATE APPROPRIATIONS FOR HIGHER EDUCATION

Appropriation Trends

The data demonstrate that among the multiple budgeting priorities and responsibilities, funding for higher education is actually only a small part of the state budget. Over the last decade or so, higher education has experienced reductions in state appropriations giving way to increased spending in other areas noted earlier. The trend toward reducing higher education funding has been significant and is worth exploring. On the surface, the data might be misleading. To begin with, funding appears to have increased for higher education in terms of the total dollars appropriated with a record $50 billion appropriated in 1997 (Hines, 1998). In fact, as Figure 5.2 illustrates, 1997 was "a banner year for state support of higher education" (Hines, 1998: 1). This figure displays a steady increase in dollars to higher education specifically during the last six years. It is important to note, however, a decline in appropriations was observed in 1993. And, equally important is the small difference in appropriations over the years 1990 through 1994.

Figure 5.2
State Appropriations for Higher Education, FY1976 to FY1998

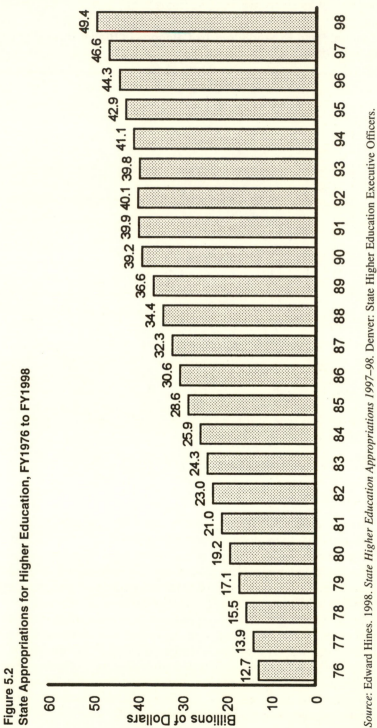

Source: Edward Hines. 1998. *State Higher Education Appropriations 1997–98.* Denver: State Higher Education Executive Officers.

Nationally, over the last decade, there has been about a 45 percent increase in total dollar appropriations, as noted in Figure 5.2, though the rate of change has occurred unevenly (Hines, 1998). Within these appropriations, for FY1996 and FY1997, two-year colleges gained more than the total amount of higher-education funding (Zumeta, 1998). Regional differences are also noted, with the West, Rocky Mountains, and the Southeast showing the strongest percentage growth for all of higher education for FY1996 and FY1997 (Zumeta, 1998), as noted in Table 5.1.

On the other hand, modest recent gains may not make up for the uneven years of funding for higher education. Zemsky and Wegner (1997) note that state funds dropped almost 9 percent between 1980 and 1993. Furthermore, Breneman and Finney (1997) indicate the percent change in higher education's share of total revenues between 1980–1981 and 1993–1994 suffered an enormous reduction of 21 percent. And according to Mortenson (1996), when one factors in a state's "ability to pay" as measured by personal income over this same period of time, state economies were stronger, yet they funneled less to higher education. Specifically, as Figure 5.3 displays, support for higher education declined, per $1,000 of personal income; in fact, except for slight gains in FY1990, the decline has been steady since FY1983.

Another important facet in determining the effectiveness of state funding for higher education over the last decade is to consider whether funding has kept pace with enrollments. Halstead notes, "One reason for public higher education's weakening claim on the budget is the fact that enrollments have not kept pace with collected revenues" (1998: 87). The pattern is clear, as displayed in Figure 5.4. State appropriations per full-time equivalent (FTE) student have fluctuated considerably. More revealing, though, is the gap between available tax revenues (per FTE student) and appropriations (per FTE student). In addition to the continuous, declining percentage of allocation to higher education, it is clear appropriations to institutions are not keeping pace with available state revenues.

Expenditure Trends within

As noted, the bulk of institutional support comes from state appropriations, tuition and fees, and federal funding. How institutions have utilized these resources among their major expenditure items is important to note. Losco and Fife provide a very detailed presentation of these expenditure trends in Chapter 3. A few key trends are noted in this discussion, as they speak to the importance of mission differentiation. It is in the best interest of the states (and citizens) to have different types of institutions that provide different focuses. Expenditure patterns provide external decision makers with a way to see how the institutions are carrying out their different missions. Some institutions may spend more on instruction for example, while other types of institutions may spend similar amounts on research and instruction.

Table 5.1
Percentage Change in Appropriations for Higher Education, FY1996 to FY1997

	General Fund	All Appropriated Funds		General Fund	All Appropriated Funds
New England	4.9%	4.9%	**Southeast**	7.3	6.6
Connecticut	4.4	4.4	Alabama	0.0	0.7
Maine	2.0	2.0	Arkansas	2.3	1.7
Massachusetts	6.6	6.5	Florida	9.7	11.4
New Hampshire	-0.1	-0.1	Georgia	7.1	7.1
Rhode Island	6.1	6.1	Kentucky	4.9	4.8
Vermont	0.2	0.2	Louisiana	9.1	8.9
			Mississippi	4.4	-1.3
Middle Atlantic	3.7	3.7	North Carolina	7.8	7.8
Delaware	0.4	0.4	Puerto Rico	*	*
District of Columbia	*	*	South Carolina	4.6	4.6
Maryland	3.5	3.5	Tennessee	4.1	4.0
New Jersey	4.2	4.2	Virginia	9.0	8.9
New York	5.5	5.5	West Virginia	5.3	4.1
Pennsylvania	0.7	0.7			
			Southwest	2.3	2.2
Great Lakes	5.0	5.0	Arizona	3.0	3.0
Illinois	5.5	5.5	New Mexico	4.5	4.5
Indiana	10.0	10.0	Oklahoma	12.6	12.4
Michigan	4.8	4.8	Texas	-0.2	-0.2
Ohio	5.6	5.6			
Wisconsin	-2.0	-2.2	**Rocky Mountains**	3.2	6.0
			Colorado	6.4	6.4
Plains	3.9	3.2	Idaho	3.0	3.1
Iowa	1.8	1.8	Montana	4.3	3.7
Kansas	1.1	-0.2	Utah	-1.3	7.7
Minnesota	2.3	2.3	Wyoming	3.0	5.6
Missouri	2.3	2.3			
Nebraska	4.1	4.1	**Far West**	7.1	6.8
North Dakota	4.1	4.1	Alaska	-0.4	-0.4
South Dakota	0.4	0.4	California	8.1	7.8
			Hawaii	-0.5	1.5
			Nevada	6.3	6.3
			Oregon	8.3	8.3
			Washington	4.3	4.7
			Total	5.2%	5.1%

Source: Ronald Snell and Arturo Perez. 1996. *State Budget Actions 1996*. Denver: National Conference of State Legislatures (November), 24–25.

*No report.

According to the National Center for Education Statistics (NCES) reports, public institutions over the last decade spent about one-third of their total current funds expenditures on instruction (NCES, 1996; Almanac, 1998). For private institutions, it is slightly less with about 27 percent. Research expenditures have

Figure 5.3
Appropriations of State Tax Funds for Operating Expenses of Higher Education per $1,000 of Personal Income, FY1976 to FY1997

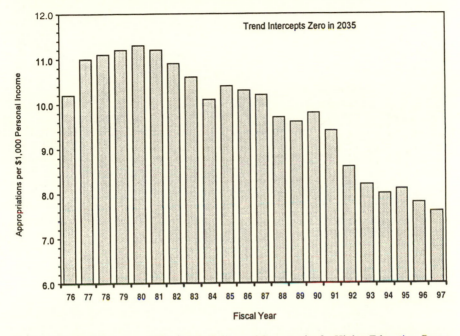

Source: Thomas Mortenson. 1998. Public Policy and Opportunity for Higher Education. Paper presented at the Scholarship foundation of St. Louis. St. Louis, Missouri, October 27.

hovered around 10 percent for publics and 8 percent for privates. Over the last decade, both public and private institutions allocated additional funding for scholarships and grants with a decline in the amount of their resources going to plant operations and maintenance (NCES, 1996; Almanac, 1998).

Salaries comprise a large percentage of expenditures. For example, overall salaries account for 52 to 63 percent of the total current funds expenditures. For instructional expenditures, salaries comprise 66 to 75 percent (NCES, 1996). Slightly less is spent on salaries for student-services expenditures (50 to 65%). Salary expenditures do vary for public two- and four-year institutions, with two-year institutions spending slightly more overall than four-year institutions for instruction.

It is important to note the differences in two- and four-year expenditures, as two-year institutions are the majority (63%) of the total number of public institutions (NCES, 1996). In FY1994, public two-year institutions spent just over 46 percent of their total current funds expenditures on instruction. Recall the overall percentage of expenditures going to instruction for all public institutions was about 33 percent; for two-year institutions it is much higher

Figure 5.4
Legislative Funding Action, 1978 to 1998

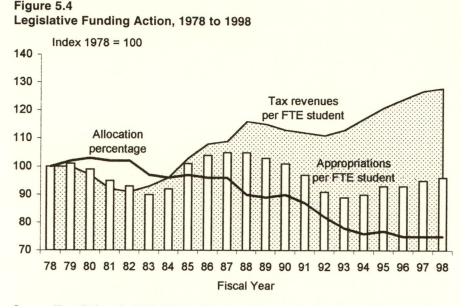

Source: Kent Halstead. 1998. *Higher Education Report Card: 1998.* Washington, D.C.:
Reasearch Associates of Washington.
Note: Amounts are in constant HEPI-adjusted dollars.

(over 46%), and it is about 30 percent for four-year baccalaureate institutions. For student services and instructional support, the two-year institutions spend about two times more than four-year institutions (NCES, 1996).

Expenditures among institutions across the states do vary somewhat. For example, instructional expenditures differed from 20 percent in New Mexico to 40 percent in D.C. Scholarship and grant expenditures accounted for about 0.9 to 8.3 percent of expenditures across the states. For two-year institutions, expenditures varied much more than for four-year institutions for instruction, with 23 percent in Delaware to more than 60 percent in Wisconsin (NCES, 1996).

In summary, it is important to note state appropriations have increased during the last few years in terms of actual dollar amount; however, the percentage of the state budget allocated to higher education has declined. The level of support for higher education has been mixed, as state revenues have increased in many regions of the country; yet real increases in actual buying power within higher education have not occurred. The "half full or half empty" view of recent funding patterns for higher education provides a growing concern for how the community can position itself for success during the next millennium. The funding patterns are increasingly important to monitor. Expectations for performance-based measures seem to be growing, as noted in the next section, and will not be going away in the near future.

HIGHER-EDUCATION ACCOUNTABILITY

Overview of Accountability Movement

Funding does not come without strings attached. This is not a new notion; and it appears it will be the focus in the future of higher education for some time. For example, according to a recent survey, two-thirds of the governors and 50 percent of the state legislators indicated that there is a favorable long-term future for accountability measures such as performance funding (Serban, 1997). Accountability measures of some sort appear to have a solid foothold in higher-education's future and relatively recent past.

National reports calling for the reform of undergraduate education appeared in the mid-1980s (e.g., Bennett, 1984; National Institute of Education, 1984). These reports were critical of higher education and provided a foundation for the assessment movement that still exists in today's higher-education environments. The need to document student performance and the need to demonstrate there was some "return on investment" fueled the desires of many state policy makers to require institutions to do "more," or at least to do things "differently." While states by and large were initially and always have been concerned with the fiscal and administrative aspects of college and university administration, the growing interest in viewing higher education as a means to achieve "state goals" created an environment for a new kind of accountability (Boyer, 1985). This new kind of accountability, firmly based on the premise that statewide return on investment was a legitimate focal point for the state, has continued to evolve in such ways as to extend state interests from fiscal and administrative matters only to broader content and curricular (i.e., "academic") interests.

In retrospect, we now know the first signs of this new kind of state-level higher-education accountability began in states such as Hawaii, Tennessee, and Washington (American Association of State Colleges and Universities [AASCU], 1998) in the mid-1970s. Tennessee is considered to be the first state to pass legislation in this area and it has the oldest currently operating performance-based funding system in the country (AASCU, 1998). Albright notes, "In some states, long-standing budgetary systems have been abandoned, being replaced by completely new funding frameworks . . . redesigned to include performance-based funding initiatives" (1998: 1).

In reviewing the recent history of the accountability movement within the higher-education community, one would be remiss to overlook a controversial and important part of the national accountability history: the State Postsecondary Review Entity Program (SPRE). Probably no one recent legislative action other than the SPRE signaled such a renewed interest in state and institutional accountability. As part of the 1992 Reauthorization of the Higher Education Act of 1965, congressional leadership sought to control the aggressive abuses of Title IV student financial-aid programs. This new program was designed to aid the federal government in its oversight of higher-education institutions that participate in Title IV programs so as to provide a mechanism for review and intervention at the state level (Lovell, 1997). This new federal program increased the states' responsibility for monitoring institutions according to an array of "triggers" set by legislative criteria (Lovell, 1996). While this was a federally mandated and created program, the states were major players in ensuring the implementation of Congress's actions. The controversial nature of such a program limited its success, and the law creating it was later terminated by the 1998 reauthorization of the Higher Education Act. Though no longer law, many of the initiatives of the SPRE program are still prevalent in many state-accountability efforts.

The funding philosophy of the state providing "up-front" funding has shifted to institution-based performances, where monies are promised in expectation of meeting certain state-wide needs or goals. The new accountability and funding paradigm has resulted in the increased use of several key terms: "performance measures," "performance funding," and "performance budgeting." "Performance measures" might be better thought of as the indicators of expected behavior. One might also think of performance measures as values. In terms of state perspectives, the goals or needs that institutions should meet are the important indicators of what the state values or how the state wants higher-education institutions to behave. Albright aptly notes, "Rather than the state meeting the institution's needs, the college or university meets the state's needs," and this sets up a change "in the funding equation by altering educators' expectations that programs or institutions are 'entitled' to a certain level of resources" (1998: 1).

"Performance funding" is often used to indicate a direct link or relationship to a certain portion of the state's appropriations to higher education according to selected performance measures (AASCU, 1998; Burke, 1997). "Performance budgeting" simply means the state uses performance measures in an indirect way in the budgeting process (Burke and Serban, 1997). Each of these terms can be used to describe a significant portion of activities states are utilizing in their increased push for more higher-education accountability.

Current Status of State Accountability

A 1997 survey by State Higher Education Executive Officers (SHEEO) indicates that most states use some type of performance measures in their accountability efforts (Christal, 1998). In the introduction of this report, James Mingle, the executive director of SHEEO, indicates that "state-level accountability and the use of performance measures have been touchstones of the 1990s" (Christal, 1998, p. vii). Specifically, performance measures of some type are in place in thirty-seven states as displayed in Table 5.2. Twenty-six

Table 5.2
Current and Future Use of Performance Measures

State	Currently In Use		Not Currently In Use	
	Used in Some Way	Plans to Expand	Not In Use	Plans to Initiate
Alabama			✓	✓
Arizona	✓	✓		
Arkansas	✓			
California	✓			
Colorado	✓	✓		
Connecticut	✓			
Delaware	✓	✓		
Florida	✓	✓		
Georgia			✓	✓
Hawaii	✓	✓		
Idaho	✓	✓		
Illinois	✓	✓		
Indiana	✓	✓		
Iowa	✓	✓		
Kansas	✓			
Kentucky	✓			
Louisiana	✓	✓		
Maine	✓			
Maryland	✓	✓		
Michigan			✓	
Minnesota	✓			
Mississippi	✓			
Missouri	✓	✓		
Montana	✓	✓		
Nebraska			✓	
Nevada			✓	✓
New Hampshire			✓	
New Jersey	✓	✓		
New Mexico	✓	✓		
New York			✓	✓
North Carolina	✓	✓		
North Dakota			✓	✓
Ohio	✓	✓		
Oklahoma	✓	✓		
Oregon	✓	✓		
Pennsylvania			✓	
Rhode Island	✓	✓		
South Carolina	✓	✓		
South Dakota	✓	✓		
Tennessee	✓	✓		
Texas	✓			
Utah	✓	✓		
Vermont			✓	✓
Virginia	✓	✓		
Washington	✓			
West Virginia	✓			
Wisconsin	✓	✓		
Wyoming			✓	✓

Source: Melodie Christal. 1998. *State Survey on Performance Measures: 1996–97*. Denver: State Higher Education Executive Officers.

of the thirty-seven states that do utilize performance measures indicated they are planning to expand or refine existing requirements.

Public colleges and universities are required to report to state coordinating boards and state legislatures on a variety of key performance indicators or measures. For example, according to the SHEEO study, more than thirty states require their public institutions to report graduation rates. Articulation, or transfer rates, are required by twenty-five states. Faculty workload and/or productivity accountability requirements exist in twenty-four states. State legislators have increasingly been focused on faculty productivity during the 1990s (Layzell, Lovell, and Gill, 1996).

Just over twenty states require some sort of student-satisfaction outcomes. Other measures or indicators include areas relating to sponsored research, remediation effectiveness, licensure-exam pass rates, degrees awarded, placement rates, admission standards, student credit-hour requirements, and accredited program requirements (Christal, 1998). It is clear by this list that states have extensive accountability measures which cover a wide range of functions. Moreover, it is also clear that states are focusing more attention on getting institutions to work on improving productivity and efficiency. Many states also require the institutions to report results of the performance measures to students and parents. Just under twenty states have some type of consumer reporting requirements (Christal, 1998). Equally revealing is that more than half of the states are planning to or are currently using performance measures in their state budgeting process, as noted in Table 5.3. Currently, most states have allocated marginal amounts for performance funding, mostly around 1 or 2 percent (Albright, 1998).

This increased accountability from states to institutions of higher education does not come without critics. Performance measures have some strengths and weaknesses, as noted by Albright (1998). She indicates that when some states report reaching a consensus on performance measures, they can sometimes build stronger support for higher education. However, getting to that consensus is extremely difficult. On one hand, performance measures can serve as an incentive to improve institutional performance; yet, measuring "quality" and learning is a process involving complex constructs. As a result, some measures reflect inadequate and oversimplified indicators. In addition to performance measures, some states have increased their responsibility for monitoring institutions through state accreditation. Yet it seems obvious from the activity of the statewide coordinating offices and in the state legislatures that accountability is not going away.

In summary, one trend that is clear from this discussion is that accountability measures are firmly established as part of our environment for now and in the future. States may change the nature of their requirements, but the environment for "proving" the institutions are conforming to legislative mandates does not appear to be changing in the near future.

Table 5.3
Use of Performance Measures in the Budgetary Process

	Direct Link To Budget	Considered, But No Direct Linkage	Not Used, But Plans to Use	Not Used, No Plans to Use
Alabama				✓
Arizona		✓		
Arkansas	✓			
California				✓
Colorado	✓			
Connecticut		✓		
Delaware		✓		
Florida	✓			
Georgia				✓
Hawaii		✓		
Idaho		✓		
Illinois		✓		
Indiana			✓	
Iowa		✓		
Kansas		✓		
Kentucky	✓			
Louisiana			✓	
Maine			✓	
Maryland			✓	
Michigan				✓
Minnesota			✓	
Mississippi		✓		
Missouri	✓			
Montana		✓		
Nebraska				✓
Nevada				✓
New Hampshire				✓
New Jersey				✓
New Mexico				✓
New York				✓
North Carolina		✓		
North Dakota				✓
Ohio	✓			
Oklahoma				✓
Oregon		✓		
Pennsylvania				✓
Rhode Island		✓		
South Carolina	✓			
South Dakota			✓	
Tennessee	✓			
Texas		✓		
Utah			✓	
Vermont				✓
Virginia			✓	
Washington		✓		
West Virginia				✓
Wisconsin				✓
Wyoming			✓	

Source: Brenda Albright. 1998. *The Transition from Business as Usual to Funding for Results: State Efforts to Integrate Performance Measures in the Higher Education Budget Process.* Denver: State Higher Education Executive Officers.

HOW RESPONSIBLE IS HIGHER EDUCATION
TO THE PUBLIC?

Who pays and who benefits are questions as timely today as they were in the 1960s and 1970s. Benefits from higher education were initially viewed as a bonus for everyone with society benefitting as much as the individuals who participated. The Carnegie Commission promoted this position with its 1973 landmark report when it noted the return on investment to society as a whole was a value society needed and therefore financial support for higher education was seen as a worthwhile investment (Carnegie Commission, 1973).

I believe this question is equally relevant again today when one considers the gains of an educated citizenry juxtaposed with costs of higher education via state appropriations. The perception is that society as a collectivity benefits from an educated citizenry. But some would argue those who really benefit are the individuals who attend and they, therefore, should bear most of the costs, not the general public through additional state appropriations. Some believe the shift in the cost of education to the individual, as depicted in Figure 5.5, is a clear sign that individual costs are more important, as the individual might stand to gain the most from the educational experiences. This shift in responsibility for the cost of higher education to the individual has continued since the early 1990s (Mortenson, 1998). Most would agree an educated population is a bonus for any state. In fact, the improved civic life, additional tax contributions, reduced welfare payments, and increased economic development (AASCU, 1998) are positive aspects to successful participation in higher education.

On the surface, the shift to the individual covering more of the costs of higher education may not seem that important. One could successfully argue this shift occurred during a time of declining state appropriations to higher education. Institutions had to increase tuition as a way to offset the decrease in state appropriations. However, if one considers the larger national political climate, one where the responsibility of services and programs is being shifted to the local level, one might believe this trend of local (or individual) responsibility will continue. Recent local elections suggest that the political climate for less government and fewer taxes is strong. Tax cuts and the returning of "excess" state revenues are common in several states (AASCU, 1998). Expenditure limits and growth limits on the state budgets imposed by citizen-sponsored constitutional amendments in Colorado, for example, are challenging issues for state legislators who are trying to cover all important service areas for the state. This scenario provides a bleak future for higher education. The state of New York is another example of a state balancing its budget by reducing state appropriations to higher education by 10 percent between FY1995 and FY1997 (NASBO, 1997) even though there was a $2 billion cut in personal income-tax rates (AASCU, 1998).

Figure 5.5
Distribution of Responsibilities for Financing Higher Education, 1952 to 1997

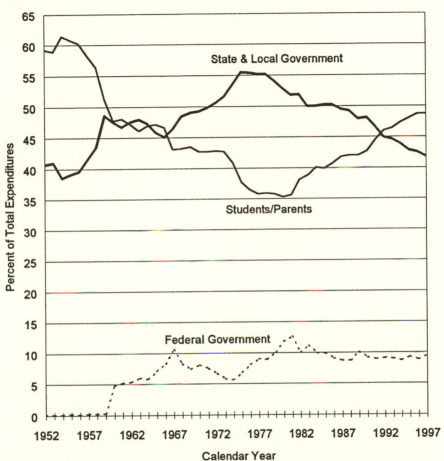

Source: Thomas Mortenson. 1998. Public Policy and Opportunity for Higher Education. Paper presented at the Scholarship foundation of St. Louis. St. Louis, Missouri, October 27.

The shift in party affiliation in state legislatures is also important in understanding the funding of higher education in the states. Split party control of state legislatures increased in the 1970s and 1980s, as displayed in Figure 5.6 (NCSL, 1998). This has continued in the 1990s. Also, the number of Republican governors has increased during the last decade as well (NCSL, 1998). Will the increased devolution activities at the national level "play out" in similar fashion at the state level? Will the individual participant in higher

Figure 5.6
Control of State Legislatures, 1960 to 1998

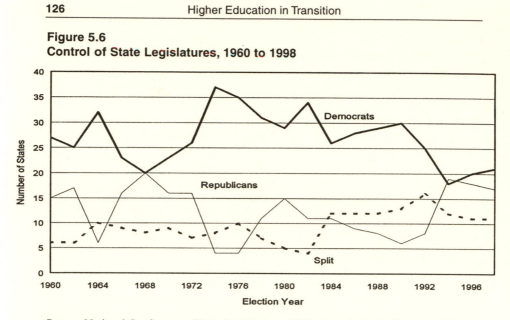

Source: National Conference of State Legislatures. 1998. Party Control of State Legislatures
1938–98. http://www.ncsl.org/statevote98/partycon.htm.

education have to share an increasing burden of the responsibilities for the
financing of higher education? These are important questions states must address for the future of higher education.

Where does this leave higher education in terms of responsibility? Does
the state defer to the individual? Does the accountability of higher education
change as a result of the shift in the financial responsibility? Does the role of
the state differ in this new environment? An option might be for the states to
adopt a new role or kind of accountability where the state has the interests of
the consumer in mind when it establishes its accountability requirements. For
example, accountability measures that take on a consumer orientation or a
consumer focus might replace accountability measures that once focused solely
on state goals. One example of this consumer focus involves broad state goals
of achieving K–16 linkages. Typically, states will include the increase of these
linkages as a state goal and will often expect institutions to demonstrate their
successes in achieving this. A more consumer-focused accountability measure might be to direct attention on statewide articulation agreements that
make the transferring of lower- and upper-division education more seamless.
A strong concern for concurrent enrollment during the last year of high school
and the ease of attending multiple institutions might be another way. With a
consumer focus, the state encourages institutions to work cooperatively to
assist students in moving, or articulating, through the education system.

Accountability issues are among the top issues states will have to address
in order to continue to provide an array of quality postsecondary options for

the citizens of a state. Other important issues the higher-education community must address for the next millennium are noted Throughout the rest of this chapter. Some of the concerns have been discussed before. A recent book edited by Callan and Finney on shaping the public policy agenda for higher education provides an excellent summary of key issues (1997). They note topics such as proprietary institutions, "just in time" education, the role of "quasi-independent" institutions, and state tuition policies are key topics for states to grapple with over the near future. Other sources have noted several key higher-education public-policy issues for states and institutions (Lovell and Gill, 1997). I offer the following important list as a way to augment the discussion on what states need to address to continue their important role in the future of higher education.

Role of For-Profit Institutions

What role can proprietary institutions play in providing an array of higher educational offerings for a state? Or for some, the question may be "do they play a role" in the higher-education community? For some states the oversight and accountability of these for-profit institutions are part of the mainstream of higher-education's responsibility with some SHEEO offices monitoring some or all aspects of the operation of these institutions. I believe most would agree that obtaining a baccalaureate degree is not necessary or encouraged for every citizen. Some have interests and skills in occupational trades that can be honed and acquired in educational settings other than a traditional educational institution. Hence, states need to have strong occupational and vocational offerings, both public and proprietary, that meet the diverse needs of its citizens. A major research institution is not the most efficient or appropriate educational provider for one to learn about data-entry occupations nor is a trade school the most appropriate educational provider for the advanced study of molecular biology. Proprietary educational institutions fill an important gap. The key question for the state, now and in the future, is to determine how to ensure high quality and sufficient diversity of educational offerings that appropriately engage its citizens. Proprietary institutions are growing in number in this country, and there are no signs of eliminating them as educational providers. The issue becomes how best to channel their offerings for consumers in a way that states can keep their commitment to providing a quality array of higher-educational opportunities.

Role of Independent Institutions

In the same spirit, states must consider better use of existing educational providers by utilizing independent institutions. In many states, independent institutions provide high-quality educational services. Some of these institutions have become central players in a comprehensive, statewide system of higher education that supports state goals of access, choice, and diversity

(Lovell, 1998). In states with burgeoning enrollments, independent institutions offer an important source of quality education. States need to determine how best to involve independent institutions and consider them as viable alternatives for future growth.

Role of State Governance

How will the state effectively manage or facilitate a comprehensive array of higher-education program offerings? What roles will independent, proprietary, and public institutions play in the future? What incentives can the state provide to encourage effective cooperation from all sectors? Can the state's new consumer focus on accountability allow for higher quality of programs? Students are attending multiple institutions in an increasing fashion. States will need to provide consumers with some level of assurance that credits can transfer, courses are consistent, and financial aid is portable with concomitant enrollment. It will become even more common for students to attend several institutions to complete their degrees; states will have to take the lead to provide a systematic governance structure that accommodates alternative attendance patterns for all consumers.

Role of Technology

What does the future hold for the use of technology? More importantly, how will the use of technology shape the future of higher education? For many state legislatures, the use of technology is seen as a way to provide greater access to higher education. Several western states have mobilized their efforts and created the Western Governors University, with the intent of expanding traditional offerings in higher education to areas of the states that might have been previously underserved. The increased access is considered equally positive in the expectation that states can at some point reduce the costs of providing higher education. The argument is that more students can benefit from a broader array of providers at a less expensive rate than the costs for the state for constructing new facilities in the underserved regions. The set-up infrastructure costs have been enormous, and it has yet to be demonstrated that cost savings will result for any state. Another question about technology that has yet to be resolved is how it enhances student learning. Much more has to be known about the effects of technology, but it is an important area of concern for states and for the future of higher education.

Role of Tuition–Fees

A significant issue for the future is what should states do about the costs of higher education? States need to examine their responsibility for the financing of higher education and determine if it is good public policy to have the consumer bearing the largest share of the responsibility. Accountability issues and meeting state goals are of paramount importance to the discussion of who pays and who benefits. Use of performance-based funding and budgeting as a method of ensuring certain institutional behaviors or outcomes has been leveraging the pressures of the states. But if the individual becomes the major provider of financial support for higher education, does the state lose its leveraging power? The responsibility for financing of higher education is a critical issue states must address for today's and tomorrow's citizens.

Role of the State in Higher-Education Policy

This is less an issue of should states play a role, and more an issue of what role they should play in the critical decision making that shapes the public-policy future for higher education. It is clear that education is a state responsibility, but what is not clear is how far states can go in coordinating education without objection from institutions. In 1992 Congress made it clear that states should play a major role in reclaiming their responsibilities in the "triad" for higher education. Yet, after contentious debate and lobbying of Congress, the same program that was to accomplish congressional objectives was eliminated. States had begun to compare their policies and their responsibilities for higher education with fulfilling their obligations for providing higher education and protecting consumers from potentially less than credible educational providers. Now once again, states are dealing with the recommendations from Congress's National Commission on the Cost of Higher Education report, calling for less state regulation and greater flexible state policies. How can states ensure a quality array of higher-educational offerings, which might require them to use their policy-making leverage, while simultaneously appeasing those who want them to do less? States will need to consider carefully their options and strategically develop relationships with institutions and educational providers that will ensure quality and meet the needs of their citizens. Establishing a clear policy role for the state is critical to the future of higher education.

Where is higher education going for the next millennium? While no one can say without some amount of guessing, I believe the aforementioned issues must be addressed by states to ensure a positive future for higher education. Education is critical to any society, and our higher-education system in the United States has made significant contributions to developments within our country and throughout the world. It will continue to play a critical role if these and other issues are addressed in a timely, comprehensive, and collaborative manner.

BIBLIOGRAPHY

Albright, Brenda. 1998. *The Transition from Business as Usual to Funding for Results: State Efforts to Integrate Performance Measures in the Higher Education Budgeting Process*. Denver: State Higher Education Executive Officers.

Almanac. 1998. *The Chronicle of Higher Education,* 45: 1, 34.

American Association of State Colleges and Universities. 1998. *1997 State Issues Digest.* Washington, D.C.: AASCU.

Bennett, William J. 1984. *To Reclaim a Legacy: A Report on the Humanities in Higher Education.* Washington, D.C.: National Endowment for the Humanities.

Boyer, Carol. 1985. *Five Reports: Summary of the Recommendations of Recent Commission Reports on Improving Undergraduate Education.* Denver: Education Commission of the States.

Breneman, David, and Joni Finney. 1997. The Changing Landscape: Higher Education Finance in the 1990s. In *Shaping the Future: National Trends,* ed. California Higher Education Policy Center. Irvine: The California Higher Education Policy Center, 27–55.

Brubacher, John, and Willis Rudy. 1976. *Higher Education in Transition,* 3d ed. New York: Harper & Row.

Burke, Joseph. 1997. *Performance-Funding Indicators: Concerns, Values, and Models for Two- and Four-Year Colleges and Universities.* Albany: The Nelson A. Rockefeller Institute of Government.

Burke, Joseph, and Andrea Serban. 1997. *State Performance Funding and Budgeting for Public Higher Education: Current Status and Future Prospects.* Albany: The Nelson A. Rockefeller Institute of Government.

Callan, Patrick, and Joni Finney, eds. 1997. *Public and Private Financing of Higher Education: Shaping Public Policy for the Future.* Phoenix: American Council of Education and Oryx Press, 61–73.

Carnegie Commission on Higher Education. 1973. *Who Pays? Who Benefits? Who Should Pay?* New York: McGraw-Hill.

Christal, Melodie. 1998. *State Survey on Performance Measures: 1996–97.* Denver: State Higher Education Executive Officers.

Congressional Budget Office. 1996. *The Economic and Budget Outlook: Fiscal Years 1997–2007* (May). Washington, D.C.: U.S. Government Printing Office.

———. 1995. *The Economic and Budget Outlook: An Update* (August). Washington, D.C.: U.S. Government Printing Office.

Gladieux, Lawrence, and Jacqueline King. 1998. The Federal Government and Higher Education. In *American Higher Education in the 21st Century: Social, Political, and Economic Challenges,* ed. Philip Altbach; Robert Berdahl; and Patricia Gumport. Boston: Boston College Center for International Higher Education, 217–250.

Halstead, Kent. 1998. *Higher Education Report Card: 1998.* Washington, D.C.: Research Associates of Washington.

Hines, Edward. 1998. *State Higher Education Appropriations 1997–98.* Denver: State Higher Education Executive Officers.

Layzell, Dan, Cheryl D. Lovell, and Judith Gill. 1996. Developing Faculty as an Asset in a Period of Change and Uncertainty. In *Integrating Research on Faculty: Seeking New Ways to Communicate about the Academic Life of Faculty,* ed. U.S. Department of Education, Office of Education Research and Improvement, National Center for Education Statistics. Washington, D.C.: National Center for Education Statistics, 93–110.

Lovell, Cheryl D. 1998. Independent Higher Education in the West: Building Access Capacity, Boulder, Colo.: Western Interstate Commission for Higher Education.

————. 1997. Ten Lessons Learned from State Postsecondary Review Entities: Policy Implications for State and Federal Relationships. *Planning and Changing* 28: 4, 194–203.

————. 1996. *State Postsecondary Review Entities: One Step Forward and Two Steps Back in State-Federal Relationships?* A Report for SHEEO Members. Denver: State Higher Education Executive Officers.

Lovell, Cheryl D., and Judith Gill. 1997. Contemporary Issues in Public Policy and Higher Education. In *Public Policy and Higher Education: An Association for the Study of Higher Education (ASHE) Reader Series*, ed. Lester Goodchild; Cheryl D. Lovell; Edward Hines; and Judith Gill. Needham, Mass.: Simon and Schuster, 10–16.

Mortenson, Thomas. 1998. Public Policy and Opportunity for Higher Education. Paper presented at the Scholarship Foundation of St. Louis, October 27, St. Louis, Missouri.

————. 1996. Headed for Zero by the Year 2035?: State Tax Fund Appropriations for Higher Education FY97 (and beyond). *Postsecondary Education OPPORTUNITY*, 53, 1–7.

National Association of State Budget Officers. 1997. *State Expenditure Report*. Washington, D.C.: NASBO.

National Center for Education Statistics. 1996. *Current Funds Revenues and Expenditures of Institutions of Higher Education: Fiscal Years 1986 through 1994*. Washington, D.C.: U.S. Department of Education.

National Conference of State Legislatures. 1998. Party Control of State Legislatures 1938–98. http://www.ncsl.org/statevote98/partycon.htm.

————. 1997. *State Expenditure Report, 1996*. Denver: NCSL.

National Conference of State Legislatures INSIDE. 1996. Devolution Calls for Expert Advice. *State Legislatures* 22:2, 1.

National Institute of Education, Study Group on the Conditions of Excellence in American Higher Education. 1984. *Involvement in Learning: Realizing the Potential of American Higher Education*. Washington, D.C.: National Institute of Education, U.S. Department of Education.

Pulliam, John. 1991. *History of Education in America*, 5th ed. New York: Macmillan.

Rafool, Mandy. 1996. The Fiscal Perspective: State Tax and Expenditure Limits. *The Fiscal Letter*, No. 5. Washington, D.C.: National Association of State Budget Officers.

Serban, Andrea. 1997. Performance Funding for Public Higher Education: Views of Critical Stakeholders. Paper presented at The American Association for Higher Education, Assessment and Quality Conference, June 11–15, Miami, Florida.

State Expenditure Report. 1997. Fighting Judicial Control. *State Policy Reports* (February), 20.

Zemsky, Robert, and Gregory Wegner. 1997. Shaping the Future. In *Public and Private Financing of Higher Education: Shaping Public Policy for the Future*, ed. Patrick M. Callan and Joni Finney. Phoenix: American Council of Education and Oryx Press, 61–73.

Zumeta, William. 1998. 1997 State Higher Education Finance and Policy Developments. In *The NEA 1998 Almanac of Higher Education*, ed. National Education Association. Washington, D.C.: U.S. National Education Association, 65–92.

6

The Professionalization of College Sports

Richard G. Sheehan

A widespread perception exists that college sports have undergone a dramatic increase in professionalization over the past few decades. Corroborating examples abound. In college basketball, players are increasingly "rented" for one year; that is, a college signs a high-school athlete with the understanding he will attend for only one year before turning professional. Even schools with strong academic reputations such as Georgetown have succumbed to this temptation. Many institutions including Colorado, Miami, and Northwestern have seen some of their athletes encounter well-publicized legal difficulties, just like their professional counterparts. Perhaps most important to the "pro" perception is the steady stream of news articles suggesting a dramatic increase in revenues going into college sports, or at least into football and men's basketball. Examples range from Notre Dame's approximately $1 million per game television contract with NBC, to Florida's $11.8 million contract for its football coach, to the addition of luxury boxes at Alabama, Georgia, and Nebraska, to Florida State's $6 million shoe contract with Nike. Nevertheless, while headline examples are common, relying on specific instances is argument by analogy, which is problematic at best.

The contention that collegiate sports have fallen prey to the evils of professionalization is not new.[1] In the early 1980s schools appearing on national television received approximately $600,000 per game, and the National Collegiate Athletic Association (NCAA) effectively took over women's sports by offering a better economic deal in the short run than the competing Association of Intercollegiate Athletics for Women (AIAW) could afford. The 1970s witnessed dramatic increases in television-rights fees, ticket prices, and booster activism. However, the most concrete indication that professionalization of collegiate sports may be an old phenomenon is simply the age of many stadiums. The facilities employed by most of the "powers" in college football date back to the 1920s, including the home fields of Michigan, Tennessee, UCLA, USC, Ohio State, Georgia, and Stanford, seven of the eight largest collegiate football stadiums.[2] The median year of completion for stadiums of teams in the top twenty-five at the end of the 1995–1996 season was 1929, although most have gone through extensive renovation and upgrading since then. By contrast, the NCAA contends that collegiate sports are amateur, and many of its policies are expressly designed to foster the image, if not the practice, of amateur athletics. For example, when accepting a grant-in-aid, all athletes must sign an NCAA form asserting that sport is only an avocation for them.

The above examples suggest that collegiate sports, at least football, are big businesses now and have been for some time. Yet few studies have adopted a comprehensive approach to the question of whether collegiate sports are dominated by professional considerations. In part, the lack of prior studies has been due to the reluctance of colleges to release financial information that would allow "outsiders" to examine their level of professionalization. Since the passage of the Equity in Athletics Disclosure Act in 1994, however, a much more comprehensive approach to this question is possible, at least from the perspective of whether colleges are making money in their sports programs.

Before analyzing whether college sports have become or are becoming professional, I need to make two distinctions. When considering the professionalization of collegiate sports, one can consider the issue from the perspective of colleges themselves or from the perspective of the athletes. I will focus almost exclusively on colleges rather than athletes, intuitively because colleges, rather than college athletes, sign million-dollar contracts and because the press has focused more on colleges' apparent financial excesses.[3] Second, there is the widespread perception that big-time college-sports programs, specifically the top Division IA football programs, are fundamentally different from other programs like Division II or III football or even other sports in Division IA like wrestling or softball. What do Michigan's or Nebraska's football programs have in common with William's or St. John's? Or what do Florida's or Ohio State's football programs have in common with their tennis or soccer programs? When considering the professionalization of collegiate sports, it is necessary to analyze the issue from the perspective of major colleges and big-time programs versus other schools and other programs. Even colleges with big-time sports programs may emphasize or professionalize some sports, typically football and men's basketball, while allowing others to be "untainted" by professionalization considerations.

Conventional wisdom distinguishes between football at Division IA schools and men's basketball at a similarly select group of schools versus all other sports and all other schools. While this distinction is convenient and intuitive, it is not without problems. Arizona's baseball program, Boston University's hockey program, North Carolina's women's soccer, or Tennessee's women's basketball programs all appear to be just as professionally oriented as many Division IA football programs. In contrast, Rice's or Temple's or Oregon State's football program at least at first glance might appear to have little in common with a professional football program. There is a second reason for not drawing too sharp a contrast between football and men's basketball on the one hand and all other programs on the other. One can ask whether those two are just the first programs down the slippery slope toward professionalization and whether others such as baseball or women's basketball are beginning a similar descent? In any event, the common perspective is that Division IA football and men's basketball have been professionalized while other sports and divisions have not. The task here is, in part, to determine whether that perspective is accurate or justified.

What exactly is meant by professionalization? From a college's perspective, professionalization is determined by the answer to the question: Is the institution focusing primarily on costs, revenues, and profits when operating its athletic program? That is, is the athletic program now run like a professional franchise, or is it now run more like a professional franchise than say ten years ago? A "yes" answer suggests that collegiate sports have been professionalized. Alternately, are colleges focusing on the overall academic mission of the institution even when guiding the sports program? Is there any substantive difference between the importance of the academic mission in the conduct of collegiate football in the 1990s and the 1900s?[4] A "no" answer suggests that college sports are not becoming increasingly professional even though they may be profitable—although one might argue that they have always been professional.

From an athlete's perspective, what is meant by professionalization? Are so-called "student–athletes" more professional in orientation, demeanor, or performance now than ten, twenty, or fifty years ago? This question is even more difficult to address than the college professionalization question. To answer it accurately would require going inside athletes' psyches and determining whether they are more attuned to their potential professional careers now than similar athletes were in years past. Obviously, that is not possible. An alternate approach to the question of athlete's professionalization focuses on the phrase "student–athlete." Is that phrase more or less appropriate now than ten or twenty years ago? Or is the phrase "student–athlete" more or less appropriate than the phrase "athlete–student" where the order reflects priorities?

The answers to the professionalization questions, in fact, have three components. First, is the professional perspective accurate now? Second, is that perspective more accurate now than, say, ten years ago? And third, what economic incentives exist that reinforce or mitigate the professional tendencies or emphasis? The outline of the chapter follows this agenda with a fourth question added: What are the implications of the professionalization of collegiate sports? In the next section I discuss measurement and methodology issues. Exactly what is meant by the term professionalization? What distinctions are relevant and important? What makes a sports program professional rather than amateur? In the third section empirical evidence is considered, both current and historical. Section four includes an examination of the economic incentives in more detail, and their implications for the future are presented in the final section.

DEFINITIONS, MEASUREMENT, AND METHODOLOGY

The key initial question is simple: Exactly what is meant by professionalization? There are two intuitive answers. First, anyone with a tremendous salary or dramatic profits is a pro. Second, people know it when they see it (e.g., Florida State's or Nebraska's or Notre Dame's football program). However, neither answer is satisfactory. The theoretical answer is much more precise and still relatively straightforward. It depends on the institution's "objective function" or goal or purpose. An institution could have a number of different primary objectives for its athletic department, including maximizing profits or total revenues, maximizing victories or the winning percentage, or maximizing the college's reputation or enrollment, endowment or even the income of its graduates.[5] In reality, a college's objective function is likely a complex combination of these factors and others, and different institutions likely place different weights on different factors. It would appear unrealistic to assume that Harvard or Harvey Mudd operate with the same objectives as Miami or Michigan. Nevertheless, it appears reasonable to assume that all institutions at least consider the question of athletic revenues and costs when determining athletic priorities, even Division III schools. Clearly, that does not make all institutions professional. Thus, I turn to the issue of the primary objective. If a college operates its athletic program—or parts of its athletic program—with the fundamental focus on revenues or profits, then I label it professional. If its prime objective is winning percentage, entertainment, alumni satisfaction, or anything else, then I contend that it is not professional—even if it is highly profitable. Stated slightly differently, in theory it is the primary pursuit of profits that makes a program professional rather than a program's success in making profits.[6]

Nevertheless, implementation of the professionalization criterion poses a substantial problem. The question of interest is, What is an administration's objective function? Without interrogating an administration at length, however, it is unlikely that anyone could uncover the true objectives. After all, what university president is going to admit in all candor that the reason his/her institution has a football program is to make money and subsidize either the rest of the athletic program or the rest of the institution? At a minimum, such candor would likely lead the Internal Revenue Service to treat their athletic revenue as taxable income. Thus, measuring the true objective or what goes on inside an administrator's head is virtually impossible, and I am left to reflect only on the results of administrative decisions. The focus therefore must be on actual profits, revenues, and costs, rather than objectives. Furthermore, actual values may differ substantially from the objectives. For example, Notre Dame's football program has had tremendous financial success, while Vanderbilt's football program has struggled financially. Thus, the numbers suggest that Notre Dame has placed great weight on financial success, while Vanderbilt has not. In fact, that need not be the case at all. Notre Dame's objective could well be to improve its academic reputation—and it may have used the football revenue to do just that— while Vanderbilt's objective could be to improve its football finances, and if not to make money, then at least to lose less. In this case, Vanderbilt would better fit the pro model than would Notre Dame![7] This conclusion is likely to be inconsistent with most people's intuition regarding the distinction between professional and amateur. This point also indicates that results presented by schools must be interpreted with great caution, although the aggregate results should be relatively insensitive to this problem.[8] In practice, rather than theory, I must employ a measure like the level of profits as an indicator of professionalization, even while recognizing this measure's limitations.

To determine whether collegiate sports are now professionalized, the primary data source is the "gender-equity" reports that each college is required to make available based on the Equity in Athletics Disclosure Act and amendments to the Higher Education Act. (Unless otherwise noted data for all tables are from university gender-equity reports compiled by the author.) This legislation requires all institutions receiving federal assistance to release data on the costs and revenues of their athletic program in general, as well as on some specific sports, including football and men's basketball. The numbers reported by the colleges are not without problems. However, they represent the best available systematic information.

Three primary problems exist with these data. First, different institutions use different definitions and accounting conventions when reporting their revenues and costs. Some take a much more comprehensive approach to what is included in costs and revenues, while others adopt a much more limited perspective. This is primarily a microproblem that sometimes makes comparisons across institutions difficult without carefully comparing revenues and costs on a line-by-line basis and without some familiarity with the institutions and their accounting practices. From my perspective this is not a major difficulty, since my primary focus is not on who is or is not professional. The second problem is the general omission of facilities expenses, infrastructure expenses, and maintenance expenses from the cost figures reported in the gender-equity reports. This omission biases upward the profits of collegiate sports franchises. I will attempt to adjust for this bias. The third problem is that the allocation of revenues as well as some costs is, at many institutions, arbitrary or rudimentary. That is not a criticism of any institution, because its accounting system is designed for internal use rather than for public consumption. Nevertheless, comparing data across institutions can be problematic. For example, some institutions include student-activities fees under unallocated athletic revenues, while others include these fees under categories like men's unallocated revenues or football revenues, and others do not include them under athletic revenue at all. If they represent fees in lieu of admission to football games, then they are appropriately included under football revenue. If they are fees for use of general athletic facilities, then typically they would not belong in the athletic department's budget. In addition, many institutions have booster–fundraiser organizations outside the direct control of the athletic department or the university, and revenues raised by these organizations may not be disclosed on a gender-equity report. Finally, many schools have institutional peccadillos that further obfuscate the true numbers. For example, the funds from Notre Dame's television contract with NBC primarily are allocated to the general scholarship fund and are not included in the athletic budget or in the revenues derived from intercollegiate athletics. In some cases revenues are understated and in others overstated; in most cases, costs are understated. The analysis below generally employs the self-reported and unadjusted numbers from the gender-equity reports. Where noted, the analysis also makes adjustments to these numbers. While profits are adjusted down, conclusions from adjusted versus unadjusted data do not differ dramatically.

THE EVIDENCE

Included in Table 6.1 is a presentation of revenue and expenditure numbers for the 1995–1996 academic year based on the self-reported gender-equity reports for all institutions having Division IA football teams with two exceptions. One exception is the three service academies. Their accounting procedures are fundamentally different from other colleges, so it makes little sense to compare them with other institutions. The second are eight institutions that have not released complete cost and revenue information.[9] That leaves a total of ninety-nine reporting institutions. Mean and median revenues and expenses are presented for football, men's basketball, and all other men's sports and women's sports.

The results indicate that the mean reported profit in Division IA football is slightly in excess of $3 million, while in men's basketball the mean profit is $1.38 million. In contrast, other men's sports and women's sports have sizable losses. The implication: Football and men's basketball appear to fit a professional model, while other men's sports and women's sports do not. The mean numbers, however, are potentially misleading, since a few programs could make substantial profits, while most lose money. The median values indicate that the median self-reported profit in football is substantially less (only $1.17 million), while the median self-reported profit in men's basketball is only $.75 million. The medians indicate that other men's sports and women's

Table 6.1
Revenues and Expenditures, 1995 to 1996 (in Millions of Dollars)

		Division 1A-Mean		
	Football	Men's Basketball	Other Men's Sports	Women's Sports
Revenue	6.27	2.40	0.24	0.59
Expense	3.26	1.02	1.28	2.42
Profit	3.01	1.38	-1.05	-1.83

		Division 1A-Median		
	Football	Men's Basketball	Other Men's Sports	Women's Sports
Revenue	4.72	1.89	0.10	0.14
Expense	2.93	0.83	1.19	2.22
Profit	1.17	0.75	-0.98	-1.68

		Number of Schools Reporting a Profit		
	Football	Men's Basketball	Other Men's Sports	Women's Sports
Reporting Profit	71	75	3	4
Total Schools Reporting	99	99	99	99

Note: All calculations are based on all Division 1A schools providing usable cost and revenue data in compliance with the Higher Education Act. All data are self-reported. The schools not providing information are Boise State, Boston College, Houston, Michigan State, Pittsburgh, Rice, and Syracuse. The three service academies also are excluded, since their accounting systems differ dramatically from those of most colleges.

sports continue to lose money and at magnitudes roughly comparable to the means. The last section of Table 6.1 indicates how many institutions report profits in each area. Seventy-two report profits in football, while seventy-five report profits in men's basketball. By contrast, only five report profits in other men's sports and only four in women's sports. In addition, given the overlap between those reporting profits in the last two categories (Central Florida, Idaho, Rice, and Stanford), it appears that for all reported profits, an artifact of accounting practices may be affecting the figures for real profits.

Based on the results in Table 6.1 it appears that virtually no institutions make money on programs other than football and men's basketball, while a substantial number of Division IA programs have profitable and potentially professional football and men's basketball programs. Thus, at least one component of conventional wisdom appears correct: Discussions of professionalization generally can ignore sports other than football and men's basketball. This conclusion should be reached with some care, however. Table 6.1 indicates that at virtually all institutions women's programs as well as other men's programs, in sum, experience a loss. Some individual programs could still be profitable, as the worksheets accompanying the gender-equity reports indicate. That is, these sums may aggregate many money-losing programs with a few profitable programs. The worksheets generally are not required to be made public under the Equity in Athletics Disclosure Act, and many schools choose not to release the information on those forms. However, almost one-half provided their worksheets, and they indicate that virtually no individual programs other than football or men's basketball make money.

On the profitability of football and men's basketball, the results in Table 6.1 present a somewhat ambiguous record. The self-reported numbers suggest that over 70 percent of all Division IA football and men's basketball programs make money. However, they leave open a number of questions. The difference between the means and medians suggests that it may be only a small fraction of Division IA schools that have substantial profits and fit the professional model. In addition, the accounting profits at a few schools in women's sports suggest that the self-reported numbers may contain some biases. And these values are for 1995–1996, raising the question of how these numbers compare with those from prior years.

Table 6.2 begins to address these concerns, comparing the 1995–1996 numbers for football and men's basketball with those from prior years. (Given the results in Table 6.1, it appears appropriate to consider other sports as nonprofessional at least for the moment.) The raw numbers for prior years are obtained from Fulks (1996).[10] Table 6.2 presents mean profits in football and men's basketball in Division IA and IAA for the years in which Fulks conducted a survey for the National Collegiate Athletics Association (NCAA). Fulks' numbers for 1994–1995 and my numbers for 1995–1996 are not strictly comparable since, for example, his are based on a survey and mine are based on gender-equity reports. Nevertheless, the numbers are consistent enough to suggest that comparisons can be made with care.

The results in Table 6.2 suggest that profits at Division IA schools in both football and men's basketball have increased steadily over the past twelve years, at least as measured by mean profits. However, Division IAA schools on average have consistently witnessed a loss of about $.5 million per year in football and have also consistently experienced a small loss in men's basketball. The implication is straightforward. Some Division IA schools are profitable but Division IAA schools are almost uniformly unprofitable. In addition, it appears that profits at Division IA football programs have increased by an average of 7.6 percent per year, while the average profits at Division IA basketball programs have increased by an average of close to 13 percent per year. These results are consistent with the hypothesis of increased professionalization in Division IA football and men's basketball. In contrast, for Division IAA average losses have increased, although the magnitudes of the increases are minor. In sum, Table 6.2 suggests that any search for professionalization in collegiate sports should likely be confined to Division IA. While institutions in other divisions may have professional dreams or aspirations, those dreams are largely unrealized.

Table 6.2
Men's Basketball and Football Profits (in Millions of Dollars)

	Football			
	Division 1A		**Division 1AA**	
	Mean	Growth Rate (%)	Mean	Growth Rate (%)
1984 to 1985	1.34		-0.25	
1988 to 1989	1.23	-2.1	-0.51	-19.5
1992 to 1993	2.27	16.6	-0.62	-5.0
1994 to 1995	2.42	3.3	-0.51	9.3
1995 to 1996	3.01	24.4	-0.53	-3.9
Average Growth Rate 1984 to 1996		7.6		-7.1
Total Division Profits 1995 to 1996	300.5		-57.7	

	Basketball			
	Division 1A		**Division 1AA**	
	Mean	Growth Rate (%)	Mean	Growth Rate (%)
1984 to 1985	0.37		-0.02	
1988 to 1989	0.69	16.9	-0.07	-36.8
1992 to 1993	1.03	10.5	-0.11	-12.0
1994 to 1995	1.38	15.7	-0.08	14.7
1995 to 1996	1.38	0.0	NA	
Average Growth Rate 1984 to 1996		12.7		
Total Division Profits 1995 to 1996	138.4			

Sources: Numbers prior to 1995–1996 were obtained from Daniel L. Fulks, *Revenues and Expenses of Division I and II Intercollegiate Athletics Programs: Financial Trends and Relationships—1995* (Overland Park, Kans.: National Collegiate Athletics Association, 1996). All other numbers are taken from data provided in compliance with the Higher Education Act.

When considering professionalization as in Tables 6.1 and 6.2 it is intuitive to emphasize profits rather than revenues or costs. Nevertheless, the revenue and costs numbers are also of interest, if only because press reports emphasize the large and apparently increasing revenues in collegiate athletics. The mean and median revenues for Division IA schools presented in Table 6.1 suggest revenues especially are not uniformly distributed across schools. In particular, it appears that the schools with the biggest revenues substantially increase the mean (relative to the median) revenue, especially in football. In contrast, the differences between mean and median costs are not nearly as great.[11]

Tables 6.1 and 6.2 focus on profits, total revenue, and total costs, but are not informative about the composition of revenues and costs. The gender-equity reports contain only limited information about the composition of revenues and expenses. Thus, I employ a decomposition of revenues and costs based on Fulks (1996). Table 6.3 presents summary information for Division IA and IAA schools for selected categories of revenues and expenses as well as the relationships between the two divisions. One limitation of these numbers is that they refer to the entire intercollegiate athletics program of an institution rather than just to the football or men's basketball program. Nevertheless, given the relative importance of those two sports, in particular in terms of revenues generated, the numbers carry strong implications about those sports as well.

What initially appears to be the most noteworthy feature of Table 6.3 is the profit implication based on Fulks's numbers. On average, Division IA athletics programs just broke even in 1994–1995. The implication is that profits in football and men's basketball were just offset by losses in other sports. However, the results in Tables 6.1 and 6.2 suggest that the averages hide a wide range of individual school performance, likely with a few programs having substantial net revenue and most having losses. In contrast, Division IAA institutions on average have a loss of almost $1 million. While some distribution about this mean is likely, the Division IAA distribution appears to be less skewed by a few outliers than the Division IA average. Thus, it would appear that most Division IAA schools lose money on athletics.

What I believe is the most interesting comparison in Table 6.3, however, at least from the perspective of professionalization, is the by-category comparison between the Division IA and IAA results. For example, total Division IAA revenues are only 27.4 percent of Division IA revenues, while total Division IAA costs are 33.8 percent of Division IAA costs. The conclusion is a reaffirmation of one result from Table 6.2. Division IA schools may be big-time professional sports, but Division IAA institutions generally are not—at least not successful professionals— although there may be a few exceptions in specific programs or schools.

The comparisons between Division IA and IAA, however, go well beyond simply the totals. Upon examining the individual revenue categories, the greatest proportional differences occur in ticket revenues, postseason revenues, conference distribution, and media. These categories are the ones most impacted by athletic success, certainly more than student-activity fees and government support. The ticket-revenue difference alone amounts to over $4 million of the approximately $11 million average difference between Division IA and IAA schools. In addition, while there has been an extensive debate about whether donor contributions are stimulated by athletic success, these results certainly suggest that having a big-time or professional sports program is accompanied by donor contributions even if it does not cause those contributions.[12] Contributions here, however, typically are direct contributions to the athletic program rather than contributions to the institution's

Table 6.3
Composition of Revenues and Expenditures, 1994 to 1995 (in Millions of Dollars)

	Division 1A	Division 1AA	Division 1AA as % of Division 1A
Revenues			
Tickets	4.54	0.52	11.5
Post Season	0.55	0.03	5.4
Conference Distribution	1.11	0.04	3.6
Student Activity Fees	1.04	0.90	86.5
Media	1.12	0.07	6.3
Donor Contributions	2.29	0.41	17.2
Direct Government Support	0.29	0.46	158.6
Institutional Support	1.38	1.21	87.7
Other	3.19	0.66	20.7
Total	15.51	4.25	27.4
Expenses			
Grants-in-Aid	2.68	1.27	47.4
Salaries/Fringe Benefits	4.84	1.70	35.1
Recruiting	0.33	0.12	36.4
Debt Service	0.48	0.02	4.2
Capital Expenditures	0.47	0.05	10.6
Other	6.69	2.08	31.1
Total	15.49	5.24	33.8

Source: Calculations are based on data obtained from Daniel L. Fulks, *Revenues and Expenses of Division I and II Intercollegiate Athletics Programs: Financial Trends and Relationships— 1995* (Overland Park, Kans.: National Collegiate Athletics Association, 1996).

general fund. As such, they are likely much more closely tied to the existence and success of a professional or big-time athletic program.

Cost differences between Division IA and IAA programs appear to be much smaller than revenue differences. However, two differences stand out, in the debt-service and capital-expenditure categories. The typical Division IA institution reports spending almost $1 million per year in these categories, while the typical Division IAA institution spends only $70,000. These categories are important because the gender-equity reports exclude them when examining expenditures. That is, profits in Table 6.1 exclude capital expenditures and debt service and consider only operating expenditures. If the $1 million figure represents the nonoperating expenditures for the typical institution, and if those expenditures are allocated entirely to football, then the median football program only breaks even. If those expenditures are allocated, for example by one-third to football, reflecting its approximate percentage of operating expenses, then the number of programs that are profitable drops from seventy-one down to fifty-nine. Given that Division IA sports other than football and men's basketball appear to have more in common with Division IAA sports in general, it would be reasonable to allocate well over one-third of the capital and debt-service expenditures to football. Irrespective of the allocation, however, just over fifty Division IA football schools are profitable—and thus presumably successful professionals.

Even this number, however, may be biased upward. It is quite likely that many of the reported cost numbers are biased downward. That is, many institutions have accounting systems that do not allocate all costs incurred by intercollegiate athletics to intercollegiate athletics. One can reasonably ask if telephone service, postage, and maintenance incurred due to intercollegiate athletic competition is actually charged to the athletic program. If it is not, then an institution's net revenues from athletics will be overstated. If only some institutions do not allocate all costs, then average costs will be understated, and average profits will be overstated. The gender-equity reports give some hint about the potential magnitude of the problem. For example, in football Florida State reports the lowest expenditures in the ACC; Penn State reports the second lowest expenditures in the Big Ten; and Texas A&M reports the lowest expenditure in the Big Twelve. Yet all three schools are consistently at the top of the conference standings in football and are consistently among the top twenty-five ranked teams. It strains my credulity that any of these teams are actually at the bottom of the expenditures despite their reported numbers. While an in-depth analysis of this point is beyond the scope of this chapter, it appears that on average football expenditures are understated by at least 25 percent and possibly as much as 50 percent. Adding these omitted expenses would reduce the number of profitable collegiate football teams to no more than forty and possibly as few as twenty-five.[13]

To this point the numbers suggest that Division IAA, II, and III institutions are generally not professional sports franchises, though some are at least successful and profitable sports franchises. In addition, the numbers suggest that not even all Division IA institutions are professional. Tables 6.4 and 6.5 address the question of who likely are the real professionals. Table 6.4 presents the average profits for football and men's basketball by conference. The presumption is that like-minded schools have joined in a conference. Schools in the Big Ten are assumed to have a similar perspective on the role of athletics in an academic setting, and schools in the MAC are also assumed to have similar perspectives. However, Big Ten and MAC schools may diverge rather dramatically in terms of goals and objectives.

The numbers in Table 6.4 suggest that as far as football is concerned, the SEC and the Big Ten are the "real pros," with average profits of approximately $9.5 million and $7.6 million respectively. In contrast, Conference USA, the MAC, and the WAC all report losses on average, suggesting that while schools in these conferences may have professional aspirations, they do not have the concomitant profits. These results should come as no surprise to anyone who follows college football.

Table 6.4
Mean Profits and Standard Deviations by Conference, 1995 to 1996
(in Millions of Dollars)

	Mean Profits	
Conference	Football	Men's Basketball
Atlantic Coast (ACC)	2.49	2.79
Big East	3.09	0.81
Big 10	7.39	3.49
Big 12	3.46	1.26
Conference USA	-0.70	1.19
Mid-American (MAC)	-0.79	-0.20
Pacific Coast 10 (PAC 10)	4.78	1.44
Southeastern (SEC)	8.60	2.60
Western Athletic (WAC)	0.22	0.48
Independent		

	Standard Deviations	
Conference	Football	Men's Basketball
Atlantic Coast (ACC)	2.93	1.83
Big East	3.56	0.68
Big 10	4.15	1.02
Big 12	2.92	1.41
Conference USA	1.75	2.83
Mid-American (MAC)	0.31	0.12
Pacific Coast 10 (PAC 10)	5.83	1.63
Southeastern (SEC)	6.34	1.54
Western Athletic (WAC)	1.15	0.76
Independent	4.38	0.31

Note: All calculations are based on all Division 1A schools providing usable cost and revenue data in compliance with the Higher Education Act. All data are self-reported. The schools not providing information are Boise State, Boston College, Houston, Michigan State, Pittsburgh, Rice, and Syracuse. The three service academies also are excluded, since their accounting systems differ dramatically from those of most colleges.

In basketball, it is a similar story, although the conferences change slightly. The ACC and the Big Ten both average profits of approximately $3.75 million, with the SEC at approximately $2.25 million. In contrast, the MAC and independents lose a small sum, while the WAC barely breaks even.

While Table 6.4 considers conferences average profits, which yield an indication of which conferences have professional tendencies or inclinations, Table 6.5 presents the profits at selected individual institutions, including the highest and lowest and a few other high profile institutions. Again, these are self-reported profits and are subject to institutional accounting peccadillos. The results confirm the suspicion made, based on the first tables, that a few

Table 6.5
Profits of Selected Schools, 1995 to 1996 (in Millions of Dollars)

	Football			Men's Basketball	
Rank	School	Profits	Rank	School	Profits
1	Washington	20.3	1	Louisville	6.9
2	Florida	19.8	2	Arkansas	6.1
3	Auburn	16.8	3	Indiana	5.5
4	Penn State	15.5	4	North Carolina	5.4
5	Georgia	14.3	5	Arizona	5.3
6	Michigan	12.1	6	Kentucky	4.7
7	Alabama	12.1	7	Ohio State	4.6
8	Notre Dame	11.6	8	Iowa	4.1
9	Tennessee	11.3	9	Nebraska	4.1
10	Texas A&M	10.4	10	Florida State	3.8
11	Ohio State	10.2	11	Michigan	3.7
28	Nebraska	4.2	17	Duke	3.5
33	Miami (FL)	3.4	27	UCLA	2.5
51	Stanford	1.1	63	UNLV	0.5
97	Ala-Birmingham	-1.7	97	Kent State	-0.4
98	Cincinnati	-1.9	98	Baylor	-0.4
99	Tulane	-3.3	99	Clemson	-0.5

Top 10 Percent of Sum of 100 Division 1A Football Schools

	Football	Men's Basketball
Profits	48.0	36.4
Revenues	28.8	27.9
Costs	11.1	16.3

Note: All calculations are based on all Division 1A schools providing usable cost and revenue data in compliance with the Higher Education Act. All data are self-reported.

schools have done extremely well. In football, Tennessee reported profits of $19 million and Florida of $18 million, while eleven schools reported profits in excess of $10 million. Note that not all highly successful on-the-field programs show up in the top rank of the most profitable institutions. For example, Florida State and Miami (Florida) both have self-reported profits of $4 million which puts them outside the Top twenty-five in terms of financial rankings. In some cases a lack of high rank is due to unusual accounting conventions (arguably Florida State); in others, it reflects a real lack of net revenues (Miami), although in some cases there are large gross revenues. Nevertheless, for a perspective on which programs are professional, the top schools in Table 6.5's rankings would be the place to start.

How far down the list does the label professional apply? The bottom of the table presents profits, revenues and costs of the top ten as a percentage of the overall profits, revenues, and costs. For football, the top-ten most profitable programs receive almost half of all self-reported profits received by Division IA schools. In contrast, their costs are only slightly more than the average Division IA school. Based on profits it appears that there are only a handful of programs that are professional. Based on costs, however, it would appear that virtually all programs at least have professional aspirations, given the near equality of reported expenditures.

ECONOMIC INCENTIVES

The results to this point suggest two conclusions. First, the distribution of profits is far from equal, with a few institutions doing extremely well and apparently typifying the perspective that collegiate sports—at least football and men's basketball—are professional sports. Second, only a limited number of institutions are profitable, and many, if not most, lose money or at best break even, even in football. Nevertheless, the results also suggest that most Division IA schools spend a substantial amount of money on football and men's basketball even if they receive no profit. In the absence of substantial average profits, why do schools continue to spend?

Two possible answers exist. First, few ask if an institution's math department makes money and few judge the library by whether it is profitable. Why should the football program be any different? This perspective is inimical to the professionalization model. However, this perspective also begs the question of whether a "big-time" football program is necessary for the academic mission of the university. Many highly reputable schools including the University of Chicago, California Institute of Technology, and Massachusetts Institute of Technology have chosen not to field a Division IA football team, but none have chosen to downplay their math department or their library. Their lack of major college football indicates that officials have concluded that football is not central to the fundamental educational mission of a university. If football is not a prerequisite for an educational institution, it would appear reasonable that it can and perhaps should be judged by a different standard than the math department or the library. Thus, football may need to generate profits in order to justify its existence at an educational institution.

Second, there may be economic factors that present an incentive for institutions to keep a sports program and fund it aggressively even if it appears to lose money. Those incentives could take either of two forms. The first is simply that having a big-time football program could be viewed as a *sine qua non* of attracting students, for example. There is no direct evidence supporting this perspective, although there is evidence indicating that winning does increase applications (Murphy and Trandel, 1994; Mixon and Hsing, 1994) and may increase admission standards (Curtis, 1995; Sigelman, 1995). It is precisely this evidence that suggests a substantial incentive to spend. The appropriate phrase would appear to be this: A college needs to spend money to make money. On that basis higher costs should be associated with higher revenues and hopefully higher profits. (A college would also expect greater spending to be associated with on-the-field success, but that is not the focus here.)

Do increased expenditures generate higher revenues? Table 6.6 presents the answer based on regressing revenues based on costs. All equations were estimated with dichotomous (dummy) variables for individual conferences with the MAC serving as the reference conference. Conference dummy variables are reported only when significant. The results for all four types of sports programs indicate that revenues increase when expenditures increase. However, the magnitude of the slope coefficients are critical. Specifically, for other men's programs and women's programs, a dollar increase in expenditures will generate only a $.26 and $.35 increase in revenues respectively. In both cases these coefficients are significantly less than one at the 5 percent level. The implication is stark. Putting money into either of these programs is not a profitable undertaking. Consider women's programs since Title IX has required institutions to increase spending on women's programs. The results indicate that each dollar of spending will generate only $.35 in additional revenue and thus will increase the athletic department's loss by $.65. The conclusion: Increased funding for women's programs is the law under Title IX, but colleges will likely have little enthusiasm for it. Title IX costs money, a result not surprising to anyone who follows collegiate athletics.

The football results are slightly different. A dollar increase in expenditures increases revenues by $.66, again less than the increase in costs. However, for football this increase is not statistically significantly different from one. In other words, these numbers can be used to argue that expenditures on football are justified based on the additional revenues generated. Supporters of big-time college football could argue that any costs of those programs do not siphon funds from the rest of the university while funds allocated to women's sports programs do exactly that. While this conclusion is consistent with the data, there is an alternative conclusion also consistent with the data—and having very different implications. Additional football expenditures have the same impact on football revenues as additional expenditures on women's programs have on their revenues. The .66 football coefficient is not significantly different from .35 women's sports coefficient. With this view, women's sports and football should be treated alike! (There is a problem with this conclusion that I will mention later.)

There is a much less ambiguous perspective with the coefficient for men's basketball. Expenditures has a coefficient of 2.04, indicating that each dollar of additional spending generates $2.04 in additional revenues. This coefficient is significantly greater than one. Thus, putting money into men's basketball generates an even greater increase in revenues and thus also increases profits. Corroborating evidence on this point is the substantial increase in the number of Division I basketball programs, though most are not included in this study. Nevertheless, the point is simply that a college appears to be able to make a greater profit in men's basketball simply by spending more money.

Table 6.6
Regression Results I

	Football	Men's Basketball	Other Men's	Women's
Constant	-.33 (0.24)	-.66 (1.58)	-.13 (1.04)	-.43 (1.40)
Expenses	.66* (2.15)	2.04** (8.38)	.26** (3.87)	.35** (3.96)
ACC	4.06* (2.14)	2.26** (3.84)		
Big East	4.72* (2.11)			
Big 10	8.88** (4.84)	3.05** (5.36)		
Big 12	5.14** (2.81)			
PAC10	6.73** (3.36)			
SEC	10.29** (5.62)	1.68** (2.98)		
R^2	.50	.68	.17	.21
n	99	99	99	99

Note: Absolute values of t-statistics are in parentheses. ** indicates statistically significant at the .01 level, and * indicates statistically significant at the .05 level. All coefficients are expressed in millions except for the coefficient on expenses. R^2 is the adjusted R square, and n is the number of observations.

The result implies that colleges have a strong economic incentive to pursue the professional model, independent of the desire to win or any other institutional goals. More spending and greater professionalization leads to greater profits—and presumably those profits can be used to subsidize the rest of the athletic department or the rest of the institution.

Before reaching the conclusion that there is an economic incentive to pursue the professional model only in men's basketball, there is one further test to undertake. Given the accounting problems noted above, it is reasonable to conclude that cost numbers in particular may be understated for a range of schools. Thus, I undertook a second set of regressions, using the conference average revenues and costs rather than the individual institution's values. The results are presented in Table 6.7.

Table 6.7
Regression Results II

	Football	Men's Basketball	Other Men's	Women's
Constant	-4.00	-.84	-.08	-.21
	(1.38)	(1.06)	(1.18)	(1.23)
Expenses	3.02**	3.12**	.24**	.32**
	(3.59)	(4.34)	(4.55)	(4.69)
R^2	.54	.64	.66	.68
n	11	11	11	11

Note: Absolute values of t-statistics are in parentheses. ** indicates statistically significant at the .01 level; * indicates statistically significant at the .05 level. The constant coefficients are expressed in millions, while the expenses coefficients are expressed in dollars. R^2 is the adjusted R square, and n is the number of observations.

With one notable exception, the results in Tables 6.6 and 6.7 are consistent. A dollar increase in other men's spending or women's spending increases revenue by \$.24 and \$.32 respectively, both significantly less than one. A dollar increase in men's basketball increases revenue by \$3.12, significantly greater than one. These findings are consistent with those from Table 6.6. The difference occurs in football, where the results in Table 6.7 indicate that an additional dollar spending increases revenue by \$3.02, which is also significantly greater than one. How can this result be reconciled with the coefficient of \$.66 in Table 6.6? I believe the appropriate explanation returns to omissions in the cost data. Specifically, the top ten programs in terms of football profits have 48 percent of the total football profits accruing to Division IA schools. They also have 29 percent of the total revenues, but only 11 percent of the reported costs. In addition, when schools like Ohio State and Florida report lower expenses than Illinois and Vanderbilt, the most logical conclusion appears to be that costs are understated for many schools.[14] Thus, regression results by school may understate the true relation, while conference averages would give a more accurate estimate.[15]

The argument that football "pays its own way" and that expenditures on football are justified by the revenue created have been around since Walter Camp, Red Grange, and Grantland Rice (Bachman, 1922; Camp, 1920; Rice, 1926; Wilkens, 1938). Are these arguments justified? For advocates of football, the regression results here have no easy positive interpretation. The individual school results suggest that, at the margin, football does not pay its own way. However, the conference results support the opposite contention. I am inclined to place more weight on the conference results, but even these are problematic for advocates of big-time football. If the conference results are more reliable, it is likely due to many institutions substantially understating the costs of their football program. In this case, the profit numbers for football in Tables 6.1 through 6.5 are biased upward. However, this change would suggest that the typical football program loses money and that most Division IA football programs are not generally profitable.

While the focus here has been on football and its profitability, supporters of the pro model have emphasized one additional point. That is, profits from football are used to subsidize other sports including women's sports programs. If this were the case, one might argue that professionalization of college football was a necessary evil. If football profits are used to subsidize women's programs, for example, we should expect higher football profits to lead to larger expenditures on women's programs. The results of testing this hypothesis are presented in Table 6.8. Expenditures for men's basketball and other men's programs and women's programs are regressed on both gross football revenues and net football revenues (profits) both by school and by conference. The two sets of results are broadly consistent. Looking at the results by school in the top of the table, an increase in gross football revenue leads to a small but statistically significant (.05 % level) increase in expenditures both in other men's programs and in women's programs. It appears to have no impact on basketball expenditures. The by-school results suggest that the magnitude of the impact is less than $.10 for each dollar of increased gross revenue. In addition, net football revenue or profit appears to have no impact on expenditures of any other program.

The conference results indicate greater responsiveness to football revenue. For example, each dollar in net football revenue increases women's expenditures by about $.32 and other men's expenditures by $.13 leaving $.55 to be spent elsewhere in the university. This result must also be interpreted with caution—and again places universities in a dilemma. For those programs like Washington, Florida, and Notre Dame where there are clear and substantial football profits, the implications are clear. More funds are available and will be spent on so-called "Olympic" or nonrevenue sports and substantial money may even be turned over to the university's general fund. For an institution like Ohio State, the results suggest women's sports expenditures will be about $3 million higher than they otherwise would be. However, what about programs like Akron, Baylor, or San Jose State that lose money on football? The implication is that the football programs at these type of institutions actually hurt the women's sports programs, for example, rather than help. The results suggest that an institution like Tulane would spend nearly $1 million less on women's sports due to the impact of football. In sum, the impact of football and professionalization on women's sports is mixed.

IMPLICATIONS FOR THE FUTURE AND CONCLUSIONS

The general conclusion is simple: Collegiate football and men's basketball appear to fit a professional model, while other sports do not. That should

Table 6.8
Regression Results III

	Men's Basketball		Other Men's		Women's	
Constant	.43**	.45**	.90**	.86**	1.38**	1.28**
	(2.49)	(2.54)	(5.11)	(5.02)	(4.12)	(3.90)
Net Football Revenue	-.02 (1.59)		.02 (1.29)		.05 (1.93)	
Gross Football Revenue		.09 (0.63)		.04** (2.73)		.07** (2.71)
R²	.27	.25	.42	.46	.38	.41
n	99	99	99	99	99	99

Dependent Variable: Expenses by Conference

Constant	.95**	.59**	.89**	.59**	-.21	1.05**
	(5.62)	(3.42)	(6.89)	(3.42)	(1.23)	(6.19)
Net Football Revenue	.03 (0.74)		.13** (4.05)		.32** (4.69)	
Gross Football Revenue		.11** (4.34)		.11** (4.35)		.21** (8.79)
R²	.06	.64	.61	.64	.68	.88
n	11	11	11	11	11	11

Note: Absolute values of t-statistics are in parentheses. ** indicates statistically significant at the .01 level; * indicates statistically significant at the .05 level. The constant coefficients are expressed in millions, while the expenses coefficients are expressed in dollars. R^2 is the adjusted R square, and n is the number of observations.

come as no surprise. What may come as a surprise is that even football is not overwhelmingly profitable. Some college programs generate substantial profits, but many do not, even when measured by self-reported profits. In addition, considerable economic incentives exist to pursue profits in football and men's basketball, even for programs that have not been fiscally successful, and it is this pursuit of profits that appears to have led to increased professionalization in collegiate sports.

What can be said about the balance between academic concerns and athletic concerns? An economist like myself is not particularly well equipped to address that question. Economists typically focus on costs versus benefits and shy away from considerations like the proper mix of goals. I effectively assumed away the question of balance at the outset by associating the professional model exclusively with profits and then noting that colleges typically have a number of objectives. I would label an athletics program professionalized on the basis of the pursuit of profit (in theory) or the realization of profit (in practice).

Do I believe colleges have the appropriate balance or the correct emphasis on sports? I must answer "no" for two reasons. First, as an economist I see the economic incentives being tilted towards sports. In what other endeavor can Duke or Florida or Notre Dame or Ohio State generate as much publicity as with their sports program? Can the library, math department, or a biology lab generate as much revenue as the football program? A negative answer suggests colleges may have an incentive in overemphasizing sports. Second, it appears that relatively little dispassionate thought has been devoted to the question of how intercollegiate sports contributes to the educational mission of a university. Developing well-rounded graduates would argue for a strong intramural sports programs; it need not translate into a strong intercollegiate football program. If collegiate sports were such an important force in molding character, one should ask, Why is it not required of all students?[16]

My focus here has primarily been on football and men's basketball and has considered professionalization from an institutional perspective, typically the perspective adopted by media coverage of collegiate sports. The results presented suggest that economic incentives have contributed to the professionalization of both sports. What impact will economic incentives have in the future development of collegiate sports? From a university's perspective vis-à-vis football and men's basketball, there is no reason to believe there will be a change any time soon. If an increase in expenditures generates an equal or greater increase in revenues, institutions will continue to have an incentive to pursue a professional model.

What remains in doubt is whether football and men's basketball represent aberrations to an amateur-sports model or whether these sports are just the first down the road to professionalization. From the perspective of colleges, there currently is no economic evidence that other sports have the same incentives. Increased spending on other sports does not appear to generate offsetting increases in revenue. However, other economic incentives appear to be pushing baseball, hockey, and women's basketball down potentially the same path as collegiate football.

Professional baseball and hockey both rely on an extensive and expensive system of minor leagues to develop and prepare talent for the "big show." Given the expense of maintaining minor leagues, major-league franchises in both sports have come to rely increasingly on college talent, and colleges are increasingly serving as minor leagues for baseball and hockey. For a professional team, this change saves player-development costs. Players also gain since they have the option of signing with a pro team after high school if the offer is sufficiently attractive; if it is not, they have a viable alternative in collegiate competition. From a collegiate perspective, however, the result is potentially increased.

Women's basketball is a different story. Within the last few years some college programs like Tennessee have become profitable, as women's professional basketball has developed into an economically viable endeavor. Both these developments have increased the exposure of women's basketball and appear to have raised the question for administrators about whether a dollar investment now may return more than a dollar in future revenue. This type of logic potentially is the first step into professionalization.

Finally, let me note the economic incentives for athletes, whose perspective I have generally neglected here. Whether collegiate athletes are professionals or are becoming increasingly professionalized is a more difficult question to address, because little direct data are available. However, indirectly one can examine professional opportunities and incentives. Once again, it is necessary to distinguish between sports, although for athletes the division between the "haves"—arguably football and men's basketball—and the "have nots"—arguably all other sports—is not nearly as pronounced.

Consider football as an example. Even the most successful collegiate sports programs like Florida State, Nebraska, and Notre Dame send slightly less than half their athletes into the National Football League (NFL). A lesser ranked program like Boston College, Kentucky, or Iowa State will be fortunate to average two per year. Thus for most Division IA schools that can sign twenty-five freshmen per year, less than ten percent make the pros—not good odds for someone with professional aspirations.[17] Once again, however, if what matters is professional aspirations rather than professional results, one could ask whether a Florida or an Ohio State, or even a Kentucky or an Iowa State, is interested in a player who does not have professional aspirations.

While the probability of playing professional ball is small even for collegiate players, professional salaries provide a strong incentive to pursue that option. The opportunities for a professional career have not changed appreciably, but the average salary has increased dramatically. For example, thirty years ago, the average NFL salary was roughly five times the average U.S. salary. Now the average NFL salary is over twenty times the U.S. average salary. The result is that many college athletes have a substantially greater incentive to strive for a professional career—which edges them, like the colleges they play for, closer to the ranks of the professionals.

For colleges I emphasized the differences between the "haves" and the "have nots." For athletes there also is a question of the distribution of "rewards." In collegiate sports there is substantial equality in terms of pay, dramatically more than in any pro sport. NCAA rules preclude the star quarterback from receiving more benefits than a third-string guard.[18] The moral is that the best players receive less than they would with open bidding for their services, while many others may actually receive more. What are the implications?

The best potentially have a greater incentive to turn pro earlier than they otherwise might. The rest, however, have a greater incentive to exploit fully their college opportunities. The net impact of these two effects on professionalization is ambiguous. Complicating the story, the distinction between the best and the rest frequently is not clear, even to the athletes themselves. It is the perspective that a little more work or a little luck will give someone the "big break," and it is likely that this perspective drives many athletes and contributes to increased professionalization of the collegiate game.[19] In that respect, it may be that colleges and athletes are identical in their tendency to promote professionalization.

NOTES

1. Koch (1971, 1986), in a series of articles, has carefully examined the intercollegiate athletics industry.

2. Penn State's facility, built in the 1960s, is the exception.

3. This approach is not without controversy. For example, an alternate definition suggested by Sperber (1990) is that anyone receiving a scholarship is bartering athletic services for an education and thus should be labeled a professional. This approach focuses on the athlete rather than on the college. Adopting this approach suggests that almost all college athletes are professionals, irrespective of sport or future career.

4. Whether colleges are focusing primarily on revenues and costs versus other issues is an intuitive statement of professionalization that need not exactly correspond to a careful definition of the distinction. This point will be examined in more detail in the next section.

5. One of the more curious points that arose in doing the background research for this chapter was the near complete lack of reflection on the role of athletics in a collegiate setting. This is true even in documents like the report from the Knight Foundation Commission on Intercollegiate Athletics (1991), which emphasizes principles like "the educational values, practices and missions of this institution determine the standards by which we conduct our intercollegiate athletics program." However, there is virtually no reflection on how the intercollegiate athletics program contributes to the "educational values, practices and missions" of the institution. The sole exception that I found was a "Statement of Principles for Intercollegiate Athletics" by the University of Notre Dame. "As a Catholic university, Notre Dame is committed to Christian values and principles as these have been expressed in our tradition throughout the University's history. These include the development of the human spirit as well as the body, the pursuit of excellence in all endeavors, the nurturing of Christian character and the call to personal integrity and acceptance of personal responsibility." However, even in this document the focus is on rules for athletes and coaches rather than a detailed examination of the role of athletics.

6. One further caveat is in order on the definition of professional. The appropriate model for the pros is extremely controversial with regard to two competing theories. One espouses the view that all professional franchises operate exclusively with a view to maximizing profits. Fort and Quirk (1995) in their review of the literature emphasize this view even while noting its controversy. The alternative is labeled the

"sportsman" approach and has been most rigorously detailed by Vrooman (1997). The sportsman view allows some owners to be concerned with wins in addition to or instead of profits. Succinctly stated, sportsmen are willing to sacrifice profits to win. With this more general view of the professional model, professionalization in the college ranks would be much broader than defined here. If the administrations at Florida, Michigan, or Nebraska were unconcerned about the profit or loss of their football team and were only concerned about winning the national championship, one could argue that they would fit the sportsman model and would be professional franchises even though they might be extremely profitable. While I believe this is the appropriate approach to study the pros, it is not the focus here, since with this view it is impossible to test whether any school could be labeled professional. In addition, making money and winning are highly correlated. There is no major college football program that regularly loses the majority of its games and also makes money. The biggest moneymakers, listed in Table 6.5, are uniformly institutions with long-term winning traditions. One could reasonably ask why any college would field a football team if it were regularly to go 0-11 or 1-10 or 2-9? Would there be student demand? Would the program cover its expenses? Would anyone argue that the football program contributes to the educational mission of the university?

7. In fact, as this chapter is being written, Notre Dame is engaged in discussion about whether to join the Big Ten conference. What may be surprising to sports fans is that this discussion is being driven by academic concerns, and if Notre Dame joins the Big Ten, it will be despite its potential negative impact on Notre Dame's sports programs.

8. The assumption underlying this statement is that some profitable schools may not emphasize profits while some unprofitable schools may indeed be primarily focused on profits, but on average, if not by school, the level of profits will reflect the level of concentration on profits.

9. The schools are Boise State, Boston College, Houston, Kent State, Michigan State, Pittsburgh, Rice, and Syracuse. Based on preliminary information available for the period of 1996 to 1997, it is unlikely that their inclusion would appreciably change the results reported below.

10. Fulks's work follows Raiborn's (1986) survey on the finances of collegiate athletic programs. The only other prior analyses of which I am aware are Lopiano's (1979) survey-based work, Sperber's (1990) study of specific acts of professionalization, and Sheehan's (1996) examination based on information available under state freedom-of-information acts.

11. The top ten schools, ranked by profits, have 29 percent of the revenues of all Division IA schools but only 11 percent of the costs. Thus their costs are only slightly above the Division IA average. This result is one more indication that costs are likely understated at a substantial number of schools, with the concomitant conclusion that profits are overstated.

12. See Sigelman and Bookheimer (1983) and Harrison, Mitchell, and Peterson (1995) for evidence on whether donations are influenced by athletic success.

13. There is one effect that works in the other direction. One can ask whether grants-in-aid actually represent an expense to the institution. That is, what is the opportunity cost of a grant-in-aid? If an institution has "excess capacity" or could admit more students, then the tuition component of a grant-in-aid represents a paper transfer from the athletic department to the general fund and has no real meaning or

real cost. This may well be the situation at an Arkansas, Michigan State, or Texas Tech. It is not the situation at Duke, Northwestern, or Stanford. Making this adjustment will increase the number of profitable schools by five to ten but will not change the general conclusion substantially. Based on Table 6.3, total grants-in-aid were $2.68 million with approximately one-third typically allocated to football. Of that amount, tuition represents approximately two-thirds of the grant at a typical state school. Thus the "savings" for football would be approximately $600,000 for those schools not at their enrollment capacity.

14. An alternate explanation would be that schools like Illinois and Vanderbilt overstate their costs. However, the opportunities to do that, given most schools accounting systems, appear relatively limited. In addition, one should ask, Does a school have a greater incentive to understate or overstate football expenses? For schools at the top of the profit rankings, one can make an argument for either bias. However, for other institutions, the political costs of admitting that the football program lost money and drained resources from the rest of the university would appear to firmly tilt the scales toward understating costs and thus understating losses.

15. There is one additional caveat to place on the regression results. It is conceivable, for example, that an increase in men's basketball revenues could lead a school to increase expenditures. Thus, higher revenues could be causing higher costs, rather than higher costs generating higher revenues. However, the latter appears to be more plausible and is the interpretation I make based on the results.

16. The roots of collegiate sports (football in particular) lie in student-organized athletic clubs. See Fleisher, Goff, and Tollison (1992) for a more detailed account.

17. The maximum number of scholarships permitted in football is eighty-five. If all players stayed for five years, including a year being "red-shirted" or not played to maintain future eligibility, then seventeen would be signed each year. The percentage making the pros at a midlevel school would rise to about 12 percent. Given the number of players who drop out or whose scholarships are not extended for another year, the average number signed each year is closer to twenty-five than seventeen. In addition, these numbers exclude the numerous "walk-ons" who are not offered a scholarship.

18. Athletes in so-called Olympic or nonrevenue sports will frequently complain about "nonprice discrimination" in terms of their treatment vis-à-vis football players in areas like use of training facilities. Nevertheless, compared to the differences in professional compensation, there are minimal compensation differences.

19. From an athlete's perspective, one could ask if an extra hour in the weight room or an extra hour studying game film will increase the athlete's skills enough to have a lucrative professional career. Unlike colleges, there are no data available to even hint at the answer, although the time and effort spent in these activities suggests that many college athletes would say yes.

BIBLIOGRAPHY

Bachman, Charles W. 1922. Is Football an Asset to the College? *The Athletic Journal*, 22–29.

Camp, Walter. 1920. Football in Business. *Collier's,* 2 (October) 30, 33–34.

Curtis Jr., Russell L. 1995. It's as Academic as American Economic Pie: Admissions Standards and Big-Time College Football. *Social Science Quarterly* 76: 2, 267–273.

Fleisher, Arthur A.; Brian L. Goff; and Robert D. Tollison. 1992. *The National Collegiate Athletic Association: A Study in Cartel Behavior*. Chicago: University of Chicago Press.

Fort, Rodney, and James Quirk. 1995. Cross-Subsidization, Incentives, and Outcomes in Professional Team Sports Leagues. *Journal of Economic Literature* (September), 1265–1299.

Fulks, Daniel L. 1996. *Revenues and Expenses of Division I and II Intercollegiate Athletics Programs: Financial Trends and Relationships—1995*. Overland Park, Kans.: National Collegiate Athletics Association.

Harrison, William B.; Shannon K. Mitchell; and Steven P. Peterson. 1995. Alumni Donations and Colleges' Development Expenditures: Does Spending Matter? *American Journal of Economics and Sociology* 54: 4, 397–412.

Knight Foundation Commission on Intercollegiate Athletics. 1991. *Keeping Faith with the Student–Athlete: A New Model for Intercollegiate Athletics*. Charlotte, N.C.: The Foundation.

Koch, James V. 1986. The Intercollegiate Athletics Industry. In *The Structure of American Industry*, 7th ed., ed. Walter Adams. New York: Macmillan, 325–346.

———. 1971. The Economics of "Big-Time" Intercollegiate Athletics. *Social Science Quarterly* 52: 2, 248–260.

Lopiano, Donna A. 1979. Solving the Financial Crisis in Intercollegiate Athletics. *Educational Review* (Fall), 394–408.

Mixon Jr., Franklin G., and Yu Hsing. 1994. The Determinants of Out-of-State Enrollments in Higher Education: A Probit Analysis. *Economics of Education Review,* (December), 329–335.

Murphy, Robert G., and Gregory A. Trandel. 1994. The Relation between a University's Football Record and the Size of Its Applicant Pool. *Economics of Education Review* (September), 265–270.

Raiborn, Mitchell H. 1986. *Revenues and Expenses of Intercollegiate Athletics Programs: Analysis of Financial Trends and Relationships, 1981–1985*. Mission, Kans.: National Collegiate Athletics Association.

Rice, Grantland. 1926. Football Pays the Bills. *Collier's,* November 27, 23.

Sheehan, Richard G. 1996. *Keeping Score: The Economics of Big-Time Sports*. South Bend, Ind.: Diamond Communications.

Sigelman, Lee. 1995. It's Academic—or Is It? Admissions Standards and Big-Time College Football. *Social Science Quarterly,* 64: 2, 247–261.

Sigelman, Lee, and Samual Bookheimer. 1983. Is it Whether You Win or Lose?: Monetary Contributions to Big-Time College Athletic Programs. *Social Science Quarterly* (June), 347–359.

Sperber, Murray. 1990. *College Sports Inc.: The Athletic Department vs. the University*. New York: Henry Holt.

Vrooman, John. 1997. A Unified Theory of Capital and Labor Markets in Major League Baseball. *Southern Economic Journal*, 63: 3, 594–619.

Wilkens, Ernest H. 1938. College Football Costs. *School and Society,* March 19, 381.

7

Administering the Modern University

Richard L. Pattenaude

Some would say the idea of university leadership is an oxymoron, like governmental efficiency. Others, slightly more charitable, view it as a tantalizing possibility—not unlike Gandhi's comment about Western civilization. One must believe this cynicism is a bit overdone. Yet there is an emerging concern about the difficulty of providing agile and decisive leadership for the modern American university or college.

The basic position taken in this chapter aligns with that expressed by Frank Rhodes, president emeritus of Cornell University, who firmly believes that universities can be led and, indeed, must be; and that the tools and the resources exist if presidents are willing to utilize them wisely and energetically (Rhodes, 1998: 12–20). This is not an easy task. Perhaps the best imagery draws from a humorous comment typically credited to Winston Churchill as he expressed his admiration for democracy: "Democratic government is like a bear that walks on its hind legs; it is not that it does it well but that it does it at all that surprises us." Intuitively we recognize that universities and colleges are not businesses in the classic American capitalistic tradition. Power is more fragmented; constituencies are more active; goals and objectives are less precise; and the clear exercise of authority has a far weaker tradition. This chapter will explore these issues in some depth, and again, with the overriding belief that leadership is possible and that higher education institutions can be responsive to changing needs. There is no choice.

THE MYTHS OF IMPOSSIBILITY AND PERSONAL COST

There is an emerging myth that the job of university or college president is undesirable and impossible to do well. This perplexes many who hold the job. Indeed, anecdotal evidence would suggest that there has been no reduction in people interested in these challenging jobs.

Advertisements in *The Chronicle of Higher Education* are numerous and written in glowing and positive terms. One must note that the expected abilities and requirements continue to expand. As one wag said, it sounds like "God on a good day." Yet in conversations from across the country, one finds a significant number of candidates seeking these positions, thus creating a highly competitive environment. The presidency of a college or university continues to be a well-rewarded, well-regarded, and actively sought position.

Occasional news stories and, to be honest, some public whining, lead one to conclude that the only outcome of being a president is to leave the job exhausted, with one's reputation in tatters and cynical about the academy. It would be foolish to suggest the job is not difficult, but when one encounters a group of presidents at meetings, there is a great deal of camaraderie, good humor, and a tremendous sense of energetic dedication to institutional purpose. It only takes one president going down in flames in public to cause a concerned alumni or a curious press to deem the job undoable.

Those who have served on corporate boards or worked closely with presidents of large corporations in the private sector seem to agree that university presidents work no harder nor in more complex environments that their private sector counterparts. Are the environments different and the challenges distinct? Absolutely! Is it less demanding or more demanding? In truth, the jobs seem quite similar. It is about resources, time, and purposes. What is perhaps different is that as university presidents rise through the hierarchy of higher education, they are seldom exposed to practices of good time management, delegation, appropriate uses of technology, or developing a clear understanding of what the limits of a presidency should be.

Presidents can be extraordinarily good micromanagers and often find this activity comforting; this is a dangerous practice if one is to be attentive to the broad needs of the institution and energetic enough to achieve them. It is important for boards of trustees to help insure that presidents are surrounded by confident and adequate staff and are informed that they are expected to take care of themselves.

Academic leadership is a long-distance run, not a sprint. One needs to use one's time and energy appropriately. Effective leadership in the private or public sector is still a sixty- or a seventy-hour week undertaking, but it is manageable. I often caution new administrators that they have to learn to draw the line; if one gives 100 percent, the organization will ask 110 percent. If one gives 110 percent, it will ask 120 percent, and so on until one lies in a heap, ineffective and exhausted. Just as universities are insatiable in their need for resources, they are insatiable in their expectations of presidents, vice presidents, and deans. The graceful art of saying "no" is an important tool for any effective leader.

The other dimension of the purported impossibility of university leadership reflects the nature of the academy. Traditions of distributed and shared governance, academic freedom, consensus-based decision making, and carefully drawn change are indeed challenges to leadership. Add to that emerging unionism, fear about downsizing, consumerism, legislative intrusions, board-of-trustee activism, and media concerns about costs and effectiveness and one can understand that there are numerous barriers to leadership and change. These barriers exist for all organizations public or private, business or academic, profit or nonprofit; one needs to use the appropriate tools for the context and setting. Still it is a difficult undertaking; as one president noted, "If these jobs were easy they wouldn't pay us so much."

The myth of impossibility and personal destruction undermines the legitimacy of university leadership and the university itself. Looking at higher education in the United States objectively and from a distance, the picture is quite positive. Clearly, the United States has the reputation of having the best higher-education system in the world; hundreds of thousands of students at all levels come to the United States each year to participate. Our research and scholarship leads the world in productivity and value. The quality of graduates continues to rise. Higher education slowly but persistently responds to the calls for action from American society. At a recent New England Board of Higher Education conference on the role of higher education in economic development, it was stunning to hear presidents list the extraordinary number of institutes, centers, credit and noncredit programs, certificate programs, and basic and applied research initiatives that have emerged in the last decade to provide a strong undergirding to the American economy. Of course this can always improve, and we must work towards that end. But to suggest that the universities and colleges of our country cannot be led is to overlook the consistent and focused evolution and improvement of higher education.

THE "GREAT MAN" DILEMMA

One of the true oddities of reviewing the literature on higher-education leadership is to hear a steady drumbeat about the lack of high profile academic leaders in America. The names drawn from the past have always been the same: Robert Hutchins, Clark Kerr, William Rainey Harper, Charles Elliott, and occasionally a few others. But then the list stops (Chait, 1998: 39–41). Perhaps there was a period of time when there were these great outspoken men (and they were all men). Certainly there were fewer competitors for headlines, and the job of the university or college president was far less demanding and busy.

A cursory review of recent literature would suggest strongly that today's presidents are far from silent. Whether the topic is alcohol abuse on campus, leadership in the modern era, the abuse of power, or the details of professional disciplines, presidents are writing and speaking at an undiminished rate. And they are speaking out more directly than ever on issues such as AIDS, gay–lesbian rights, domestic violence, and racism. Principled statements by presidents abound whenever a violent or a tragic event occurs. The marketplace of ideas and the media environment are more crowded than before; often these voices do not reach beyond their localized audience.

One must conclude either that society has changed significantly, and thus the role for a few outspoken and authoritarian individuals has diminished, or that information channels are so clogged that it is rare for any one voice to reach across the breadth of our diverse and active interests. One should look closely at the speaking, writing, and publishing records of individuals such as Derrick Bok, Nannerl Keohane, Steven Joel Trachtenberg, Robert Birnbaum, Leon Bottstein, Frank Rhodes, and Claire Gaudiani, and a myriad of others, to ask if presidents are not speaking out on a wide range of topics. The lamenting for a time that barely was is of little value when assessing the needs of leadership in the future.

THE ERROR OF SINGLE-CELL ANALYSIS

In the current literature about higher-education leadership, there is a homogeneity to the commentary that does not mirror the reality of higher education. The themes running through *The Presidency* and *Change* have a consistency that suggests a single institutional environment. The rich texture of our system defies the efforts to look for a single style of leadership or a single set of ideal behaviors. We actually have a complex matrix of universities and colleges in the United States.

One can build that matrix from a variety of perspectives, using such characteristics as public versus private; proprietary versus nonproprietary; community college, liberal-arts college, regional university, research university; small, medium, or large enrollments; and selective, highly selective, or open admission. The traditional approach is to utilize the Carnegie classifications across one dimension of the matrix, and then along the other dimension, select another set of characteristics appropriate to analysis at hand—typically public versus private or total enrollment. The result is a multicelled matrix into which one places the thirty-six hundred or so colleges and universities in America. In each cell there are nuances, contexts, and events which influence leadership and administration. It is at great risk that simple analysis is done, and sweeping generalizations announced, although inferences are obviously possible. The other risk is to be overwhelmed by complexity in an attempt to fill each cell; the complexity of that task is equally unwise.

This chapter is not about a detailed analysis of leadership style. But it is important to acknowledge that much of the commentary one reads or hears is somewhat indifferent to the existence of a variety of leadership settings. Some of the generic issues raised within this chapter will address this diversity, but the effort here is more to look at the nature of the university in the coming millennium and the ways in which leadership must respond.

WHO ARE TODAY'S PRESIDENTS?

There is considerable conjecture about who is becoming a president at the modern college and university. Anecdotal evidence should not suffice for analysis about the identity of the modern university or college presidency. Luckily, we have research to address that issue and give us a clearer picture of the changes. The fundamental conclusion must be that the trends we have seen over the past ten years will continue to evolve.

The American Council on Education has engaged in a long-term exhaustive study, documenting presidential career patterns and demographics. Called the National Presidents' Study, it has issued three reports over the last decade, providing us with both snapshot details and longitudinal analysis. The most recent report, *The American College President*, was published in 1998 (Ross and Green, 1998). The following descriptions draw directly from that report.

Based on interviews and surveys of 2,297 presidents (76% response rate) from public and private, doctoral, comprehensive, baccalaureate, two-year, and specialized institutions, the resulting data present a fairly comprehensive picture.

In 1995, the typical president was described as follows:

- fifty-six years old.
- Caucasian.
- Male.
- Seven point three years of continuous service.
- An external candidate.
- An academic vice president at one time.
- From a similar institution.
- Holds a doctorate or highest degree in field.
- A full-time faculty member at some point.

There are few surprises here. What is of interest is that changes are underway. Tendencies are emerging that provide a view of things to come.

Comparing 1995 with 1986, the following points emerge as salient:

- Presidents are older (55.9 years old versus 52.3).
- There are more women presidents (16.5% versus 9.5%).
- There are more minority presidents (10.4% versus 8.1%).
- There is a longer period of service for presidents (7.3 years versus 6.3 years).
- There are more former college presidents (19.9% versus 17.3%).

• There are fewer nonacademics (8.6% versus 10.1%).

These trends, measured over a ten-year period, came into sharper focus when looking at the characteristics of recent appointees, that is, all presidents taking office between 1991 and 1995. There are

• More women (21.6% of all appointees).
• More minorities (18.2% of all appointees).

So there is a slow but steady movement towards more women and minorities being appointed as presidents. Still, given the current rate, it would take forty years for women and minorities to reach a proportion of presidencies equal to their proportion of the professional staff populations on American college campuses (Ross and Green, 1998). Another strengthening factor contributes to this. It is a surprise to learn that of presidents appointed in 1995, 19.9 percent came directly from another presidency. And for 7.9 percent, this was their third presidency. These figures compare to 17.3 percent and 5.9 percent in 1986.

Search committees seem to gravitate toward a common, comfortable model. The presence of more women and minorities, particularly in two-year institutions, is the most notable shift and the one most likely to continue.

ISSUES CONFRONTING UNIVERSITY LEADERSHIP IN THE TWENTY-FIRST CENTURY

Another emerging truism is that colleges and universities will face extraordinary and unparalleled challenges in the twenty-first century. There is no doubt that it will be a difficult time, but to see it as more distressing than earlier times seems to overlook our shared history. I can think of nothing more difficult than leading a college or university during the Vietnam era, when the fundamental legitimacy of the institution and its decision-making authority were challenged on a regular and hostile basis. Also, the crippling inflation of the late 1970s and early 1980s tore away at the financial footing of all institutions. The destructive recession of the late 1980s and early 1990s created internal havoc at universities and colleges as it drove up tuition at double and triple the inflation rate. Each decade or period brings challenges that must be accommodated, understood, and solved. The twenty-first century will be no different.

One could build an endless list of things to consider. Let me try to be somewhat more concise. In a recent editorial in *Change* magazine, revered university sage and analyst Clark Kerr examined what he considers to be the challenges to university leadership (1998: 10–11):

Higher education has entered a new stage in its history with new challenges for leadership. These include

1. To help find a new set of urgent priorities in service to society. A generation ago, there were three great priorities shared with the nation at large: to become the world leader in academic research, which entailed making good use of a great increase in federal funds for research and development; to supply the new labor market with people of high skills as the need for more "human capital" became evident; and to create new programs to improve equality of opportunity. The first two of these once-upon-a-time priorities have been fulfilled to perfection. The third needs new thought and energy. Also, what are the new, shared priorities?

2. To assist the reunification of the academic world. The academy has been so split by political ideologies, race and ethnicity, and methodologies that it has become a multiverse of discourse—a Tower of Babel—instead of a universe of knowledge.

3. To make the campus, once again, more of a human community, around which many lives are centered, and less a place of occasional one-dimensional contacts, despite the electronic revolution and two-career families.

4. To concentrate on the more effective use of resources, equally with their more effective procurement. Today we concentrate so much on short-run resource procurement that, to paraphrase Shakespeare, our wits are in our bellies and our guts are in our heads.

Clark Kerr's list is an important statement, but there are, from the operational level, several additional issues that call for our attention.

- Balancing consumerism with the core values of the university. The growth of corporate education, such as that at the University of Phoenix and similar institutions, and the rise of Internet-based instruction all send a clear message: higher education needs to be more responsive and convenient. These new approaches are valuable but are seen on most campuses as direct threats to the contemplative and reflective aspects of education. Too often this results in degree programs being offered in areas where there are no libraries or sophisticated computer facilities available. Faculty bridle at the idea of the university becoming simply a trade school for the economy. Finding ways for these equally valuable viewpoints to coexist will call for rethinking priorities and bringing about gentle but persistent changes in our culture.

- The rise of technology. Technology has become intrusive to all aspects of university and college work, whether it is in the classroom, the business office, the dormitory, the faculty member's office, or, perhaps most importantly, the budget. It is essential and vital, but wholesale adoption of every technological innovation that comes along threatens to make the personal computer more of a fad than a substantive and valuable tool. The cost of bringing technology to the classroom, the laboratory, the library, or administrative offices is unlimited, and therefore careful decision making must occur to avoid a technological hegemony that is not justified. At the same time faculty have to continue their efforts to incorporate technology into both the content and the processes of their classroom. Students will live and work in a technological world, and there is no logic for the university's world to be different. It is too easy to simply give in to the technologist's acronym-laden diatribe (often laced with intellectual guilt) that results in unwarranted investments in obsolete, obsolescent, or superfluous technology.

- The demand for opportunity and access. It is possible to structure an argument that says everyone in the United States must have a college degree. Clearly that is not true. High-school graduates and technical-school graduates will have very important roles to play in the new economy. Yet high-school counselors and parents feel incredible pressure to urge all students to immediately pursue baccalaureate education. This is a disservice and results in many students in our classrooms who are ill prepared for college work. Yet, given the history of our society, it is not in our nature nor in our values to deny opportunity to anyone. By working with high-school leaders and human-resources professionals, we can figure out what college and university experiences add to an individual's life and how we should support individual aspirations. Within this sorting out is the equally compelling problem of emerging class elitism based upon the capacity to pay. Cost controls and greater financial aid are going to be paramount if we are to avoid pricing people out of opportunity.

- The vision thing. Not unlike Clark Kerr's last point, but from a slightly different perspective, the ability to give the participants within the university and the supporters from outside the university confidence that there is a clear direction for each institution will be the key test of leadership. Multiple forces inside and outside the institution push and pull the university or college in diverse ways. Gaining an intellectual, budgetary, and administrative alignment of these forces will be critical if the institution is to evolve in positive ways, respond to institutional and social needs, and use its resources effectively.

THE BUSINESS CHALLENGE

Businesses are asking universities and colleges to respond more quickly to the changing world and the changing needs of industry, and legislators and the public are seeking greater accountability for funds expended; as a result, there has emerged a strong challenge to the traditional pattern of leadership development in higher education. This call was brought to a sharp focus in a report issued by the Association of Governing Boards of Universities and Colleges (AGB) in 1996 entitled "Renewing the Academic Presidency: Stronger Leadership for Tougher Times" (Commission on the Academic Presidency, 1996). This document contains an important statement about leadership in the coming decades.

The authors suggest that the traditionally prepared university president is ill-suited for the leadership challenges facing universities and colleges in the coming years. The lack of business training, financial sophistication, and outcomes orientation troubles groups such as AGB. The argument proceeds that individuals who are leaders in other fields such as business, politics, and government might better serve the needs of students and other constituencies in the future. Traditionally, serving as the academic dean or vice president is the typical prerequisite for leadership in higher education. To some degree we see increasing selections from alternative groups within the institution, such as from development, as well as selections from outside the academy. It would be difficult to say that this is an emerging trend; the majority of evidence brought forth is fundamentally anecdotal and focuses on those situations that have been deemed highly successful.

AGB summarizes its recommendations to the president and boards as follows:

Key recommendations to presidents:

- Formulate a vision of the institution's future, build consensus around it, and take the risks required to achieve that vision, on campus and off.

- Lead the board and faculty through a process of clarifying the precise nature of shared governance on each campus and of reducing ambiguities in authority and decision-making processes.

- Exercise the authority already inherent in the position. Presidents must resist academia's insatiable appetite for the kind of excessive consultation that can bring the institution to a standstill.

Key recommendations to boards:

- Select presidents who are truly capable of leading their particular institutions as change agents and risk takers. While many candidates will be found on campuses, the new challenges facing higher education may lead institutions to consider candidates from nontraditional backgrounds.

- Require the president to develop a vision and clarify how shared governance should operate on that campus. The board must work with the president to accomplish these goals.

- Support and stand by presidents, publicly and effectively, as long as they hold the confidence of the board. While mindful of their dual roles as supporters of the institution and guardians of the public trust, boards must back effective presidents when they are under siege by internal or external constituencies (Commission on the Academic Presidency, 1996: xi).

Upon closer reading there emerges another distinct set of concerns. Trustees and legislators often fixate on the governance structure of the university, specifically the reliance upon shared government and its basis in the traditions of academic freedom and autonomy. After declaring that "without a stronger presidency, these demands and challenges stand little of being met," the AGB authors nonchalantly declare, "This conclusion will arouse passionate resistance in some quarters as an assault on the tradition of shared governance" (Commission on the Academic Presidency, 1996: x). Indeed, that would be a reasonable conclusion.

Articles appearing recently in *The Presidency*, a new journal devoted to college and university presidents, also raise this topic. A regular reading of AGB's *Trusteeship* reveals an ongoing concern about consensus management, tenure, academic freedom, and rate of change. All make links to the somewhat archaic but deeply ingrained tradition of shared governance. Certainly the consensus-driven model does not help colleges and universities by being strikingly agile and decisive, particularly at a time when the rate of change in the commercial world is accelerating.

In light of this, the AGB conclusion to bring in presidents from outside the academy is problematic. This seems an illogical conclusion, given the reality that shared governance, tenure, and academic freedom will be around for a considerable period of time. Leadership failure often occurs when there is a clash between the values of the leader and the values of the culture where that person is supposed to lead. This could not be any clearer than the situation where a business leader is brought into the academy and then asked to move the institution to a higher level of performance. It would seem more logical to spend time and energy providing new presidents drawn from the academy with workshops and seminars on business skills and practices.

As this final point suggests, it would be folly to reject the AGB argument out of hand. Universities do need presidents who are strong and able to lead. And this will become more difficult as challenges become more complex and special interests better organized and more articulate. Perhaps most importantly, strong presidents are needed, because we also need strong universities. As Frank Rhodes has observed, the key source of human comfort and wealth in the future will be knowledge, and it is from universities and colleges that knowledge is produced and shared (1998: 12). Society needs the university to be strong and, hence, the president to be strong. The issue is how do we get there.

It is possible that the AGB recommendation inadvertently results in a Catch-22 that will strike down the energetic and aggressive president. If a board urges a new president to "draw a line in the sand" and hammer out a definition and operational specifics of shared governance, and to reassert his or her authority, one fears that for the next three to four years that president will be battling process and definitional issues. It has all the markings of an inevitable "us-versus-them" deadlock. How then is the president to focus on the challenges facing the university and the outcomes expected by all constituencies? It is hard to be responsive, decisive, and agile when one is involved in a situation that appears so frequently in *The Chronicle of Higher Education* under headlines like "President Under Fire; Projects Put on Hold." Short of that kind of doomsday thinking, one must also recognize that the capacity of the academy for intransigence, moral outrage, and passive–aggressive foot dragging is immense. It is only at great risk that the president, new or experienced, pushes all the buttons simultaneously.

How then would it be plausible to address this governance aspect of presidential leadership? A positive approach might be to act with somewhat greater subtlety. A careful evaluation of policies, union agreements, and governance agreements often reveals clear means of authority that have gone unused or underutilized. Knowing what the rules are can be very powerful; people have great respect for rules in academia. The expenditure of great amounts of time on communication and listening will reassure people, particularly faculty, that they have been heard and that the process is indeed a process. (This carries with it the responsibility of actually changing things if good ideas come forward as they always do.) Finally, at least in this brief analysis, one needs to use the presidency as a bully pulpit and exhort the institution to move to new and better levels of performance, drawing always upon the norms, values, and language of our traditions. The reins of power exist within the university; they must be used if the president is to be effective.

The AGB Commission's report on college Presidencies does have a good point. It is also important that stronger management skills be part of the portfolio of the newly emerging modern president (Commission on the Academic Presidency, 1996: 22). But to simply reach out and snatch up governmental or business leaders to be the new heads of universities and colleges suggests a much greater level of success in the private sector and governmental sector than current evidence would support. In leadership-selection processes, great attention must be given to the potential for culture clash and for guerrilla wars over shared governance. They will hobble any president and are not prone to providing solutions within the context of a single institution.

LEADERSHIP—A BRIEF ASIDE

Research on effective leadership has a long and somewhat frustrating history. Considerable effort has been spent trying to determine the core characteristics or traits of leaders, such as intelligence, task knowledge, dominance, self-confidence, energy, tolerance for stress, integrity, honesty, and emotional maturity (George and Jones, 1999: 405–406). This and other traditional approaches have not yielded much insight on the actual processes of leadership.

Behavioral analysis assists in understanding the context of leadership effectiveness and the key behaviors of leaders. These studies, as well as contingency models and decision-style models, do provide a more informed understanding of decision making and leadership, yet they are often too complex for either operational use or for training of new leaders.

Recognizing there are numerous models and theories available, one particular contemporary approach that offers promise is Bernard Bass's work on transformational and charismatic leadership (Bass, 1990). In this approach the charismatic leader has a vision of a better organization, convinces subordinates of the importance of their tasks and the organization's goals, communicates and supports the need for personal growth and development, and motivates individuals to work for the greater good of the organization. This analysis focuses on leader–follower interactions and seems particularly helpful in thinking about the highly personal nature of leadership in universities.

Amidst the research efforts, numerous writings, theories, pop theories, and personal reflections on leadership, one of the newer ideas has particular value for understanding and dealing with leadership in the university: chaos theory. (Yes, there is some humorous irony in selecting this theory.) At its core, the theory suggests that there is structure and persistent patterning in all systems

(Mossberg, 1998: 6–8). One needs to step back from daily events to perceive these patterns; sometimes the complexity of systems makes analysis very difficult. But, assuming that all systems work according to some logic, then one can place events in an analytic perspective that is useful.

As Mossberg notes,

- Energy is a destabilizing force. Even positive acts with the best intentions create turbulence immediately.
- Control is not realistic as an achievable goal for more than the short term. Stability can be achieved only as a long-term concept.
- In a system, everything belongs. Diversity is not antagonistic to stability. Instead, walling things up, separating out, discounting, and dismissing facts as irrelevant or "controlling" are detrimental to cohesion.
- Understanding "the whole" and aiding in how "the whole" works is the leader's unique role (Mossberg, 1998: 5–6).

The perspective, patience, and optimism intimated by chaos theory is intellectually reassuring. Drawing operational lessons will be more challenging.

The object lesson is that serious, continuing, theoretical, and empirical research on leadership continues unabated. It is useful for reflection and broad insights. One should not expect this body of literature to tell one how to administer universities in the new millennium. One can, however, be cognizant of this work, assimilate its broad lessons, and apply it when possible.

THE POWER AND IMPORTANCE OF LANGUAGE

As presidents proceed with their careers, their learning context changes. They attend American Association for Higher Education (AAHE), American Association of State Colleges and Universities (AASCU), American Council on Education, or National Association of State Universities and Land-Grant Colleges conferences far more often than their discipline-based professional conferences. They start reading *Change, The Chronicle of Higher Education*, and now, *The Presidency* and *University Business*. More time is spent with business leaders, legislators, alumnae, and administrative peers. Inevitably this impacts how one formulates and expresses one's ideas.

Specifically, management terms and images begin to creep into speeches and documents. Plans become strategic plans; common purpose becomes mission–vision–values; student success and faculty scholarship become outcomes measures and accountability; and academic rigor becomes quality improvement, to cite a few simple examples. These terms, and the deeper imagery they mobilize, can alienate faculty. It is critical to always recall that faculty became members of the academy because of deeply held values: a love of learning, a desire to advance knowledge, a joy in teaching, and a concern for the intellectual rigor of our society. To have these ideals converted into management terms creates an immediate alienation and a resistance to change.

The informed university leader will respect the values of the faculty, honor their deeper motivations, and engage them in a dialogue that embraces the higher purposes of the academy. By doing this the president is able to confront the challenges facing the institution in a way that makes sense to the members of the institution and to invite them to join in a common struggle for advancing and sharing knowledge, supporting student success, stewarding resources wisely, and insuring the university or college is maintaining or improving its academic reputation.

Care with language, respect for process, and a legitimate concern for the important values of faculty and staff is not a weakening of leadership. It is a more effective and more thoughtful way to bring all members of the academic community into the dialogue and to ensure that needed improvements will take place.

WHY DO PRESIDENTS SUCCEED OR FAIL?

There are numerous pundits eager to provide advice for presidents (current company included) that is often not grounded in experience or fact. Yet there are those experienced few who can provide useful perspectives on presidential success or failure.

Again, it is important to begin with Frank Rhodes. Pithy and confident, he suggests the following as core activities for effective presidents:

1. Define and articulate the mission of the institution.
2. Develop meaningful goals.
3. Recruit the talent, build the consensus, create the climate, and provide the resources to achieve them (1998: 15).

He also notes, "The effective president will embody a level of energy, and enterprise, of optimism and openness, that is infectious. It is this spirit, and the teamwork it promotes, that achieves success" (1998: 15).

As for failure or frustration, Rhodes observes that several traps await the unwary:

1. Personal exhaustion resulting from a lack of discipline or good time-management skills.
2. Muddled priorities or, even worse, no priorities.
3. Neglecting family and those close to you.
4. Personal isolation that limits one's ability to trust, to empathize, to enjoy.
5. Intellectual starvation, resulting in a loss of spiritual nourishment and creativity and engendering a personal hollowness.

He concludes, "One final thing: the president must lead. Everything I have written so far is prelude to leadership. But it is not a substitute for it" (1998: 18). This is very well put and accurate.

Others help in assessing the opportunities and risks. One of the most thoughtful and systematic observers of the university and college presidency has been Robert Birnbaum. In his book, *How Academic Leadership Works* (1992), one of the key subthemes is understanding success and failure.

The following are Birnbaum's "Ten principles of good academic leadership"

1. Make a good first impression.
2. Listen with respect and be open to influence.
3. Find a balance for governance.
4. Avoid simple thinking.
5. Do not emphasize the bureaucratic frame or linear strategies.
6. Emphasize strong values.
7. Focus on strengths.
8. Encourage leadership by others.
9. Check your own performance.
10. Know when to leave (1993: 16–20).

These are useful principles for leadership in any complex setting. Equally attractive is Birnbaum's summary, which echoes much of Frank Rhodes' sentiment:

There are no quick fixes or magic bullets for presidential leadership in higher education. Ten-minute managers, pop psychologists or charismatics with fixed ideas about what it takes to be a good college president need not apply. Good presidents come to their positions with useful competencies, integrity, faith in their colleagues, and a firm belief that by listening carefully and working together they can all do well. In a turbulent and uncertain world, what happens after that is as much in the laps of the gods as in the hands of the president (1992: 196).

As far as broad general principles of leadership go, it is hard to improve upon the insights of Rhodes and Birnbaum. Yet, as we come to the millennium, there is a need to think even more contextually and strategically.

KEEP YOUR EYE ON THE BALL

Presidents face the prospect of leading their universities and colleges in a century that shows no hint of relief from the pressures currently mounting. With all the demands, distractions, and opportunities that will inevitably arise, how does one, to quote an old saying, "Keep your eye on the ball!"

First one has to know what the "ball" is. The best response to this is simple; no matter how detailed or fancy the job description, the president's job is clear—make the school a better institution! No excuses, no diatribes about legislators or alumni, no long asides about the impact of a highly-tenured and unionized faculty—one simply has to bear down, figure the situation out, and start making the place better. And that means improve the quality and reputation of the college or university one has been honored to be chosen to lead.

Being a university president is a privilege: One has a solid income, good living conditions, considerable public respect, and significant responsibility. So why does whining and hand wringing persist? Maybe because it is a very demanding job that tests the mettle, patience, and sanity of all who do it. But it is a "volunteer" position; no one is forced to be a president. And, unfortunately, it is going to get tougher. But it is no worse than being CEO of a corporation, superintendent of schools in a large district, or city manager of a medium-sized city. The work of all these positions is grinding, frustrating, and fraught with risk, as well as wonderfully rewarding. But, there appears to be a large number of people eager to step forward and do the job, if one chooses to walk away.

Further, the evidence seems clear that universities and colleges will exist in a world that is

- *More expensive*: Salaries, benefits, technology, facilities, deferred maintenance, and new service expectations will create an inexhaustible appetite for resources.
- *More complex:* Office and classroom technology, federal mandates, challenges to affirmative action, interstate competition, and the call for more collaborative ventures will make decision making more challenging.
- *More competitive:* The University of Phoenix and its ilk, the decline of the high-school pool, demographic shifts, the continuing expansion of corporate education, and the need to increase enrollments to increase income will put greater pressure on marketing and retention efforts.
- *More fragmented:* Every group wants its voice heard, and the democratization of the organization will continue to erode centralized authority.

This suggests that there is a need for leadership advice that extends beyond the somewhat generic, though useful, ideas this chapter has so far shared. Risky as it is, the following are presented as strategies to help the energetic president make his or her university or college a better, more respected place.

STRATEGIES FOR THE NEW MILLENNIUM

Have a plan: Planning helps build consensus and gives marvelous opportunities for campus-wide dialogue. The decision-making focus it provides ("No, I'm sorry, we can't do that right now, it's not in the plan") is immensely useful. And the requisite vision of what the institution is, or is not, allows for more efficient use of resources, clearer messages to all, and an enhanced sense of controlling one's own destiny.

Keep the faith with the faculty: Whatever a university or college is or is to become results from the work of the faculty. If they are not "on board," the school is not going anywhere. More importantly, they are the guardians of the core purposes of higher education and, to put it awkwardly, they are the "production capacity" of the school. Considerable energy must be spent engaging faculty, dialoguing, and partnering. This does not mean catering to faculty or giving up appropriate authority. It means treating the faculty with the same care, respect, and strategic sense one would give to the education committee of the legislature or the academic affairs committee of the board. A president who does not enjoy the company of faculty is in trouble.

Do not sacrifice quality: Being responsive, agile, decisive, accountable, and pragmatic does not mean working to the lowest common denominator. One can pursue new goals, new partnerships, new activities, (e.g., Internet courses or instruction at the worksite) with all the rigor and quality one musters for a research facility in biotechnology. At the end of the day, quality wins. It may be necessary to rethink quality, or our definition of it. For example, rather than viewing diversity efforts as an add-on or a mandate, it is useful to see diversity as a key component of quality—which it is. A more diverse institution is a higher-quality institution because it enhances student growth and learning. One must not abandon institutional quality in the name of other pressures.

Get your hands on the budget: The demand to control costs *and* manage resources efficiently will be a mantra for all presidents that will grow louder in the years to come. One cannot do this unless one understands the budget, controls the budget, and imposes one's will on the budget. Does this make the president the chief financial officer? No! A president can and should delegate considerable power to the CFO, but only on terms dictated by the president. Budgets are the ultimate expression of policies, goals, priorities, and action. The president must make the budget a key tool for implementing the plan.

Be entrepreneurial and creative: It is up to the president to help the university or college engage new ideas, adopt new practices, and "think outside the box." This means the president has to be learning, listening, thinking, and growing. Success will greatly depend on new ways to raise support, to build facilities, to launch programs, and to establish critical partnerships. Presidents need to protect and reward innovators and risk takers (but not give them too much base budget control). The president has to open the doors of the institution to the forces of competition and change, while preserving values and traditions. By reading widely, listening carefully, questioning assumptions regularly, and always asking for better performance, the president can lead (and nag) the institution forward.

Build your own team: Presidential exhaustion and ineffectiveness often are a by-product of the president trying to do it all. Good management practices such as careful delegation, regular accountability, and performance reviews are often alien to senior academic officials or viewed as suspect, drawing too heavily on business practices. All this conspires to keep the president from being the president. University and college presidents need to have the best senior managers they can afford and then need to use them appropriately; specifically through energetic delegation with clear goals and accountability. There has to be a shared set of values, a confidence in capacity, an agreement in outcomes, a high level of focused energy, and a strong loyalty if the team is going to provide the president and the school with the critical mass of leadership energy needed to make the school better.

REFLECTION

Like the humorists say, university or college leadership is like herding cats: hard to do, but not impossible. And, given the critical importance of a rigorous and responsive higher-education sector to the future of this nation, thoughtful and effective leadership of our colleges and universities is absolutely essential. Boards of trustees must insist upon and demand evidence of it. Any president who cannot do the job must be told to move on.

BIBLIOGRAPHY

Bass, Bernard. 1990. *Bass and Stogdill's Handbook of Leadership: Theory, Research and Managerial Applications*. 3d ed. New York: Free Press.

Birnbaum, Robert. 1993. Why Presidents Succeed (and Fail). *AGB Trusteeship*, 1: 4, 16–21.

———. 1992. *How Academic Leadership Works*. San Francisco: Jossey-Bass.

Chait, Richard. 1998. Illusions of a Leadership Vacuum. *Change* 30:1, 39–41.

Commission on the Academic Presidency. 1996. *Renewing the Academic Presidency: Stronger Leadership for Tougher Times*. Washington, D.C.: Association of Governing Boards of Universities and Colleges.

Ellis, Patrick. 1998. The Managerial Presidency According to the AGB. *Change* 30:3, 44–46.

George, Jennifer M., and Gareth R. Jones. 1999. *Understanding and Managing Organizational Behavior*. 2d ed. New York: Addison-Wesley.

Goleman, Daniel. 1998. What Makes a Leader? *Harvard Business Review*, 76: 6, 93–102.

Greenberg, David. 1998a. The College President as CEO. *The Washington Post*, July 26, 1.

———. 1998b. Small Men on Campus. *The New Republic*, June 1, 16–20.

Keohane, Nannerl O. 1998. More Power to the President? *The Presidency* 1:2, 12–18.

Kerr, Clark. 1998. Clark Kerr's Perspective on Leadership Challenges. *Change* 30:1, 10–11.

Mossberg, Barbara. 1998. Why I Wouldn't Leave Home without Chaos Theory. *The Inner Edge* 1:4, 5–8.

Rhodes, Frank H. T. 1998. The Art of the Presidency. *The Presidency* 1:1, 12–20.

Ross, Marlene, and Madeleine F. Green. 1998. *The American College President*. Washington, D.C.: American Council on Education.

8

Desegregation and Diversity in Higher Education

Reginald Wilson

Affirmative action legislation was initiated when it became clear that action undertaken to end discrimination, such as *Brown v. Board of Education* (1954), which ended legalized school segregation was not sufficient to end exclusion. In response to pressures from civil rights organizations, a string of executive orders, court rulings, and voluntary practices was initiated in the 1960s and 1970s that was intended to address this failing.

—Walter Feinberg (1998: 7)

As Feinberg so forthrightly states, the link between desegregation and affirmative action has a long and complex history, and the connection between the two is as close as the two faces of a single coin. Most commentators in speeches and books have treated the two issues as though they were discrete phenomena, but as history shows, both have had similar goals, and remarkably similar travails and at the moment, have suffered similar fates.

Both desegregation and affirmative action were implemented as conservative, partial, and incomplete measures to take the nation from its two hundred-year history of slavery, legalized discrimination, and racism into a new era of equality. That they fell short of that lofty goal should come as no surprise. But that they have occasioned some retrogression of their initial intent is a matter of some disquiet. It will be the burden of this chapter to delineate the tangled and separate lives of desegregation and affirmative action and their effect on people and the nation.

BROWN AND ITS PROGENY

On May 17, 1954, when the *Brown v. Board of Education* (1954) decision was announced, Thurgood Marshall, the lead attorney for the plaintiffs, stated that he thought schools would be completely desegregated in "five or six years" (Higginbotham, 1998)—wildly optimistic and tragically wrong. Few anticipated the "massive resistance" that followed—from outright refusal to obey the decision to closing public schools rather than to desegregate them. The resistance was so strong that it occasioned *Brown II* (1955) with its famous order that desegregation must proceed "with all deliberate speed." Ironically, the emphasis in most states was on "deliberate" rather than "speed."

Yet, despite the historic importance of *Brown* and the furor it caused throughout the nation, very little had changed. Except for the highly publicized confrontations, principally in the south (especially in Little Rock, which resulted in the 1958 case, *Cooper v. Aaron*), most school boundaries historically followed segregated housing patterns, and thus "neighborhood schools" essentially remained predominantly one-race schools despite *Brown*. The long history of segregated housing, restrictive covenants, inferior schools, discriminatory jobs, and the resultant poverty left the promise of *Brown* a mockery for most of the nation. For more than ten years the Supreme Court observed the resistance and inaction of the country to live up to the mandate of *Brown*— that "segregated schools are inherently unequal." The Court then delivered perhaps its most controversial decision in *Green v. County School Board of New Kent County* (1968). *Green* reversed the order of simply "prohibiting" an unlawful act (segregation) to "ordering" a desired one (desegregation). The school boards had indeed eliminated their segregated schools but the history of segregated school boundaries had left white and black schools virtually intact. The justices ruled in *Green* that "school desegregation should be judged by its effects." If *Brown* did not eliminate segregation, then it was required to "remedy" the effects of prior unconstitutional segregation. Critics of *Green* have said that the Court, in mandating an activist role in assigning pupils to schools by race, has led to all the pernicious and litigious acts that have followed—for example, busing, charter schools, magnet schools, and white flight. On the other hand, others fault the Court for concentrating on racial balance rather than ordering quality education, which was the original motivation that impelled black people toward *Brown*. Not that removal of the ugly stain of segregation was not a worthy national goal, but that what flowed from it was even more of a blight—inferior schools, impacted neighborhoods, and poverty. Thus, *Green did* change markedly the landscape of school desegregation efforts in a more activist direction and indeed led to a series of decisions spelling out the direction of the intent of the courts.

One such case, *Swann v. Charlotte—Mecklenberg Board of Education* (1971), a North Carolina case, was successful in ordering large-scale deseg-

ing. What also was crucially important was the relative calmness of the community in the implementation of the plan. It continues to represent one of the most successful desegregation efforts in the country.

Several Supreme Court orders—Houston in 1975, Milwaukee in 1976, and Buffalo in 1976—resulted in the establishment of magnet schools, with varying degrees of success. Several states—Connecticut, New York, California, and Massachusetts—required school districts to have a specific level of racial balance, but to little avail as white flight accelerated. The California court was quite prophetic, in *Hernandez v. Stockton Unified School District* (1975), when it was observed that "the greater the reduction in race imbalance, the greater the white loss. Central city school districts above 30–35 percent minority . . . never regain lost whites."

Of course, the loss of whites from central cities meant the loss of tax base, the dispersion of jobs, the impacting of a relatively poor lower class, and the consequent impoverishment of schools. A recent Census Bureau report shows that 39 percent of African American children lived in poverty in 1993, up from 32 percent in 1969 (Bennett, 1995). In the schools, particularly, this usually means poorly trained and uninspired educators, adversarial labor relations and mismanagement. Linda Darling-Hammond writes "most classrooms serving poor and minority children continue to provide students with significantly less engaging and effective learning experiences" (1996: 7). In 1997, a Boston teachers' union threatened to strike when school leaders tried to increase the school day's instructional time by fifteen minutes (DeMitchell and Fossey, 1997).

In the meantime, busing had been used to an increasing degree to achieve racial balance. But this too failed as white flight continued and minority parents became disillusioned with the busing of minority children to increasingly minority schools. The plea of inner-city school leaders to end busing began to receive a sympathetic ear from the courts.

The final blow to attempting to achieve some desegregation of inner-city schools came with the decision of the Supreme Court in *Milliken v. Bradley* in 1974. It was an attempt to relieve racial isolation in the Detroit schools by cross-district busing to the suburbs in the metropolitan area. Although the District Court was sympathetic, the Supreme Court flatly rejected the imposition of a cross-district desegregation plan in the Detroit metropolitan area, unless it could be shown that suburban school districts had been intentionally drawn for the purpose of segregation (Feldman, Kirby, and Eaton, 1994).

Of course, the people who had moved to the suburbs (and their children) had done so primarily as a result of the increased "darkening" of the city's population. And the schools minority proportion had been accelerated by *Brown*. The suburbs had no reason to impose segregation, as there were few, if any, minorities residing in them. The idea to extend busing beyond the city limits, although it may have been costly and cumbersome in implementation, would have put the states on notice to finally confront the fact that they have an obligation to provide "adequate and efficient" schools for all children regardless of their race or where they reside.

Although substantial research (e.g., Schofield, 1996) has shown that desegregation of elementary and secondary students results in a positive effect on reading and mathematics scores of minority children, and in later life, influences friendships, graduation rates, and income, it appears that court decisions coupled with demographic changes have placed this remedy, for the most part, outside the realm of possibility. Richard Fossey (1998: 16) has said it most starkly: "*Brown's* promise has been broken in the inner cities and may not be fulfilled in our lifetime." This unfulfilled promise at the K–12 level has a profound effect on higher education.

ADAMS AND HIGHER EDUCATION

The *Adams v. Richardson* case (1973) was among the first to take a comprehensive look at segregation in higher education. This segregation had a long history that stemmed from the same sources as that which resulted in *Brown*. But an added complication is that this had led to the creation of historically black colleges and universities (HBCUs), American Indian community colleges (called collectively AIHEC), and some designated institutions serving large numbers of Hispanics (called HSIs).

The black colleges were founded after the Civil War for the express purposes of educating the recently freed slaves and maintaining them in separate colleges from the white colleges. The Indian- and Hispanic-serving colleges were designated much later for many of the same reasons, but they were not founded as a response to legal segregation as were the black colleges. Thus, the emphasis in college desegregation history has been on desegregating the public black and white colleges.

Indeed, in its early history, the litigation that culminated in *Brown* was built primarily on a series of higher education cases (Davis and Graham, 1995). These cases were the first ones to create a wedge in the wall of segregation that led to *Brown* but the decision also implied that white colleges, primarily in the South, would soon be subject to the same demand for equality of access. For example, in the *Missouri ex rel. Gaines v. Canada* (1938) case, Lloyd Gaines was ordered admitted to law school at the University of Missouri, which had previously denied him because of his race. In the *McLaurin* (1950) case, McLaurin was admitted to the University of Oklahoma to pursue a doctoral degree but was segregated to an assigned seat in the classroom, the library, and the cafeteria. The Supreme Court ordered that the restrictions be removed and that he be treated like all other students. It was through the incremental victories such as these that the civil rights attorneys finally were victorious in *Brown*, though ultimately paving the way for attacks on segregated higher education. The G.I. Bill, after World War II, enormously accelerated the demand for higher education particularly by the low-income students. But the G.I. Bill, despite its good results, merely enhanced segregation in the already racially separate universities.

Initially, the higher-education cases were almost entirely focused on the segregation that had historically excluded blacks from mainstream universities: for example, the *Board of Trustees of the University of North Carolina v. Frazier* (1956), and a previous case, *Tureaud v. Board of Supervisors of Louisiana State University* (1954). Both cases ordered the admission of black students to colleges who were turned down because of their race. Nothing was said about affirmative action or test scores; the students were simply denied entry because they were black. The Justices were faced with one issue: "the constitutionality of segregation in public education. We have announced that such segregation is a denial of equal protection of the laws" (*Brown v. Board of Education of Topeka, Kansas,* 1954).

Three federal acts subsequently paved the way for a more broad assault on higher-education desegregation. The first was the passage of the Civil Rights Act of 1964 by Congress under the pressure of President Lyndon Johnson. President Johnson then issued Executive Order 11246—the "Affirmative Action" order—which required any employer with $100,000 in government contracts or employing fifty or more employees to have an affirmative-action plan with goals and timetables, and must make a "good faith effort" to achieve those goals. At the commencement address at Howard University on June 4, 1965, President Johnson stated, "You do not take a person who, for years, has been hobbled by chains and liberate him, bring him up to the starting line of a race and then say 'you are free to compete with all others' and still justly believe you have been completely fair." This was followed by the passage of the Higher Education Act of 1965, which forbade any institution receiving federal dollars from discriminating on the basis of race, sex, or national origin. Armed with these powerful tools, colleges around the country—some reluctantly, some eagerly—began to integrate their student bodies (they were, for various reasons, less successful with faculty). But some colleges (primarily in the South), despite these laws, made little movement.

John Quincy Adams, a black man, was the lead appellant in a lawsuit brought by NAACP Legal Defense Fund against the Department of Health, Education and Welfare, alleging that ten states had not attempted to desegregate and yet continued to receive federal funds. *Adams v. Richardson* (1973) was soon expanded to the nineteen states that maintained dual systems of higher education. *Adams* was a landmark decision which required all public institutions in these states to file desegregation plans and be in compliance with Title VI of the Civil Rights Act by a certain date, which varied from five to ten years. Suffice it to say, at the end of their various terms, *no* state institution had fully complied with its own desegregation plan, and no institution lost federal funds as a result. On the other hand, the *Adams* litigation did prod some states to make progress in desegregating their higher-education facilities. Gary Orfield, a Harvard desegregation researcher, has said "even after the Office of Civil Rights was ordered by the federal courts to require equity and desegregation plans in the states that had intentionally segregated students, it never used its power to cut off funds" (1998: 5).

Mississippi, the most reluctant of the southern states, was not making progress despite *Adams* and the Civil Rights Act. Thirty years after *Brown*, the state still maintained five all-white universities and three that were virtually all black. In *United States v. Fordice* (1992), the justices of the Supreme Court examined four policies: admission standards, institutional missions, program duplication, and the continued operation of all-white universities. The Court ruled that these were policies of the states prior to the *de jure* system of segregated higher education. Yet, despite these rulings, the Court recently held that admission standards must be uniform for all Mississippi colleges and universities, which resulted in more than a twenty percent drop in black enrollment at black Jackson State University and Mississippi Valley University (Orfield and Miller, 1998). The Court did provide for summer development programs for those students who did not initially fully qualify, but (1) the cost to participants could be prohibitive; and (2) particularly low-income and black students would be affected.

DeFunis v. Odegaard (1974) promised to be the first definitive case testing affirmative action in higher education. Marco DeFunis sued the University of Washington Law School for denying him admittance while accepting minorities with lower LSAT scores. He was admitted to the law school while his case journeyed through the courts. When his case reached the Supreme Court, he was about to graduate, and his case was declared moot. Nevertheless, his case foreshadowed that future cases would increasingly focus on test scores and the definition of "merit."

It was *Regents of the University of California v. Bakke* (1978) that defined affirmative action and remained the law governing college admissions, even during fierce attacks by the conservative Reagan administration which investigated admission practices at a number of universities, particularly attacking race-conscious admission practices, and calling for raising entrance requirements and doing away with civil-rights measures. These practices, coupled with the huge rises in tuition and sharp cuts in Pell Grants led to a drop in minority students entering college during the early 1980s (Orfield and Miller, 1998).

The *Bakke* case arose at a time of severe turmoil and social upheaval in American society, with students demonstrating on American campuses. *Bakke* was also deliberated with a serious ideological split on the Supreme Court. The first bloc consisted of Justices Brennan, White, Marshall, and Blackmun, who believed that race should be considered in the admission process. The second group was made up of Justices Stevens, Rehnquist, Stewart, and Chief Justice Burger, who thought that the admission programs, which Allan Bakke challenged, violated the law (Davis and Graham, 1995).

The University of California at Davis had set up a minority-admissions program in which sixteen of the one hundred slots for the entering class in its medical school were reserved for minority students. Bakke challenged this program because some of the students admitted had lower Medical College Admission Test (MCAT) scores than he had, and he had been rejected. Bakke only challenged the minority applicants, despite the fact that eight white applicants who were admitted had lower scores than he had. Nevertheless, it remained for Justice Lewis Powell to break the tie between the two blocs of the court, and he did it with a Solomon-like decision.

On the one hand, citing the Fourteenth Amendment, he found the special admission program to be a quota that was forbidden by the equal protection clause and struck it down. On the other hand, he invoked the "robust exchange of ideas" as warranting diversity in the classroom and felt that race could be a "plus" factor in determining admission. In support of that notion he cited the Harvard College admission program. There were, as expected, many dissents and concurrences among the justices. Justice Thurgood Marshall's eloquent dissent was especially informative when he said, "It is unnecessary in 20th Century America to have individual Negroes demonstrate that they have been victims of racial discrimination; the racism of our society has been so pervasive that none, regardless of wealth or position, has managed to escape its impact" (*Regents of the University of California v. Bakke*, 1978). Feinberg noted that "[B]y ignoring the historical basis for affirmative action, *Bakke* began the shift away from race and gender based affirmative action that we are witnessing today" (Feinberg, 1998: 11).

Bakke remained the law for approximately twenty years, although it was increasingly restricted by subsequent Supreme Court decisions. For example, in *Adarand Constructors v. Pena* (1995), a construction case in which contractors challenged the provision that they were to set aside 30 percent of their subcontracts for minority firms, the Supreme Court ruled that any time race is invoked in a legal action, it required "strict scrutiny" of its intent. Moreover, any preferences granted to minorities must show a "compelling state interest" and be "narrowly tailored" in their remedy of the alleged violation. The Court overturned the set asides. In addition, in 1995 in *Podberesky v. Kirwin*, the Fourth Circuit Court of Appeals ruled that Daniel Podberesky, a student of Hispanic origin, had been unconstitutionally barred from the Banneker scholarship program (a program for blacks) because of his race. The University argued that it had a long history of exclusion of blacks which it was attempting to overcome with this program. The Court ruled that the program was not narrowly tailored enough because the University had some non-Maryland recipients of the scholarships. The program is now no longer confined to black students, who currently receive less than 30 percent of the scholarships. The Supreme Court refused to review the decision. These rulings, among others, restricted the application of *Bakke* more and more, compelling institutions to more carefully adjust their admission criteria for fear of lawsuits.

HOPWOOD AND PROP 209

The two states with the largest number of Hispanics in their population passed restrictive measures that defeated affirmative action and severely lowered the access of Hispanics, and blacks as well, to selective universities in their states; one was the result of a court challenge, the other was by citizen petition. Cheryl Hopwood, a white student, sued the University of Texas for denying her admission to law school while accepting Hispanics and blacks with lower grades and LSAT scores, through a two-tiered admission process. In *Hopwood v. Texas* (1996), the Fifth Circuit Court of Appeals found that other whites who had lower scores than Hopwood had also been accepted but nevertheless ruled in her favor that race could not be used in a two-tiered process for admission. In the meantime the admission process had been discontinued because the university found it weak; therefore, the Supreme Court refused to review the case on appeal because it declared the issue moot (Fossey, 1998). Since the Fifth Circuit governs the states of Texas, Louisiana, and Mississippi, the ruling caused considerable confusion. For example, Mississippi is under a Supreme Court ruling in *United States v. Fordice* requiring it to desegregate its institutions of higher education and thus must keep track of race—a direct contradiction of the *Hopwood* ruling. Louisiana, on the other hand, is also under a court order to merge some programs between predominantly white Louisiana State University and Southern University, the HBCU. Therefore, for all intents, the *Hopwood* ruling only has effect in Texas. Compounding this confusion, the attorney general of Texas, Dan Morales, said he interpreted the *Hopwood* ruling as applying to *all* admissions in all state schools, not just the law school. Furthermore, he said it applied to all race-based financial aid as well. Finally, he said, he would not defend anyone who challenged the court's ruling. He later modified this rule to let the University of Texas appeal the ruling, but only if it used a private attorney. But the Supreme Court justices declined to hear the appeal.

The harsh nature of the *Hopwood* ruling and its broader interpretation by the attorney general prompted the Hispanic and black caucuses of the legislature to join with their colleagues to successfully pass the "10 Percent Law," which basically says that anyone in the top 10 percent of their high-school graduating class is automatically admitted to the University of Texas and Texas A&M University. This may tend to blunt some of the worst effects of *Hopwood*, but several scholars have conjectured that it could lead to the "best" students at the "worst" schools being accepted and then finding that they are unable to compete with the "best" students from the "best" schools. These commentators were also concerned that minorities below the top ten percent at the better schools would miss out, while less-prepared minorities would be chosen (Orfield and Miller, 1998). This is speculative at the moment, it is too early to have definitive data.

In California, the Regents of the University of California under the leadership of Regent Ward Connerly (following the lead of his mentor, then Governor Pete Wilson) persuaded the regents to pass SP-1, after a contentious and emotionally charged meeting. SP-1 forbids the University of California to use race or sex as criteria in any of its programs: admission of students, awarding of contracts, and the like. The passage of SP-1 produced highly vocal demonstrations and marches of students on campuses and in the streets.

Mr. Connerly, flush with his success with SP-1, started an organization with strong financial backing to put a measure on the ballot, known as Proposition 209, that places the same restrictions as SP-1 on the entire state as well. The measure was known as "The Civil Rights Initiative" (Orfield and Miller, 1998).

With the infusion of considerable funds and personnel, the measure passed with 54 percent of the vote and became a part of the constitution of the state of California. Some critics have suggested that in exit interviews ten percent of those voting for the measure thought it was *supporting* affirmative action (Fossey, 1998).

Connerly has since taken his organization around the country and in concert with the conservative Washington, D.C.- based Center for Individual Rights, has won a similar ballot initiative in the state of Washington with Proposition 200. He has said he is now looking at vulnerable states such as Colorado and Michigan for his next drive (Broder, 1999).

THE FUTURE

It is certain that the histories of affirmative action and desegregation have shown a rise and are now experiencing a fall that may end in their demise. Orfield (1998) has said, "Threatened by court decisions, referenda, political attacks, and law suits, colleges are struggling to foresee the consequences of abandoning affirmative action and to devise viable alternatives for promoting and preserving campus diversity. . . . These changes can create a vicious circle of resegregation" (1998: 10). The first examples are already apparent. In California the black enrollment has dropped by 63 percent at the law schools, and the Latino enrollment has dropped by 34 percent. At the University of Texas Law School, enrollment was less than 1 percent black (1998). In assessing why we have come to this stage in seeking equality for minorities in American society, we need to examine two phenomena that have played a major role in this scenario: the federal courts and the leaders of higher-education institutions.

During the twelve years of the Reagan and Bush administrations, these presidents had the opportunity to appoint the majority of all federal judges now sitting on the bench (Orfield and Miller, 1998). These consciously conservative appointments and their narrow vision are seen in the steady narrowing of desegregation and affirmative-action cases. From the defining of *Bakke* to the ending of *Hopwood*, the downward trend has been slow but steady (Justiz, Wilson, and Bjork, 1994). Reagan and Bush similarly placed conservatives on the Supreme Court. The Court currently enjoys a solid 6 to 3 conservative majority on most cases. President Clinton has been able to name two justices to the Court—Ruth Bader Ginsburg and Stephen Breyer—but they have mainly replaced retiring justices without changing the ideological balance of the court.

The possibility for success of the courts is with the state courts, not the federal courts. The litigation in *Sheff v. O'Neill* (1996) offers some intriguing possibilities. Milo Sheff, a black student, with sixteen of his fellow students is suing the state of Connecticut in the state courts over the state constitution's guarantee of a "minimally adequate" education (Fossey, 1998). Federal courts, because of binding legal precedent, were inadequate to do this, but state courts seem to offer an opening to promising litigation. The state Supreme Court ruled in favor of the plaintiffs and ordered the state to provide equal educational opportunities to the Hartford children, where pupils are 93 percent black and Hispanic. The case is still in the implementation phase but should be watched closely for its possibility of opening up in other states this kind of litigation.

The leaders of higher-education institutions, for the most part, went into affirmative action cautiously and hesitantly and found that the sky did not fall. Then they rushed into it as they found that diversity added richness to their campus, despite the problems and glitches that often occurred with its implementation. I think it is safe to say that most presidents of higher-education institutions genuinely believe in affirmative action, but they have lived and believed so long in the meritocratic model that it is difficult to dislodge it from their minds, and thus they have not been forthright in speaking out for affirmative action. The need to rethink how we measure competence and determine merit is greater now because the attacks on affirmative action have made it necessary. This rethinking is something higher-education leaders should have been doing a long time ago. But it was much simpler to go with the scores on the LSAT and SAT and call them "merit."

The experiment with alternative strategies that has been tried at the University of California–Irvine also has intriguing possibilities (Orfield and Miller, 1998). It uses a two-stage process of admission. Sixty percent of students are admitted on academic qualifications alone. Forty percent are admitted on a combination of academic qualifications and personal characteristics such as leadership, overcoming adversity, poverty, and background. Irvine officials have found that using these criteria has allowed them to enroll a class nearly as diverse as the year before (Orfield and Miller, 1998). Moreover, the Regents have approved the plan because it does not use race as criteria.

The two studies cited above are simply the latest innovations that civil-rights lawyers and heads of institutions are trying out in this time when the end of affirmative action appears near. They are both aware that what they are doing is in the best interests of the country and its economic future regardless of what the federal courts do or what public opinion stipulates. This is similar to a belief that many leaders of educational institutions had when the G.I. Bill was passed: It would let the "rabble" into their institutions. They found, however, that it was the greatest positive transformation of our collegiate institutions. Our leaders today are faced with another challenge in which a rapidly growing segment of our population is being shut out of our educational institutions. We must find solutions as dramatic as the G.I. Bill to save us from ourselves.

BIBLIOGRAPHY

Bennett, Charles E. 1995. *The Black Population in the United States*. Washington, D.C.: Bureau of the Census.

Broder, David S. 1999. Campaign against Affirmative Action Widens. *Austin American—Statesman*, January 31, E1.

Darling-Hammond, Linda. 1996. The Right to Learn and the Advancement of Teaching. *Educational Researcher* 25, 5–17.

Davis, Abraham, and Barbara Graham. 1995. *The Supreme Court, Race and Civil Rights*. Thousand Oaks, Calif.: Sage Publications.

DeMitchell, Thomas, and Richard Fossey. 1997. *The Limits of Law-based School Reform: Vain Hopes and False Promises*. Lancaster, Pa.: Technomic Publishing.

Feinberg, Walter. 1998. *On Higher Ground: Education and the Case for Affirmative Action*. New York: Teachers' College Press.

Feldman, J.; E. Kirby; and S. E. Eaton. 1994. *Still Separate, Still Unequal: The Limits of Milliken II's Educational Compensation Remedies*. Cambridge, Mass.: Harvard Project on School Desegregation.

Fossey, Richard. 1998. Facing the truth about Urban Schools. In *Reading on Equal Education*, ed. R. Fossey. Vol. 15. of *Race, the Courts, and Equal Education: The Limits of the Law*. New York: AMS Press, 5–19.

Higginbotham Jr., A. Leon, 1998. Breaking Thurgood Marshall's Promise. *The New York Times*, January 18, Sec. 6, 3.

Johnson, Lyndon B. 1965. Commencement address delivered at Howard University, June 4.

Justiz, Manuel J.; Reginald Wilson; and Lars G. Bjork. 1994. *Minorities in Higher Education*. Washington, D.C.: American Council on Education.

Orfield, Gary. 1998. Campus Resegregation and its Alternatives. In *Chilling Admissions: The Affirmative Action Crisis and the Search for Alternatives*, ed. Gary Orfield and Edward Miller. Cambridge, Mass.: Harvard Education Publishing Group, 1–16.

Orfield, Gary, and Edward Miller, eds. 1998. *Chilling Admissions: The Affirmative Action Crisis and the Search for Alternatives*. Cambridge, Mass.: Harvard Education Publishing Group.

Schofield, Janet W. 1996. Review of Research on School Desegregation's Impact on Elementary and Secondary Students. In *Forty Years after the Brown Decision: Implications of School Desegregation for U.S. Students*, Vol. 13, ed. K. Lomotey and C. Teddlie. New York: AMS Press, 71–116.

COURT CASES

Adams v. Richardson, 480 F.2d 1159 D.C. Cir. (1973).

Adarand Constructors v. Pena, 512 U.S. 200 (1995).

Board of Trustees of the University of North Carolina v. Frazier, 350 U.S. 979 (1956).

Brown v. Board of Education of Topeka, Kansas (*Brown I*), 347 U.S. 483, 98 L.Ed. 873, 74 S.Ct. 686 (1954).

Brown v. Board of Education of Topeka, Kansas (*Brown II*), 349 U.S. 294, 99 L.Ed. 1083, 75 S.Ct. 753 (1955).

Cooper v. Aaron, 358 U.S. 1 (1958).

DeFunis v. Odegaard, 416 U.S. 312 (1974).

Green v. County School Board of New Kent County, Virginia, 391 U.S. 430, 20 L.Ed. 2d 716, 88 S.Ct. 1689 (1968).

Hernandez v. Stockton Unified School District, Case No. 101016, Superior Court of California (1975).

Hopwood v. Texas, 78 F.3d 932 (5th Cir.), cert. denied 116 S.Ct. 2581 (1996).

McLaurin v. Oklahoma State Regents, 339 U.S. 637, 94 L.Ed. 1149, 70 S.Ct. 851 (1950).

Milliken v. Bradley, 418 U.S. 717, 41 L.Ed. 2d 1069, 94 S.Ct. 3112 (1974).

Missouri ex rel. Gaines v. Canada, 305 U.S. 337, 83 L.Ed. 208, 59 S.Ct. 232 (1938).

Podberesky v. Kirwin, 38 F.3d 147 (4th Cir.), cert. denied 115 S.Ct. 2001 (1995).

Regents of the University of California v. Bakke, 438 U.S. 265 (1978).

Sheff v. O'Neill, 678 A.2d 1267 (Conn.) (1996).

Swann v. Charlotte-Mecklenberg Board of Education, 402 U.S. 1, 28 L.Ed. 2d 554, 91 S.Ct. 1267 (1971).

Tureaud v. Board of Supervisors of Louisiana State University, 347 U.S. 971 (1954).

United States v. Fordice, 505 U.S. 717 (1992).

9

Technology in Higher Education: Issues for the New Millennium

Karen Hardy Cárdenas

There is little doubt that technology will have a significant impact on higher education in the future. However, this observation raises at least as many questions as it answers: What will the impact of educational technology be? What problems can technology solve for higher education? What problems might technology cause? Will the traditional campus with its "hallowed halls of ivy" be replaced by computers that connect isolated learners to a distant instructor? Will technology enable both students and teachers to learn and teach in exciting new ways?

Amidst all the attention that has been given to educational technology recently, central questions have been ignored. It is easy to proclaim technology as "the wave of the future" and celebrate its every manifestation in the higher-education community. It is equally easy to dismiss technology as useless. It is somewhat more difficult to acknowledge the value and the limitations of technology.

In order for the higher-education community to faithfully discharge its responsibilities to its students, to the general public, and to itself, it must pose and answer critical questions about appropriate and inappropriate uses of technology in fulfilling its mission. The issues are becoming more complex every day. It may be useful to examine the problem of technology and its presence in college and university communities from four separate perspectives: (1) students, (2) faculty, (3) programs, and (4) support.

STUDENTS AND TECHNOLOGY:
CURRENT STATUS AND FUTURE CHALLENGES

Institutions of higher education exist (or should exist) primarily for the benefit of the students who attend them. Thus, it is important to decide how much college students know about technology and how much they need to know. It is equally important to determine what the role of higher education should be in preparing these students for the challenges of the future.

Some would have us believe that the current preoccupation with technology in higher education is student driven. Those who promote technology (often for the sake of technology) insist that faculty must use instructional technology in all phases of every class because they are teaching to a generation that grew up on television. Students will expect lectures to be accompanied by cartoons, video clips, and Power Point presentations. They are all computer literate and will expect each class to have a webpage and to require extensive use of the Internet.

Well, maybe that is happening somewhere. But popular and professional magazines and newspapers are reporting something entirely different. According to statistics published in the August 28, 1998 issue of *The Chronicle of Higher Education*, only 56.7 percent of fall 1997 freshmen indicated that they used a personal computer extensively (more than six hours a week). 58.2 percent of men and 55.5 percent of women answered the question in the affirmative. Even for someone who considers herself a novice user of technology, I found this statistic shocking. I had assumed that the vast majority of students came to college prepared to use a computer. I even assumed that more than 56.7 percent of entering freshmen would have their own computer.

Although this statistic could be interpreted in several ways, it certainly suggests that the computer-literacy courses required by most high schools are not producing technophiles in overwhelming numbers. In fact, it suggests that obligatory instruction in computer use is producing computer users in a ratio only slightly higher than the study of Shakespeare is producing dramatists and poets. Just because a person can use a computer does not mean that he or she will.

Two other articles appearing recently also suggest that students are somewhat less enamored of technology than we have been led to believe. Eisenberg and Adams (1998) noted with some amusement and amazement that, despite high salaries and a dearth of applicants in the field, only 4.6 percent of the students taking the 1998 ACT examination indicated that they were considering a career in computer science. This compares to 20 percent who plan to pursue a career in health sciences.

Students also seem to be a bit less than totally enthused about the use of websites in the recruitment and admission process. Students are continuing to use university websites in growing numbers, according to Guernsey (1998a). The study, based on the responses of five hundred college-bound high-school seniors across the country, indicated that about 78 percent had used campus websites to get admissions information and other general information such as program descriptions. However, "when the students were asked to rate the importance of four recruitment tools—printed catalogues, websites, CD-ROMs and videotapes—the paper format won. About 62 percent cited printed catalogues as 'very important,' while websites were ranked that high by only 34 percent of the students" (Guernsey, 1998a).

This survey contributes two more interesting insights into students' comfort level with technology. First, the study demonstrated that the popularity of on-line applications to colleges had actually declined. In spite of predictions that the paper application was doomed, only 21 percent of the students surveyed said that they preferred on-line applications. This number was down 34 percent from the previous year. Students cited confidentiality as one reason to balk at applying on line. They also indicated that they thought a college would take applications received by mail more seriously than those sent on line (Guernsey, 1998a).

In response to another question, 75 percent of students indicated that they planned to take a computer to college. (Parents, beware! Only 56.7 percent will be using them!) In light of the fact that many schools are requiring students to purchase a computer, 95 percent of the students in the survey said that they would attend an institution even if they were required to make such a purchase.

Obviously, there is a segment of students that arrive on campus with a computer and a vast amount of computer experience. According to Stone, there are more than 9.8 million children using the Internet. This number is projected to triple in the next four years. The same author cited research by CNN and *USA Today* that indicated that "28 percent of teens said they could live without their TV, but only 23 percent said they could get by without a computer (1998: 72).

But how are they using their computers? Are they experimenting with programming? Is there a significant amount of industrial-design work occurring in the family computer room? Are young people designing computer games that are not particularly academic but that still require a significant degree of knowledge? Well, no, not generally. There are teens who are doing all these things and more. However, they constitute the exception that proves the rule. And the rule is that most young people are "into" passive Internet browsing and getting into chat rooms. According to Stone, "Perhaps the most sobering statistic of all: at the peak of *Titanic* mania, AOL says, there was a message posted about Leonardo DiCaprio *every 10 seconds*" (emphasis theirs) (1998: 72).

It is a given that the freshmen entering our colleges and universities have more knowledge about the computer than did their predecessors, but they have scarcely mastered it as a working tool. It is difficult to imagine how to accommodate the skills, needs, and sensibilities of a generation that can post a message about Leonardo DiCaprio every 10 seconds. This is going to require extensive critical analysis.

It is also important to consider the fact that the children referred to as the "keyboard kids" may live in your neighborhood or mine. However, they may not live in the neighborhoods from whence our students come. A recent national television news story on computer use by young people revealed the not-so-surprising fact that computer use by African-American and Hispanic children is only half of what it is among white children. Computers and access to the Internet have been proclaimed for their potential to level the playing field by allowing everyone the same access to knowledge. At this point, however, they seem to have contributed to an Orwellian situation in which all the animals are equal; but some are more equal than others.

Let us accept, just for purposes of discussion, that, despite all the rhetoric, the students we will have in our classrooms, regardless of the influence of technology in their lives, are not proficient at using computers. To the extent that they as a group have some competence, these abilities are not shared uniformly. Some are good; some not so good. Some have extensive background; some little at all.

The question which must be addressed by leaders in the field of higher education at this juncture is, So what? What do students' computer skills (or lack thereof) imply for the missions of our various institutions? How vital are computer skills (and by extension, familiarity with other forms of technology) to students' academic success and to their success in their professional or personal life after college? And, are such skills more important to academic and professional success than acquiring knowledge and critical-thinking skills?

A knowledge of keyboarding will enable students to submit papers and projects that are neater than those written in longhand. And, it is fairly certain that the student with the most advanced computing skills and the most sophisticated knowledge of technology will have an edge in procuring a job in a field which requires such skills. But if a professor requires that all assignments be produced on a word processor or that all students download assignments from a website, how should such requirements be justified? If a student can demonstrate an understanding of course content but can neither keyboard nor download, does the student deserve a lower grade?

Of course, incorporating technology into instruction as one of the requirements of the course (even if the course does not really need to use technology) may be defensible if one of the goals of the institution is to produce students who can function in the high-tech workplace of the future. However, in order to justify an artificial use of technology (what some have called "technology for technology's sake"), an institution would have to prove that technological expertise would be required of their students as they seek entry-level positions. The institution would also need to explain why a college or university should be the place where they acquire such expertise.

Suppose, for example, that businesses of the future are looking for workers who can reason and conduct an intelligent debate on an issue. Suppose that industry would prefer to have a student who has been trained to be a lifelong learner over one with technological expertise. While it is incumbent upon colleges and universities to produce students who are marketable, to what extent does the academic community want to compromise other essential aspects of students' education to make sure that they are computer competent?

Computer competence or literacy may prove to be a bit like our students' competence in written and spoken English. Academics believe that it is essential that students be competent communicators. They supposedly come to college with this competence. However, as anyone who has taught at a college or university knows, the fact that students have studied both English and speech as secondary-school and university students does not mean that they can speak and write effectively.

Just as many institutions have expanded the teaching of composition into the various disciplines through programs in writing across the curriculum, so may students' computing skills come to be developed through their major field. It is certainly the professors in the major field who have the strongest vested interest in their students' viability in the marketplace. And they, more than anyone else, should know what the marketplace will require of their graduates in terms of technological preparation.

In asking (1) how much technology should be emphasized in a college–university setting at the expense of other kinds of knowledge, and (2) who should be ultimately responsible for assuring that a student is technologically marketable, an informed professoriate is beginning to define the concerns that will determine the role of technology in higher education in the next millennium. Frustrating though it may be, it is clear that these are not questions that higher education can answer alone. It has been obvious for some time that no segment of education exists in a vacuum. However, even though experience has shown otherwise, there is still a tendency to believe that a single group of institutions—for example, primary schools, middle schools, secondary schools, colleges–universities, and businesses—bear a particular burden, such as technological preparation, alone.

If those who influence the direction of higher education are truly serious about the importance of producing graduates who can function in the high-tech workplace of the future, they need to abandon the notion that this responsibility lies solely with higher education. Addressing this need will require a truly collaborative effort among educational institutions at several levels and between education and business. Preparing students with a significant degree of usable technological expertise will require some changes in how all concerned view the educational process and its relationship to the real world.

Before I pose some models of how education may need to change to respond to this challenge, let me note that we should avoid panic in devising approaches to address our students' need for technological competence. Education in general (and higher education, which used to be an exception, but no longer is) has an unfortunate tendency to seize simple, quick solutions to extremely complex problems. That is, it tends to be trendy and faddish. And, beyond that, it tends to allow the current fad to control educational processes far beyond what is reasonable or seemly.

However, for the sake of argument, assume that having students who are well educated in every traditional sense and in the creative uses of technology is a plausible goal for society. Accomplishing that goal is not solely the responsibility of higher education. Higher education can take a leadership role is helping primary, middle, and secondary schools develop their students' expertise in this area. Higher education can also form active partnerships with business and industry that will lead to developing students with truly marketable skills. However, higher education must not assume that preparing students who are functionally proficient in the various uses of technology is a significant part of its mission.

If technological expertise is the *sine qua non*, without which our students will be incapable of fully productive professional lives in the future, then their technological expertise must be developed beginning in the elementary grades. A working knowledge of technology, like a working knowledge of a foreign language, is not something that is acquired overnight. If technology is to be an important aspect of their future, students must begin to be computer literate before they leave grade school.

In middle school or high school, all students should have had some direct contact with an industry or a business where technology is used. At the middle-school level, this might take the form of a field trip to see how people use technology in the work place. At the secondary level, students might be encouraged to have brief internships, during the school year or during the summer, in order to experience technology in action in a business or industry that interests them. In the future, students at the secondary level might even be required to have such a "hands-on" experience. Even if students do not plan to enter a field in which technological competence is crucial, an internship will enable them to understand how technology works in the "real" world.

Now our hypothetical students are entering college. If higher education has taken a leadership role in helping all preuniversity students attain a reasonable level of technological expertise and experience, the groundwork has been laid. Higher education should continue to provide appropriate experiences for all students in the area of technology. It should encourage internship experiences for various majors in areas in which technology is important. However, under no circumstances should it place technology above learning.

If the future requires students to have a knowledge of technology that cannot be obtained through a reasonable amount of college–university coursework plus internships, then higher education might resort to a five-year program. Students might spend their first year or two acquiring the basics of higher education, and then two more years on the major and minor fields. Then in a fifth year, they might devote themselves to a variety of sophisticated technological applications appropriate to their field of endeavor.

The important concept here is that technology is a means to an end. It is not, nor was it ever intended to be, the end or the goal itself. If and/or when higher education "deifies" technology, it will have lost its sense of mission. No amount of technological expertise can substitute for students' ability to critically analyze a problem and to clearly articulate a response to it.

FACULTY AND TECHNOLOGY: TODAY AND IN THE NEXT MILLENNIUM

In considering the issue of faculty and technology, it is important to ask the same questions as we did regarding students: (1) What do faculty currently know about technology and what should they know? and (2) What kinds of expertise will be required of faculty in the future? Not too surprisingly, the answers to these questions regarding faculty differ significantly from those regarding students.

College–university faculty in general (not counting the "technowhizzes" and troglodytes on every campus and in every discipline) are more technologically proficient than their students. There has been a tremendous amount of pressure on college–university faculty nationwide to at least become competent in word processing and electronic correspondence if only for their own benefit. There has also been a strong interest in using techology in teaching. Whether teaching in a small classroom, a large lecture hall, or via electronic media to one or more distant sites, faculty have been encouraged to become proficient in teaching with technology. In addition, faculty with particular research interests have acquired knowledge of databases, spreadsheets, and other more sophisticated programs.

Even if there were no pressure from administration for faculty to become conversant with technology for personal, teaching, or research purposes, faculty members should make an effort to acquire such knowledge. "But why?" protest my more traditional colleagues (also known as "straw people"). "I've been writing all my lecture notes on legal pads since I got my doctorate in 1973, just as my professors did. I can give the secretary my handwritten letters to colleagues at other institutions. My discipline really doesn't require any significant use of technology for research purposes. So, why do I have to change the way I have been doing things for the last twenty-five years?"

Well, the simplest and most direct answer to this question, which I have heard from dozens of colleagues in the last ten years, is that it is a professional obligation. Time marches on. It is not necessary to pursue each of the latest fads to meet one's obligations as a professional. However, if there are innovations that might provide us with easier, faster, and more effective ways of doing what we have done in the past (research, service, and teaching), professionals in the field must give some of these ideas an honest try before dismissing them as useless. Computers allow university faculty to update lecture notes from semester to semester. E-mail allows them to keep in touch with colleagues across the country with whom they share research interests or professional affiliations.

But perhaps the more compelling reason for faculty to become at least somewhat proficient in the use of appropriate technologies is that professional educators must do so for their students. Not all students are receptive to the use of certain kinds of instructional technology. Recently one student asked me if we would have Internet assignments in the Spanish course she was taking. I said no—in this particular course students would be given extra credit for some Internet work; however, no one would be required to "log on." I was amazed when she said, "Good. I get so tired of having to waste my time with Internet assignments that have nothing to do with the course." That same day, however, another student asked if he could download my syllabus from my website. Perhaps these two students cancel each other out.

Even if all students are not technology *aficionados*, faculty still need to make an effort to know what technology can do for them and for their students. All experienced educators know that there are many learning styles. Some students exposed to a traditional lecture–discussion classroom will never really learn the material. Or rather, they will not learn it as well as they would have if other teaching techniques had been employed.

In one of my many efforts to improve my teaching skills, I attended a professional development seminar a few years ago. The speakers were not in my field, and I was not sure what I could learn from them. I was pleasantly surprised. They reported on research they had done with students taking large lecture courses in the social sciences. In the past, students had done rather poorly in these courses. Regardless of the instructor's professional and instructional expertise, most students did not retain enough of the information to receive an acceptable grade in the courses. The two professors who spoke related two techniques that had helped their students retain the information more effectively.

One had used a Power Point presentation that showed the important points of the lecture on a screen as the professor spoke. This professor indicated that student achievement in her classes had soared since she began using this technique. And, to those who would complain that this is "teaching to the test," I would counter that this is simply effective teaching. Providing vast amounts of information to students with no indication of what parts of that information are most important is justified only if instructors are solely interested in preserving their reputation as demanding teachers. However, it is not effective teaching.

The other speaker at the seminar had handed her students a brief copy of the main points of her lecture. However, the handouts the students received had words missing. The students' job was to fill in the sentences as the instructor spoke. At the end of each period, the instructor displayed the information the students had received on an overhead (today it might be an Elmo).

Together the teacher and the students filled in the missing words and reviewed the most important points of the lecture together.

If effective teaching is our goal, faculty must be constantly seeking ways to make teaching more effective. If teachers are aware, as they should be, that most students do not perform best in a traditional lecture–discussion course, they must look for ways to help students learn in such a setting. Using technology to help students absorb information more rapidly and effectively should not be equated with "dumbing down" a course or a program of study—quite the contrary. When teachers find ways in which technology can help their students learn more effectively, they can make their courses even more demanding.

Students lay the burden of technological proficiency on us in another way. Within the last year or so my colleagues and I have discovered that a significant number of our students are relying on the Internet in doing research for our classes. The first time this happened in one of my classes, I was enchanted. Instead of the typical dry, uninspiring paper on the topic I had assigned, I received a paper with fresh insights and color illustrations.

This particular paper was sound in every regard. However, in subsequent papers using only Internet sources, I began to find problems. In some cases the facts were simply wrong. In one paper, I found that numbers in dates had been inverted so that something that happened in 1763 was declared to have happened in 1673. In other cases, assertions were made which could not be supported. The Internet source had not supported the assertion; but, students assumed that no support was necessary.

In the "information age," faculty have acquired a new responsibility. They must still perform their traditional duties, including the assignment of research papers. But, teachers must also be aware that anyone can establish a website. Information posted on the Internet may be as accurate as information available through other more traditional means. On the other hand, it may not be. The information age, which has been heralded as the great equalizer, allowing all access to information, must be regarded with caution, if not suspicion.

Our students need to be aware that the fact that something appears on the Internet is not proof that it is true. Many, if not most, students naively believe that all the information they receive, be it from a book, a journal article, or a source on the Internet, is equally valid. It is the responsibility of the faculty to help them distinguish between what is valid information and what is not.

It is extremely difficult to know what technological challenges the next millennium will pose for faculty. Based on the last decade, my best guess is that it will be more of the same but at an increasingly intense level. Currently my students can access an enormous amount of information (some of it unreliable) via the Internet and e-mail. They can also use e-mail to correspond with students in other countries. In the future, they will receive even more information on the web, and their contact with people in other cultures may involve video and audio transmission in addition to simple e-mail.

This increased and increasingly immediate access to information and people will make the jobs of faculty more challenging. One can easily envision a group of enterprising faculty in different disciplines leaving teaching in order to devote themselves to providing information about the reliability of certain websites. Universities may find it necessary to establish protocols regarding when it is safe for students to move from e-mail contact to full video and audio exchanges.

In their classrooms and in their research, faculty will also find themselves with a veritable plethora of products and choices. Administrators who are truly committed to the use of technology in all areas of academic life may find themselves obliged to provide release time to faculty for the investigation and development of technological resources. Without such release time, few faculty will be able to successfully discharge their obligations to their profession and to their students.

ACADEMIC PROGRAMS AND TECHNOLOGY: SERIOUS ISSUES FOR THE NEW MILLENNIUM

In considering the relationship between academic programs and technology, one enters an entirely new dimension. In part, the concern with current and future uses of technology in the delivery of programs is very similar to the concerns that have been raised regarding student and faculty skills in this regard. However, when we discuss academic programs, we are entering the realm of administration.

Education in the late twentieth century is not solely about teachers and learners. It is also about fiscal accountability. Within most educational institutions or systems, faculty are no longer free to design programs solely because they feel that they will be in the best interest of their students. Faculty may feel that they should be only accountable to their students and to the students' education; but, they are accountable first to the bottom line. As a faculty member, I may offer any course or program of study I wish—as long as each of my courses enrolls a minimum of ten students. I should also offer courses with sufficient frequency to insure that students receive the courses they need in a timely and predictable fashion.

The paragraph above should not be interpreted as a protest of what higher education has lost in the age of fiscal accountability. When I look back on the courses I taught in the 1970s and 1980s that consisted of only two or three students, I am amazed that such things were allowed. Certainly as state legislatures began to scrutinize higher education more closely, it was inevitable that the luxuries we enjoyed in "the good old days" would be questioned.

Often our programs in the past were less the result of solid planning than of a collection of individual whims. I once interviewed for an administrative position at a small university. In the course of the interview, I expressed some interest in the upper-division curriculum, which seemed to have a wealth of courses in some areas and a dirth of courses in others. I was informed that Professors X and Y insisted on offering courses in their specialties (for example, eighteenth century Spanish essay and nineteenth century Latin American drama) each semester. Even though these courses were woefully undersubscribed year after year, there was little room in the curriculum for other specialized courses, regardless of how many students may have needed such courses.

Demanding that faculty be fiscally accountable may have forced them to be more accountable to students as well. When faculty in my department (the Department of Foreign Languages at South Dakota State University) were asked to revise the curriculum of each major language in order to insure that students received the best education possible and that no course enrollment fell below the magic number of ten, it was amazing what we found that we could live without. Some of the courses we eliminated were very popular. Indeed some had been added to the curriculum to increase our enrollments. But, when forced to decide, we discovered that many of the faculty's pet projects were not really necessary.

Although this may seem to be unrelated to the topic of technology, it is not. The same administrators who asked departments and disciplines to take a hard look at their course offerings have also asked if alternative delivery systems for courses and programs might not be feasible. Actually, "asked" is probably not the right word, as those familiar with current academic administration can attest. In South Dakota, the French and German majors at three institutions were threatened with extinction when the faculty were "asked" if they would be willing to offer these programs cooperatively via technology.

Not too surprisingly, the faculty chose cooperation over extinction. To some extent, faculty and students in these two programs should be grateful to administrators and to technology for allowing two important programs to continue. However, it is important to note that, from the outset, the use of technology in these cooperative programs was mandated.

The French Studies Program development committee was charged with developing a program that (1) had a practical focus, (2) involved cooperation among faculty at the three institutions, and (3) incorporated inventive uses of technology. The Office of the Board of Regents had determined the ground rules by which the three institutions must play in order to preserve their programs. It was made clear that other alternatives would not be acceptable. Focusing on (impractical) literature was not an option. Reconstructing programs on each of the three campuses by whatever means possible was not an option. Cooperation without the use of technology was also not an option.

Since serving as the coordinator for the cooperative French Studies and German majors over a two-and-a-half-year period and publishing two articles about that experience, I have received a great deal of correspondence and inquiries from other campuses. I have concluded that, in many ways, we were fortunate. Although we were ordered to cooperate and to use technology, we were allowed to determine, at least initially, how best to cooperate and what kinds of technology were most appropriate.

We decided to use a two-way audio, two-way video technology called PictureTel which most closely resembled what would go on in an actual classroom. Although our cooperative classes leave something to be desired in terms of replicating the intimacy and the interaction of a "real" classroom, they are vastly preferable to what some institutions have been required to create.

I recently received a phone call from a department chair in another state. He had read one of my articles and wanted to ask me some questions about what we were doing. He wanted to know if we had considered the fact that distance education was not necessarily the best way to develop communication skills in a foreign language. I indicated that we had thought of that. He also asked if we were aware that by offering courses cooperatively via electronic means we would be tying up expensive facilities for a handful of students. I noted that we were aware of that also. After he had raised every possible objection to offering foreign language courses via electronic means and I had affirmed the validity of his objections, I explained why we were proceeding as we were. Essentially, we were given few choices. We could offer cooperative courses via electronic means or we could lose our majors in French and German. It was not that technology was the godsend we had prayed for; it was our "*pioresná*" (*peor es nada*, or, better than nothing).

It was then that my caller told me that the goal in his system was to create programs which were independent of time and space. I might have laughed at the idea that an entire program, much less a foreign-language program, could have been limited by such constraints. However, I did not laugh. I had heard the phrase before.

The concept of creating courses and programs independent of time and space is the clarion call of those administrators who envision the higher-education "client" of the future to be vastly dissimilar from today's student. According to these administrators, future students will no longer wish to devote four years in one place to their undergraduate education. They want the latitude to pursue their education at their own pace in their own space. Therefore, all courses must be asynchronous. That is, they must not require all students registered in a course to be in the same place at the same time.

Although it is important to retain an open mind regarding all of the movements and theories currently affecting the delivery of higher-education programs, one is advised to be wary when asynchronous delivery becomes the desired goal of all programs. For years I worked on such programs. In those days we did not use such exalted terms as "asynchronous delivery." We called them correspondence courses.

This may be proof that everything old is new again. However, it is more likely that faculty and administrators, with their desire to find new solutions to persistent problems, have neglected to observe the relationships between the new interactive Internet courses and the old, outmoded correspondence courses. Of course, there are differences as well.

When I designed a correspondence course in Spanish, I attempted to develop communicative skills by requiring all students to submit part of their assignment on tape. Now, students can go into the "cafeteria" or "student lounge" area of their webcourse to visit with other students (although communication in a language other than English is still somewhat problematic since some Internet communication systems do not allow students to use accents, tildes, and other diacritical marks). With each of my correspondence courses, I sent students a bound notebook with all of the information and the assignments they needed for the course. Today students must download such information from the course website.

Although webcourses may provide some students with instruction that they could not access otherwise, they do not offer the same quality of instruction as traditional courses. (Having said that, it should be said that a really good webcourse is better than a really poor teacher). The third-world students (and this is where the webcourse is most popular) whose only access to a higher education is through the web may be grateful to have such a resource. And, the single mother who has a minimum wage job and is hoping to upgrade her skills so that she can make a decent living can also profit from substance courses such as accounting or bookkeeping.

If a student cannot come to a campus, even for an evening or weekend course, then webcourses may be a very valid alternative to a more traditional mode of teaching and learning. There is even some evidence, albeit anecdotal, that some traditional students do better with webcourses than with traditional courses because they are less inhibited when they are keyboarding their ideas than when they have to speak in class. However, this does not mean that webcourses are better for all students. And, it certainly does not mean that all subjects can be taught via webcourses.

Yet faculty at many institutions are being vigorously encouraged (if not being downright forced) to develop webcourses and to use technology as extensively as possible in every segment of their courses. At this point, it is important to consider whether concerns with technology are not, in reality, concerns with the administrative obsession with technology. Neal notes that "faculty members are [also] put off by the artificial urgency of the whole campaign to adopt technology, especially with regard to distance learning. 'Adopt now, or die!' seems to be the prevalent sentiment." (1998: B5) Neal asserts, quite accurately, that it is not the faculty who are pushing the various uses of technology. It is manufacturers of software and hardware and administrators who want to make the higher-education experience more accessible and affordable. Neal indicates that faculty are suspicious of the claims being made for the need for technologically assisted or supported higher-education courses, and rightly so.

At the beginning of his article, Neal alludes to the period in the 1960s and 1970s when we were told that instructional television would irrevocably change the way that higher education was delivered. A book cited in the article predicted, back in 1966, that in the future "as much as 50 percent of the college degree programs will be available for credit via television" (1998: B4). For veteran professors previous predictions of vast and momentous changes in higher education, and their failure to materialize constitute another reason for their hesitancy to rush into the creation of webcourses.

Certainly in the field of foreign languages, faculty have been told for years that technology would make the individual instructor obsolete. When I was teaching at a junior-high school in the mid-1960s, I was fortunate to have a reel-to-reel tape recorder with six headphones in my classroom. The theory at the time encouraged me to allow students to use this equipment as much as possible, since drill (repetition and manipulation of basic sentence patterns) was regarded as the *sine qua non* of language instruction. Eventually machines, which could drill students much more effectively and much more tirelessly than mere human beings, would make teachers expendable.

If today's college and university faculty view technology askance, it may be because they remember earlier periods when they were urged to embrace technologies which did not fulfill the promise of their promoters. It could also be that much technology simply does not answer as many problems as it raises. And, it may well be that faculty suspect that the promotion of technology is aimed primarily at the bottom line. That is, faculty suspect that administrators are hoping that technology will allow an institution or a system to become less reliant on people.

One cannot fault administrators for being concerned with providing the most effective education via the most economic means. However, administrators who are promoting technology seem to be very vague when it comes to comparisons of electronic versus nonelectronic course-delivery costs. Delivering a course via the web would seem to be fairly economical. It may provide a poorer quality of instruction; but it is economically effective.

However, there are some courses that develop interactive skills. These courses do not lend themselves to Internet delivery. So, some form of synchronous teaching via technology is required. If a lower-grade (SwiftSite) PictureTel unit costs $40,000, and telephone-line charges are approximately $8 per site per hour, how many students must take advantage of courses shared via PictureTel to make them justifiable from an economic standpoint? And, if this delivery system is not economically efficient, what are the alternatives? Is it possible to acknowledge that, for some disciplines, technology, or at least distance education, is not the best alternative?

Could we use the funds being used to fund distance education to provide more faculty for the campuses involved? Or, will disciplines such as foreign languages be forced to use increasingly inferior technology (webcourses) in order to be "efficient." And, what do we mean by efficient? If I can offer a really bad course more cheaply than a really good course, where is the efficiency?

In attempting to examine educational technology as it currently exists in American colleges and universities with a view toward the future, it is clear that some changes will have to be made. We must accept that technology will be an increasingly important part of our personal and professional lives. However, we need to look closely at how technology policy should be determined. At present, faculty may be creating exciting technological applications and products that will benefit their students. However, in far too many cases, the uses of technology on a campus or within a larger higher-education system are not determined by the knowledge of the faculty or the needs of the students.

Technology has become the bandwagon *du jour* of higher education. Faculty, regardless of their discipline or technological expertise, are being urged to hop on board the bandwagon. However, the driver of the bandwagon has not, most probably, been in a classroom for some time, if ever. Faculty do not control the funds that have been invested to make technology an essential part of the higher-education experience. And that is truly regrettable, because faculty around the country are coming up with some very exciting uses of technology to benefit their students and their profession.

TECHNOLOGICAL SUPPORT IN CHANGING TIMES

This brings us to the final issue to be treated in this chapter: support. Assuming that technology can make a positive contribution to higher education in the new millennium (and I believe that it can), what kinds of support will be required? Based on the current situation, a great deal of support of various kinds will be necessary.

A very brief and informal survey of faculty that I conducted with a small group of faculty around the country with whom I am connected via e-mail (see the Appendix) revealed a great disparity in the kinds of support faculty members receive on various campuses throughout the United States. On some campuses faculty reported that they had some assurance that the personal computer in their office would be upgraded at a reasonable (two to three year) interval. However, many of the faculty included in the survey indicated that there was no clear policy regarding computer acquisition and upgrades on their campuses. It was basically a situation of survival of the fittest (or the loudest).

The situation regarding support for training in the use of hardware and software was equally inconsistent. Some faculty were satisfied with the way in which computer-support personnel made themselves available to help them with new hardware and with software applications. However, several reported a reluctance to ask for assistance from computer-support personnel because these individuals were somewhat less than helpful.

Support in terms of highly specialized instructional technologies in labs and classroom settings showed the same degree of unevenness as support for individual faculty. On some campuses, including my own, "smart" classrooms equipped with VGA projectors controlled from a central panel and connected to an Elmo, a satellite feed, a computer connection, a VCR, and a laser disk have been installed at an impressive rate. On other campuses such facilities are rare and reserved for certain disciplines or available only to those who can find the grant money to equip "smart" classrooms.

Neal comments on a phenomenon which is both common and controversial. He notes that, "although higher education is under stringent fiscal constraints, money for technology is abundant" (1998: B5). This particular observation was particularly meaningful since, on July 22, 1998, *The Brookings Register* contained the following article:

Regents' Panel Embraces Plan

PIERRE (AP)—Few industries change as rapidly as the computer sector, and the Board of Regents is being asked to make sure that state universities don't fall behind, said Tad Perry, Regents' executive director.

The Budget and Finance Committee of the regents has recommended that another $13.6 million be spent each year to regularly update computer equipment and software at the six schools, Perry said Tuesday.

The suggestion will be acted on Aug. 8 when the full board meets at Spearfish, he said.

"We need to capture the dollars that we need to keep ourselves current over time with technology," Perry said.

The university system already spends $10.1 million a year on computer systems. The recommendation of the budget panel would add $13.6 million in order to replace computer equipment and software on a three-year rotation. (A3)

To be fully appreciated, however, the *The Register* article should be reread with the following remarks by Ed Neal in mind:

Eager vendors, hoping to corner the educational market, provide cut-rate products and services. Legislators pass budgets with large sums for educational technology, because they fear that students will be unprepared for the future unless they use technology every day in school. As a result, well-meaning administrators often seize upon technology as a solution to their budgetary problems. No doubt, some administrators also see technological initiatives as a route to their personal success, a way to make their mark on an institution and advance their own careers.

Faculty members are the ones who have to implement new technology, and they should decide whether or not to experiment with it or adopt it. Yet often they are not consulted about the practical problems and barriers they confront when they do want to experiment with using technology in their own particular courses. They need effective assistance–of the type they desire, not what software developers deign to provide–to determine which applications yield the best results. (1998:B5)

In these comments, Neal is not objecting to technology as much as he is criticizing those who currently have control of technology. And, he addresses two very important issues: funding and faculty control. Neal is by no means the only person to have raised his voice in protest against the amount of money that naive legislators and well-meaning administrators are throwing at technology. Healy sees the willingness of legislators to spend money as closely tied to the technology hysteria that has gripped every level of education:

Why do we so desperately need to believe in computers? After surveying current attitudes for the nonprofit organization Learning in the Real World, William Ruckeyser told me, "The nearest thing I can draw a parallel to is a theological discussion. There's so much an element of faith here that demanding evidence is almost a sign of heresy." Witness the federal government's initiative to wire all schools for telecommunications by the year 2000, under the simplistic assumption that connecting kids to 'information' will somehow make them more able to read and use it intelligently. Meanwhile, library and sometimes even school budgets are cut across the nation.

Eighty percent of people who plan to buy a personal computer soon will cite children's education as the main reason. Ninety percent of voters in the United States are convinced that schools with computers can do a better job of education, and 61 would support a federal tax increase to speed the introduction of technology into the schools. In 1995 the American Association of School Administrators published the results of a survey that asked parents, teachers, leaders from various fields, and members of the general public what skills would be important for students graduating in the twenty-first century. "Computer skills and media technology" ranked third in a list of sixteen possibilities, outvoted only by "basic skills" (reading, writing, and math) and "good work habits." Computer skills were deemed more important than "values" (e.g., honesty, tolerance) by every group but the leaders. "Good citizenship" and "curiosity and love of learning" were considerably further down the list, and such topics as "knowledge of history and geography" and "classic works (e.g., Shakespeare, Plato)" were near the bottom (highly valued by only 29 and 21 percent of business leaders, respectively). (1998: 19–20)

Healy's book also contains a number of quotes which pertain to the subject of technology and money: "Penetration of the education market with computer-based technology has depended more on effective conditioning of the market through a barrage of advertising and ideology than on the effectiveness of the technologies themselves" (Douglas Noble, author of *The Classroom Arsenal*) (1998: 79).

Mingle also questions the amount of money being poured into technology:

The level of technology support state governments provide to higher education continues its upward trend. In 1995–96, states earmarked at least $350 million for higher education technology, an amount that rose to nearly $370 million in 1996–97. Legislative earmarks in 1996–97 include $18 million in Georgia, $12 million in Ohio, $10 million in Illinois, and $100 million in bonds authorized in New Jersey over the next seven years. . . .

The productivity payoffs from technology must come from improved student learning. Given the added costs of incorporating technology into instructional programs, our goal should be to use technology when and where it has the highest potential to improve student learning. . . . Without learning gains in such areas as math, science, and communications, technology may prove to be part of the cost problem and not the productivity solution. (1997: 1–2)

Although it is heartening to see someone like James R. Mingle, executive director of the State Higher Education Executive Officers, supporting a critical rethinking of expenditures on technology, many faculty would question that "state board members and campus trustees" should be in control of this important process. Young (1998b) addressed this concern in an article regarding webpages at the University of California, Los Angeles (UCLA).

The author reported on the reaction of faculty members to an initiative which required all courses to have their own individual webpages. Some faculty objected on the grounds of academic freedom and protection of property rights. Some students protested because they were assessed a per-course fee to pay for the creation of the webpages. UCLA administrators indicated that their goal had been to make technology an increasingly central part of the students' university experience. And, predictably, opinions were mixed regarding the value of the webpages.

Although some of the letters in response to the article lauded UCLA for providing professors with assistance in making webpages, others saw only the arrogance of an administration that had decided what faculty would do and how they would do it. The UCLA case is a good example of what should have been a discussion of technology becoming a discussion of administrative style. The issue of the effectiveness of webpages and what they actually contribute to a class was almost lost in the debate regarding faculty rights. And, unfortunately, as long as administrators regard the choice of implementation of technology to be their responsibility, the situation is apt to remain unchanged. As higher education enters the new millennium, issues regarding administrative style may be inseparable from, and even more important than, those related to technology.

Y2K, as the start of the new millennium has been dubbed, is most commonly associated with problems. *Newsweek* publishes a regular feature about once a month called "The Y2K Watch," which keeps readers posted on our state of unpreparedness for that fateful day when our computers will see a date that ends in a double zero and promptly go haywire. Ron Bass, one of Hollywood's most successful screenwriters, has commented that "this crisis has arisen out of the hilarious incompetence of the computer geniuses who've made us dependent on their inventions" (Brown, 1998: 14).

Y2K probably will not be technology's finest hour. And, we are too close to the magic year of 2000 to expect the problems with technology in higher education to have been miraculously solved by that time. However, it is not too late for those of us who believe in technology to begin planning our new millennium's resolutions.

Higher education's first new millennium resolution must be to get control of technology in higher education back into the hands of the people who must use it: the faculty. The current situation, in which decisions that affect teaching are made by people who have not been in a classroom for years (if ever), is unacceptable. The fact that administrators are often unduly influenced by hardware and software vendors makes the situation even worse. Not only are faculty being frustrated in their search for the technologies that suit their purposes, education institutions and systems are losing vast amounts of money on technologies that simply do not work.

The second Y2K resolution should be to shift funding for technology in higher education from central control to local control. And, through local control, higher education should strive to support faculty who are exploring the uses of technology in innovative ways. *The Chronicle of Higher Education* regularly contains articles on how technology is solving a problem for students and/or professors in some discipline on some campus somewhere. Although, in some cases, the faculty have had some grant support for their activities, in many cases they have not. The research and the development of their programs have been paid for by the faculty members themselves—with their time, energy, and money.

Higher education's third resolution should be to determine, once and for all, how software development is to be considered insofar as promotion and tenure are concerned. Although this issue has not been discussed in the body of the article, it is important. If administrators hype technology on the one hand, but deny that software development can be considered research and publication on the other, they have sent an important, discouraging message to faculty. The same message is being sent by institutions and systems that claim all rights to programs created by faculty. Institutions may have a right to some of the profits from work done while a faculty member was under contract. However, if institutions are going to claim total ownership of such inventions, there is little incentive for faculty to do this kind of work (which is usually done on evenings and weekends).

The final two resolutions have to do with the basics of all education: students, teaching, and learning. This is what counts most; indeed, it may be all that counts. There are challenges involved in teaching students during a technological age, which have to do with seeing how many technological applications can be used in a single class period. And, there is also the need to simply make sure that students are computer literate. Now, more than ever, our students need training in critical thinking. In the information age, with all its scary freedoms, where anyone can set up a website, our students need to develop the good, old-fashioned ability to detect lies and half truths. Students should be able to spot fallacies in a line of reasoning.

If faculty require any sort of research at all in their courses, they are probably already aware of the fact that students are using search engines more and the library less. And, there is no Internet police to make sure that information provided by this resource has any resemblance to the truth. I have had students hand in papers in which there were massive errors in fact as well as in interpretation. If administrators are going to push technology, they have an obligation to make sure that students know how use it responsibly. This burden cannot be borne solely by faculty in subject matter courses. Along with composition, algebra, and speech, students in the new millennium may need a freshman-level course in analysis of information. At the very least, they should be taught to confirm the information they have gathered from the net against more traditional sources.

Finally, faculty and administrators throughout higher education must resolve to submit technological applications used in the classroom to the same kind of rigorous analysis that any other teaching technique would receive. There are many teaching methods, including rote memorization, that are no longer used in education for the simple reason that they do not work as effectively as other methods. Why should we, after critical analysis, discard methods of teaching used in the past, when we accept every new fad that comes along uncritically? We should constantly be asking what is happening in the students' minds as they use a particular kind of technology. Whether it be PictureTel, Power Point, or even simple video, we should be analyzing the impact on teaching and learning that uses any kind of technology.

Do students who are not visual learners suffer in a dimly lit classroom when the entire lecture is accompanied by a Power Point presentation? How does the dim lighting needed to use an Elmo effectively affect students? When technology directs the students' attention consistently to the front of the room and to the teacher and the message he/she has to impart, what happens to the knowledge that students can gain from each other? If it is true that certain kinds of students do better in a virtual classroom than they do in a traditional classroom, how can this technology be used to maximize such students' traditional learning experiences? How can a website enhance a course? Will it necessarily be a benefit for all students in a given course or only those with certain learning styles or aptitudes?

The questions are endless; the answers are not simple. In suggesting that all technology be evaluated carefully in terms of its effectiveness as a teaching/learning device, I am not proposing a technological witch hunt. I am not suggesting that, if held up to scrutiny, most technical applications will be found wanting. Quite the contrary. In foreign languages in the last ten years, we have undergone a wrenching paradigm shift. Everything I ever did as a young teacher has been subjected to a rigorous reexamination in terms of its ability to contribute to a student's proficiency in actually using a language.

In the course of reexamining what I had been doing for years, I have learned a tremendous amount about my students, myself, and about what really works. I use technology every day in my classrooms and, among foreign language professionals, I am not exceptional. In fact, compared to some of my colleagues, I am a novice. I use the Elmo and an audio tape recorder almost daily. I use the video-cassette recorder and the overhead projector once or twice a week. I rarely connect my classroom to live satellite transmissions from Spanish-speaking countries or use my computer in class. Many of my colleagues do all of the above—and more.

My colleagues did not set out to be technowhizzes. They were not attempting to impress the department head, the dean, or someone else who was pushing technology. They use slides of places in foreign countries, tapes, or CDs of music from these countries and videos that show typical holiday celebrations. They also use live satellite transmission to put their students in contact with the news of the day and a computer link to a website to instruct students in how to obtain information from that resource. And, they do all of this because, when one teaches a foreign language, it is important to bring students into the most immediate contact possible with both the language and the culture being taught. An instructor should not use technology for technology's sake; rather, because it works.

In examining all of the challenges technology will present for higher education in the next millennium, this one is paramount. Our greatest challenge, as faculty and administrators alike, will be to examine each new technology and each new application of technology critically to see what it can offer us and our students. This cannot be a knee-jerk process. That is, the first time I see a new technology, I cannot dismiss it out of hand because, at that point, it seems cumbersome, awkward, or expensive. Many of the techniques I routinely use in my courses did not work well the first time I used them. I need to grant technology the same degree of latitude that we would for any other teaching method.

When one thinks of how technology has already changed so many aspects of our lives for the good, it is hard not to be enthusiastic about what the next millennium holds for us. There may even be a new technology out there that will help us reach the young man or woman in the third row that we never seem really able to teach effectively. There will be problems. Sadly, if things do not change, faculty may well have to battle their own administrators to see that technology is used well and not just in ways that the administrators advise. But, new centuries are a time for optimism. With faculty and administrators working together instead of at cross-purposes, what will we not be able to achieve in the new millennium?

APPENDIX

Technology in Higher Education: Informal Satisfaction Survey

1. How often can faculty on your campus/in your state system expect to get an upgrade for their office computer, printer, etc.?

    _____ 1–2 yrs.   _____ 3–4 yrs.   _____ 5–6 yrs.   _____ Other, explain

2. When faculty are allowed an upgrade, how would you describe the options they have?

_____ Complete; they can choose any computer they like with no additional charge to their department.

_____ Limited; they can choose any computer provided their department is prepared to pay the difference between the basic model and the computer chosen.

_____ Limited; they are restricted to a few models.

_____ Other, explain.

3. How satisfied are faculty with the computer equipment they have in their own offices?

_____ Very satisfied   _____ Satisfied   _____ Dissatisfied   _____ Other, explain.

4. How satisfied are faculty with the support they receive for keeping their computer, etc. working?

_____ Very satisfied   _____ Satisfied   _____ Dissatisfied   _____ Other, explain.

5. How satisfied are faculty with the support they receive for learning new applications for their office computer equipment and classroom teaching technologies?

_____ Very satisfied   _____ Satisfied   _____ Dissatisfied   _____ Other, explain.

6. How would you describe the process of acquiring a new computer on your campus?

_____ Slicker than oil   _____ Speedy   _____ OK   _____ Unsatisfactory, explain.

7. Please describe any frustrations or successes you and your colleagues have experienced in the acquisition or use of instructional technologies.

8. Please add any additional comments.

BIBLIOGRAPHY

Adler, Jerry. 1998. Online and Bummed Out. *Newsweek*, September 14, 84.

Biemiller, Lawrence. 1998a. Lonely and Unhappy in Cyberspace?: A New Study Prompts On-Line Debate. *The Chronicle of Higher Education*, September 18, A31.

———. 1998b. U. of Utah President Issues a Pointed Warning about Virtual Universities. *The Chronicle of Higher Education*, October 9, A32.

Blumenstyk, Goldie. 1998. A Philanthropy Puts Millions into Asynchronous Learning. *The Chronicle of Higher Education*, November 13, A23–A25.

The Brookings Register. 1998. Regents' Panel Plan, July 22, A3.

Brown, Corie. 1998. Searching for a Plot, Hollywood Looks to the Millennium. *Newsweek*, June 29, 14.

Cárdenas, Karen Hardy. 1998a. Saving Small Foreign Language Programs: Is Cooperation the Answer? *AFDL Bulletin* 29:3, 11–19.

———. 1998b. Technology in Today's Classroom: It Slices and It Dices, But Does It Serve Us Well? *Academe* 84 (May-June), 27–29.

The Chronicle of Higher Education Almanac. 1998. The Nation: Attitudes and Characteristics of Freshmen, August 22, 22.

Eisenberg, Daniel. 1998. Foreign Language Instruction through Interactive Television at Northern Arizona University. *AFDL Bulletin* 29:3, 20–23.

Eisenberg, Daniel, and Kathleen Adams. 1998. What Are They Thinking? *Time*, September 7, 88.

Gajilan, Arlyn Tobias. 1998. Live from the Dorm Room. *Newsweek*, September 14, 82.

Guernsey, Lisa. 1998a. College-Bound Students Use the Web, but Value Printed Information More. *The Chronicle of Higher Education*, July 17, A32.

———. 1998b. The New Players in College Admissions: One-Stop Shops for Students. *The Chronicle of Higher Education*, October 9, A30.

Healy, Jane M. 1998. *Failure to Connect: How Computers Affect Our Children's Minds—for Better and Worse*. New York: Simon and Schuster.

Kelly, J. Terence, and Robin Leckbee. 1998. Reality Check: What Do We Really Know about Technology, and How Do We Know It? *Syllabus* (August), 24, 26, 53.

Krantz, Michael. 1998. Click till You Drop. *Time*, July 20, 34–39.

McCollum, Kelly. 1998a. A Computer Requirement for Students Changes Professors' Duties as Well. *The Chronicle of Higher Education*, June 26, A22–A23.

———. 1998b. High School Students Use Web Intelligently for Research, Study Finds. *The Chronicle of Higher Education*, December 4, A25.

———. 1998c. NSF Grants to Help Universities Connect to New Networks at Home and Abroad. *The Chronicle of Higher Education*, October 2, A29.

Mingle, James R. 1997. New Technology Funds: Problem or Solution? http://www.sheeo.org.

Monaghan, Peter. 1998. U. of Washington Professors Decry Governor's Visions for Technology. *The Chronicle of Higher Education*, June 19, B4–B5.

Neal, Ed. 1998. Using Technology in Teaching: We Need to Exercise Healthy Skepticism. *The Chronicle of Higher Education*, June 19, B4–B5.

Samuelson, Robert. 1998. Down with the Media Elite! *Newsweek*, July 13, 47.

Stone, Brad. 1998. The Keyboard Kids. *Newsweek*, June 8, 72, 74.

Young, Jeffrey R. 1998a. An Artist Unexpectedly Finds Herself Transformed into a Technology Advocate. *The Chronicle of Higher Education*, June 12, A23–A24.

———. 1998b. A Year of Webpages for Every Class. *The Chronicle of Higher Education*, May 15, A29–A31.

Index

About the Editors and Contributors

Alexander W. Astin is Allan M. Cartter professor of Higher Education and Director of the Higher Education Research Institute at the University of California, Los Angeles. He is also the founding director of the Cooperative Institutional Research Program, an ongoing longitudinal study of the American higher education system involving more than 9 million current and former students, 200,000 faculty and administrators, and 1,500 institutions.

Karen Hardy Cárdenas is Professor of Spanish at South Dakota State University. She is the coauthor of the introductory Spanish text, *Para Empezar* and has worked with educational technology as both an instructor and an administrator. She is currently working on developing professional webcourses for teachers.

Brian L. Fife is Associate Professor of Public and Environmental Affairs at Indiana University–Purdue University Fort Wayne. He is the author of *School Desegregation in the Twenty-First Century: The Focus Must Change* and *Desegregation in American Schools: Comparative Intervention Strategies* as well as several articles on education policy in the United States.

Joseph Losco is Professor of Political Science at Ball State University. He has published in the areas of political theory and public policy and is the author of *Human Nature and Politics*.

Cheryl D. Lovell is Assistant Professor of Education and Coordinator of the M.A. program in Higher Education and Adult Studies at the University of Denver. She was previously Director of the State Higher Education Executive Officers–SPRE Technical Assistance Network in Denver and Research Associate with the National Center for Higher Education Management Systems in Boulder.

Michael D. Parsons is Associate Professor of Higher Education at Indiana University–Purdue University Indianapolis. He is the author of *Power and Politics: Federal Higher Education Policymaking in the 1990s*. In 1999, he lectured and conducted research as a Senior Fulbright Scholar at Karaganda State University, Karaganda, Kazakhstan.

Richard L. Pattenaude has been president of the University of Southern Maine, the largest university in Maine, since 1991. He received his Ph.D. in Political Science from the University of Colorado.

Gary Rhoades is Professor and Director of the Center for the Study of Higher Education at the University of Arizona where he studies academic labor, restructuring of higher education, and institutional policy. His most recent publication is *Managed Professionals: Unionized Faculty and Restructuring Academic Labor*.

Richard G. Sheehan is Professor of Finance and Business Economics at the University of Notre Dame where he specializes in monetary policy as well as the economic impact of sports. He is the author of *Keeping Score: The Economics of Big-Time Sports*. He is also currently Chair of Notre Dame's faculty senate and President of the South Bend school board.

Reginald Wilson is Senior Scholar *Emeritus* at the American Council on Education and is the co-author of its Annual Status Report on Minorities in Higher Education. Prior to his appointment at the ACE, he was president of Wayne County Community College in Detroit for ten years. He received his Ph.D. in clinical and educational psychology from Wayne State University and holds honorary degrees from several institutions.

ISBN 0-89789-637-8

9 780897 896375

HARDCOVER BAR CODE